Hollywood 9/11

Hollywood 9/11

Superheroes, Supervillains, and Super Disasters

Tom Pollard

Paradigm Publishers

Boulder • London

Copyright © 2011 Paradigm Publishers

Published in the United States by Paradigm Publishers, 2845 Wilderness Place, Boulder, CO 80301 USA.

Paradigm Publishers is the trade name of Birkenkamp & Company, LLC, Dean Birkenkamp, President and Publisher.

Library of Congress Cataloging-in-Publication Data

Pollard, Tom.
    Hollywood 9/11 : superheroes, supervillains, and super disasters / Tom Pollard.
        p. cm.
    Includes bibliographical references and index.
    Includes filmography.
    ISBN 978-1-59451-759-4 (hardback : alk. paper) — ISBN 978-1-59451-760-0 (pbk. : alk. paper)
    1. Violence in motion pictures.   2. Heroes in motion pictures.   3. Villains in motion pictures.   4. Psychic trauma in motion pictures.   5. Terrorism in motion pictures.   6. Motion pictures—United States—History—21st century.   7. September 11 Terrorist Attacks, 2001—Influence.   I. Title.

PN1995.9.V5P585 2011
791.43'655—dc22

2011010322

Printed and bound in the United States of America on acid-free paper that meets the standards of the American National Standard for Permanence of Paper for Printed Library Materials.

Designed and Typeset by Straight Creek Bookmakers.

15 14 13 12 11   1 2 3 4 5

Contents

v

Preface and Acknowledgments

This book surveys the major film genres and subgenres stimulated by 9/11 and related events. In previous work, I focused on the often complex relationships between the U.S. military and Hollywood filmmakers. During wartime, studios invest in combat films, but their rate of return depends on the wars' justification, conduct, and ultimate effectiveness. I noticed that the events of 9/11 and the wars that followed affected an entire generation of filmmakers and inspired an important new film movement. Today critics widely acknowledge the existence of a "post-9/11 movement" and "post-9/11 films." This new movement promises to be as seminal and influential as the classic film noir movement was in the 1940s and 1950s. In studying this subject, I realized that it called for a book-length study, and I became increasingly excited about the prospect of writing about it. The result is *Hollywood 9/11: Superheroes, Supervillains, and Super Disasters*.

I wish to acknowledge the assistance of Sue Dickey, lifelong partner and inspiring reader. Her patience in reading the manuscript and suggesting improvements helped immeasurably. I also wish to thank Carl Boggs, Ph.D., my close friend and collaborator, and Michael Parenti, Ph.D., who offered insightful feedback. Thanks also to Daryl Mitchell for his research assistance. I thank my parents for introducing me to movies and encouraging me to indulge in my passion for films. They, along with my brothers, Stephen and Michael, made going to the drive-in theater the highlight of many summer evenings.

In 2001, when television viewers tuned in to the images of the 9/11 attacks, the emotions engendered proved far more powerful than normal feelings. Large segments of the viewing population expressed shock, grief, horror, rage, paranoia, and a powerful thirst for vengeance against those responsible for the attacks. The first seven chapters on this study focus on the heightened emotional states stimulated by 9/11. **Chapter One: Shock**, the most common emotion manifested immediately after the terrorist attacks, explores Hollywood's initial reactions to these traumatic events and presents theoretical approaches to understanding those. **Chapter Two: Grief** analyzes a cycle of films, made in 2003 onward, that documented the terrorist attacks themselves and the wars that followed. It also analyzes movies dramatizing the wars in Iraq and Afghanistan. **Chapter Three: Horror** focuses on horror and revulsion in films, particularly the horror genre, which experienced unprecedented popularity after 9/11. This chapter analyzes the reasons behind the dramatic rise in the popularity of horror films after September 11. **Chapter Four: Rage** reveals post-9/11 war films set in locations other than Afghanistan and Iraq. These films provide indirect but often telling commentary on the "war on terror." They depict armed conflicts in Vietnam, Burma, Sierra Leone, and other exotic locations, but as combat films they invite comparisons with 9/11 wars. **Chapter Five: Vengeance** showcases superpowerful protagonists possessing extraordinary powers. These characters eventually triumph over all their antagonists, no matter how powerful, unlike the U.S. military. Hollywood films now routinely resonate with a powerful thirst for vengeance against the antagonists, indirectly referencing contemporary feelings of revenge against terrorists. This chapter explores the reasons superhero films spiked in popularity after 9/11. **Chapter Six: Terror** highlights terror as an emotion and depictions of terrorism and terrorists in post-9/11 thrillers. Post-9/11 terrorist films reveal profound fear and distrust of the intelligence agencies that failed to predict or stop the September 11 events. Villains morph into shadowy rogue U.S. intelligence agents, renegade Wall Street brokers, or government officials. **Chapter Seven: Paranoia** examines a remarkable cycle of recent science fiction films depicting death and destruction on a massive scale. Sci-fi films normally derive much of their dramatic tension through fear, but fear accelerates into panic and then into paranoia in post-9/11 movies. Post-9/11 sci-fi depicts intergalactic warfare, plagues, alien invasions, and cataclysmic climatic upheavals. **Chapter Eight: Post-9/11 Hollywood** summarizes 9/11's impact on Hollywood across all genres, from terrorist films and depictions of the war on terror to horror films, superhero movies, science fiction, war films, and thrillers, revealing areas of commonality and recurrent themes and patterns. This chapter also speculates on future directions in the post-9/11 film movement.

—Tom Pollard

CHAPTER ONE

Shock

The terrorist attacks of September 11, 2001, shocked the world and led to the U.S. invasions of Afghanistan in 2001 and Iraq in 2003. These dramatic events transformed the United States politically, socially, and artistically. But did this transformation lead to changes in the film industry? It may take scholars years or even decades to fully assess the impact of 9/11 on films, given the complexity of the changes unleashed by the terrorist attacks, the normal progression of technology in the film industry, and the fact that new styles, themes, and issues related to the attacks continue to unfold. Initially, many expected Hollywood to decrease graphic movie violence, while others wanted filmmakers to use the opportunity to lay bare underlying volatile sociopolitical issues. Both predictions proved wildly inaccurate. Hollywood's direct and indirect responses to the attacks initially seemed bewildering and unpredictable but upon deeper reflection appear perfectly reasonable and even inevitable. The attacks uniquely affected Hollywood compared to other events in U.S. history. Some genres that previously appealed to small, cultlike followers suddenly transformed into box office bonanzas appealing to the masses. Other genres became "blended" genres, whereas others disappeared completely. Hollywood melodramas and comedies alike assumed a comic-book quality with larger-than-life heroes and villains battling each other, often with humanity's very survival at issue.

The September 11 attacks became a historical watershed. The world transformed abruptly from one that appeared relatively "normal" and "sane" into one that seemed dangerous, unstable, and deadly. Gun and ammunition sales spiked to all-time highs, and the general public began expressing significantly more positive feelings about war and violence. Nicholas Carnagey and Craig Anderson studied public attitudes toward violence,

1

This snapshot of people fleeing the World Trade Center on September 11, 2001, flooded the news media and contributed to the shock many people felt about the attacks, as well as grief for the victims. Billowing smoke from the collapsing World Trade Center Tower testifies to the intensity of the fires burning in the building. Conspiracy theorists speculated that the Towers fell as a result of explosives secretly placed by government agents. (AP Photo/Amy Sancetta)

aggression, and war before and after 9/11. Their broad, long-term study revealed that the terrorist attacks not only "significantly altered relevant attitudes, especially war attitudes," but also "resulted in self-reported increases in aggression, anger, and hostility."[1] Pre-9/11 films now appear naïve and optimistic compared with today's pessimistic genres, which include revenge thrillers, violent combat films, torture porn, and dark sci-fi. Critics refer to films produced since 9/11 as "post-9/11," many of which bear unmistakable signs and references to the 9/11 attacks and their aftermath, often presented obliquely through tone, metaphor, symbolism, and innuendo.

December 7, 1941

Hollywood's immediate responses to the attacks on the World Trade Center and the Pentagon bear striking similarities to its responses to the 1941 Japanese bombing of Pearl Harbor and the U.S. entry into World War II. Both December 7, 1941, and September 11, 2001, unleashed massive military campaigns. Both events affected people profoundly, galvanizing widespread public support for military retaliation and quickly spawning massive military campaigns. And both events launched new film genres with altered film styles, resulting in many important films. Substantive differences, however, remain between audience preferences in these two eras. The films created by Hollywood depicting the Japanese attack on Pearl Harbor, including Fred Zinnemann's *From Here to Eternity* (1953); Richard Fleischer, Kenji Fukasada, and Toshio Masuda's *Tora! Tora! Tora!* (1970); Otto Preminger's *In Harm's Way* (1965); and Michael Bay's *Pearl Harbor* (2001), exude a sense of historical outrage over the Japanese "sneak attack" that precipitated American entry into the war. December 7, 1941, stood out as the most infamous date in American wartime history until rivaled by another date, September 11, 2001.

While World War II continued to inspire combat films, another style and genre emerged: film noir. It arose as an artistic response to the war's carnage and destruction, as well as to other disturbing events of the era, including the Great Depression. Films like Boris Ingster's *Stranger on the Third Floor* (1940), *The Maltese Falcon* (1941), *Double Indemnity* (1944), *The Big Sleep* (1946), *Gilda* (1946), and *The Third Man* (1949); Robert Aldrich's *Kiss Me Deadly* (1955); and Orson Welles's *Touch of Evil* (1958) reference the war. Sometimes the films refer to the war directly, whereas at other times their bleak subject matter, doomed heroes, sleazy settings, and dark style invoke it indirectly. These films, later labeled "film noir," display a pessimistic, at times almost nightmarish quality expressed by setting, lighting, mood, and dialogue. The protagonists consist of powerless, emotionally scarred characters who attempt to survive in a hostile environment. The horrors and losses of World War II (including the Holocaust), the victories and defeats, inspired an entire generation of audiences and filmmakers. The "classic" film noir cycle spanned nearly two decades during and after the war, encompassing the Korean War, the cold war, the rise of nuclear weapons, and McCarthyism. The existing issues and anxieties helped fuel audience demand for the film noir thrillers populated with down-and-out protagonists struggling for survival in a chaotic world.

The Vietnam War, the civil rights movement, the rise of feminism, along with other disturbing events of the 1960s and 1970s, including the rise of urban crime and drug addiction, inspired a later film noir cycle. As Americans watched on television and witnessed almost firsthand daily battlefield carnage and stacked body bags, as atrocities against civilians became exposed, as massive civil rights and antiwar marches unfolded across the country, the bleak, pessimistic cinema labeled "neonoir" appeared. The neonoir genre includes such films as Martin Scorsese's *Taxi Driver* (1976), Roman Polanski's *Chinatown* (1974), and Lawrence Kasdan's *Body Heat* (1981), along with more recent films, including *The Usual Suspects* (1995), *In the Cut* (2003), and *Mystic River* (2003).

Violence

A new film cycle also emerged soon after the events of 9/11 and the "war on terror." Though critics refer to it as "post-9/11," it could be labeled "post-9/11 noir." The post-9/11 movement retains elements of the older film noir and neonoir movements but adds some new elements. As in these earlier cycles, post-9/11 noir emphasizes emotionally flawed, depressed protagonists trapped in threatening, potentially deadly situations, dark settings, and social dislocations. Gender battles, long a film noir hallmark, also figure prominently in the newer cycle. Like World War II and the Vietnam War, the events of 9/11 inaugurated an important film cycle featuring bold plots, strong heroes, and dangerous villains.

The post-9/11 genre exudes violence, cynicism, and paranoia about disturbing, violent events, often including various forms of terrorism. Examples include Spike Lee's *25th Hour* (2002), Paul Greengrass's Bourne series (2002–2007), David Cronenberg's *A History of Violence* (2005), James McTeague's *V for Vendetta* (2006), Paul Greengrass's *United 93* (2006), Oliver Stone's *World Trade Center* (2006), Christopher Nolan's *The Dark Knight* (2008), Zack Snyder's *Watchmen* (2009), James Cameron's *Avatar* (2009), and Paul Greengrass's *Green Zone* (2010). Each of these films references the 9/11 attacks and war on terror either directly or indirectly, and each possesses elements of post-9/11 style, which resembles darker neonoirs. These films, and many others, belong to the post-9/11 film movement.

After the shock of the 9/11 attacks, filmmakers wondered if audiences had lost their taste for violence and terrorism in movies, concerns that prompted a massive production freeze on a variety of violent thrillers. However, producers' fears proved groundless. Instead of the predominantly light "family values" fare predicted by some critics, post-9/11 audiences preferred violent horror, sci-fi, and thrillers that only indirectly referenced 9/11 and the war on terror. Some audiences supported docudramas shown in art house theaters or on television that directly depicted the 9/11 events. However, most showed little interest in those films directly depicting 9/11 or the wars in Afghanistan and Iraq and, based on box office sales, continue to prefer the oblique, indirect references to these events. By 2006 the actual 9/11 attacks formed the subject matter for a few significant films, but no trend started as box office receipts proved disappointing.

Few films probed for possible causes behind the anti-American and anti-Western ideas, attitudes, and feelings exposed by the 9/11 attacks. Villains resembled terrorists, whose depictions followed the pre-9/11 pattern of flat characters with base and ignoble motives such as ego and greed—not politics. Any attempt to present the viewpoints of violent opponents of U.S. foreign policy could appear treasonous as long as the wars in Afghanistan and Iraq remain unresolved. Currently, audiences remain uninterested in realistic depictions of the issues behind today's conflicts between East and West.

As movies became more violent, their heroes grew vastly more powerful. In fact, post-9/11 films often feature superheroes, either classic heroes of the past, such as Superman and Batman, or more modern characters like X-Men, Spider-Man, the Hulk, and the Fantastic Four. When combined with vampire and werewolf films (which also feature superheroes) and action films (Rambo and other action heroes come close to possessing superpowers), today's movie protagonists wield far more power and unleash far more destruction than heroes did before 9/11. Their powers increase in response to the growing dangers and potency of villains threatening them.

Post-9/11 Emotions

Few dispute that 9/11 unleashed powerful emotions. Millions stared at their televisions in stunned disbelief as two jetliners plunged into the World Trade Center in New York City. Audiences gazed helplessly at images of Tower I and then Tower II collapsing as fires raged and hundreds of fear-crazed people stampeded in panic from the smoking buildings. Images of planes embedded in the World Trade Center, of victims leaping out of windows to their death, and of towers reduced to rubble remain in our memories years after the events occurred.

Nineteenth-century biologist Charles Darwin first identified six primal emotions he believed humanity shared. Today biologists and psychologists still rely on Darwin's set of basic emotions. Darwin's six "normal emotions" include anger, happiness, sadness, disgust, fear, and surprise, immutable emotions enabling humans to cope with life's vagaries.[2] After the September 11 terrorist attacks, violent, painful emotions much more powerful than those Darwin and his followers named appeared, including shock, grief, rage, horror, paranoia, and terror. Darwin's primal emotion of "surprise" fails to portray the feelings of bewilderment and numbness with which many greeted the news of the 9/11 attacks, whereas "shock" matches actual feelings better. "Sadness" inadequately describes the intensity of reaction to 9/11. As the extent of the deaths in the Twin Towers became known, many experienced powerful outpourings of sorrow and grief for more than 2,700 victims. The entire world grieved for those who died from the terrorist attacks, and many films continue to reference that emotion. And "disgust" cannot fully describe the emotional outpouring over the violation and destruction from the attacks. Feelings of disgust transformed into feelings of horror and outrage.

Darwin also identified "anger" as one of the primal emotions, but that word appears too mild to describe the wave of emotion that rose after 9/11. Anger quickly transformed into intense feelings of outrage, and many demanded revenge against the perpetrators. Darwin's "fear" quickly transformed into panic and outright paranoia. Terrified homeowners stockpiled weapons and supported expanded military budgets; demands to "secure the border" and institute draconian methods to control illegal immigration testified to residual fears originally stimulated by the 9/11 attacks.

Terror, an emotion closely related to horror and revulsion, also exploded after 9/11, and films often depict frightened, terrified individuals, families, and communities resulting from domestic or international terrorists. The terrorists causing the panic happily deliver mayhem and murder that eventually results in paranoia. Today's melodramas typically include some kind of terrorist. Movie terrorists may originate from distant planets or closer to home. In fact, they may arrive from any location except, it seems, from the

Middle East. Contemporary films rarely depict Islamic terrorist organizations, instead selecting rogue intelligence officers, disgruntled Wall Street day traders, gangsters turned legitimate businessmen, and a variety of others who mimic many of the actions and tactics used by real terrorists.

Post-Traumatic Stress Syndrome

Individuals often repress extremely unpleasant or painful emotions. The events of September 11, 2001, disrupted normal emotional states, according to psychologists. A 2009 study found that after 9/11 "7.5 percent of New Yorkers and 20 percent of those who were near the World Trade Center when the attacks occurred suffered from Post-Traumatic Stress Disorder (PTSD)" (also known as post-traumatic stress syndrome, or PTSS), a powerful psychological illness in which emotions often run wild, disrupting victims' lives while leaving them vulnerable to deep depression. Follow-up studies revealed that instances of 9/11-induced acute PTSD lasted for many months and that those affected by the tragedy developed "coping mechanisms" to help them heal from their emotional damage, including renewed emphasis on social networks, redefinition and adjustment of personal priorities, and discussion with others about the September 11 events.[3]

Those exposed to media coverage of the 9/11 terrorist attacks continued to experience significant cases of PTSS long after the attacks had ceased. A 2006 study undertaken by Harvard Medical School discovered that in the weeks and months following September 11 a significant number of children and adults exposed to media coverage of the attacks developed full-fledged cases of PTSD (over 5 percent). In addition, an astonishing percentage of children (18.7) and adults (10.7) developed some symptoms of PTSD but did not develop full-blown cases.[4] All of these studies provide evidence of substantial and long-lasting emotional damage from the 9/11 attacks.

Another study, undertaken by clinical psychologists Michael Cohn, Matthias Mehl, and James Pennebaker, analyzed the emotional responses in more than one thousand journals of online writers over several weeks prior to and after 9/11. They found that in the first two weeks following 9/11 a high proportion of writers expressed powerful negative feelings, far stronger and more negative than before the events. Although this expression of negative emotions leveled off and even declined with time, many subjects continued to express "psychological distancing" (decreased use of singular personal pronouns and of the present tense in verbs, considered prime markers of psychological distress and discord) for up to six weeks after 9/11.[5]

Repressed emotions often find symbolic expression in dreams and art, just as the emotional intensity occasioned by the 9/11 events quickly found expression in pop music, comic books, and movies. From the first docu-dramas and documentaries depicting the terrorist attacks to mainstream thrillers, science fiction, combat, and horror, Hollywood embarked on a cycle of films reflecting the heightened emotions evoked by the September 11 attacks. These post-9/11 films constitute a powerful cinematic move-ment and add a new chapter in film history. Since 9/11, audiences have gravitated to horror films containing graphic media images of mangled, wounded, and dead bodies and buildings and even entire cities reduced to rubble. Like combat films, contemporary horror movies feature massive amounts of blood, gore, and mangled body parts.

Contemporary films often call up fears of terrorism indirectly, depict-ing not real terrorists but some cataclysmic events threatening the complete destruction of earth or at least large segments of it. Instead of Islamic ter-rorists, the new threats arise from asteroids, global climate change, plagues, massive earthquakes, aliens, robots, zombies, and other monsters. These films perfectly express the paranoia that many audiences still experience.

Hollywood's Initial Reactions

Critics speculated that the devastation wrought by 9/11 remained too sensi-tive for cinematic depiction and seemed destined, like footage of the atomic bombing of Hiroshima and Nagasaki and scenes of the Nazi death camps, to remain taboo for years, even decades. Hollywood studios suspended produc-tion on a number of feature films that suddenly seemed too sensitive. David Sterritt reported that Hollywood was "scrambling to regain its balance." Nor-mally bold Warner Brothers quickly pulled Andrew Davis's thriller *Collateral Damage,* starring Arnold Schwarzenegger as a firefighter battling Colombian terrorists in New York, a film slated for release on October 5, 2001. Sterritt predicted that the film, depicting terrorists bent on blowing up a New York skyscraper, would never reach the screen. In fact, after the attacks Warner Brothers pulled all advertising, which included a mock newspaper clipping alongside Arnold Schwarzenegger's face featuring the word "bombing" and the tagline "What would you do if you lost everything?" To Warner Brothers this seemed far too close an analogy to 9/11. The studio also revamped advertising featuring a shot of an explosion in the background and Schwarzenegger's face in the foreground minus the original tagline. In addition, Warner Brothers completely transformed the film's Web site, and the planned video games and other materials disappeared. The original movie included the famous Colombian actress Sofia Vergara, who played an airplane hijacker, but producers scrapped the hijacking scene and deleted other potentially sensitive scenes.[6] The film finally appeared in a truncated version on Friday, February 8, 2002. Even then, *Collateral Damage's* release evoked strong protests. Reverend Brian Jordan, ministering to the people at Ground Zero, charged that "making the main character a firefighter who becomes a vigilante is an insult to the firefighters who became heroes after the terrorist attacks." Roger Ebert speculated that Hollywood would refrain from making films like *Collateral Damage* "for a long time" because "we're at the end of the tunnel, the light is out, the genre is closed. *Collateral Damage* may stir unwanted associations for some viewers. Others may attend it with a certain nostalgia, remembering a time (was it only five months ago?) when such scenarios fell under the heading of entertainment."[7]

Collateral Damage distinguished itself from other pre-9/11 terrorist films by overtly presaging the terrorist attacks. In Davis's film terrorists set off a powerful explosive in New York City. Gordon "Gordy" Brewer (Arnold Schwarzenegger) nearly perishes along with his wife and child in a bombing perpetrated by terrorist Claudio "El Lobo" Perrini (Cliff Curtis). In the film El Lobo issues a warning: "As long as America continues its aggression in Colombia, we will bring the war home to you, and you will not feel safe in your own beds!" Gordy, in true pre-9/11 fashion, tracks El Lobo to his lair in Colombia and follows his trail back to New York, where he eventually kills him and his accomplice.

El Lobo, with his band of dedicated followers, seems vaguely reminiscent of Osama bin Laden, whereas Gordy presages the post-9/11 popularity of superheroes who preserve the peace by relentlessly seeking out and destroying terrorists, vigilante-style. The nationalistic terrorists in *Collateral Damage,* like the 9/11 attackers, stop at nothing in their drive for media attention. Although the Army of Colombian Liberation, not Islamic terrorists, serves as the film's villains, *Collateral Damage* justifiably made studio executives nervous—it resonates with political statements. At one point in the film Congress capitulates to the terrorists after El Lobo warns Gordy,

"Colombia is not your country. Get out now!" Cravenly caving to fear, Congress heeds the warnings and orders CIA operatives out of Colombia, weakening the fight against the Army of Colombian Liberation. Although Davis's film seems to anticipate anger over attacks on American soil, it also demonstrates a profound distrust of the U.S. government's will to fight terrorism. The film presents the United States as a paper tiger in a vicious world in which only a superwarrior like Gordy, not the U.S. government, stands between the terrorists and American civilians. The triteness of this message moved reviewer Todd McCartney to muse that "in an ideal universe Warner Bros. should simply not release this film overseas, so perfectly does it project the myopic, simplistic and uninformed mindset many people have long accused Hollywood of possessing anyway."[8]

Other filmmakers launched efforts to revise their films in the wake of the terrorist attacks. Barry Sonnenfeld eliminated a dramatic World Trade Center climax in *Men in Black 2,* a sequel to the popular 1997 comedy *Men in Black.* Similarly, Disney shelved *Big Trouble,* another Sonnenfeld film scheduled to appear in late 2001, until the spring of 2002 because its key plot element—a suitcase nuclear bomb headed for a plane—suddenly seemed too sensitive. Disney eventually released it with little fanfare and sparse advertising. Roger Ebert commented, "These are terrorists and bombs from a simpler and more innocent time." He also observed, "The movie is a reminder of an age when such plots were obviously not to be taken seriously. It's nice to be reminded of that time."[9]

In an effort to distance its film from 9/11, Sony pulled posters and coming-attractions trailers for *Spider-Man* (2002) because they showed New York's Twin Towers reflected in the hero's eyes. The studio also pulled a trailer featuring the superhero ensnaring a helicopter used by bank robbers as an escape vehicle in a giant web positioned between the Twin Towers. In a related development, Tri-Star Home Entertainment withheld release of *A Knight's Tale* on VHS because the video contained trailers from *Spider-Man* showing the superhero rappelling from the Twin Towers.[10]

Miramax Studios delayed Martin Scorsese's *Gangs of New York,* scheduled for September 2001 release, because studio executives became concerned that its "violence in New York" theme might offend viewers. The film finally appeared in December 2002. Although Scorsese shot his film before September 11, and even though it depicts nineteenth-century gangland warfare, not Islamic terrorism, Scorsese's film seemed to evoke many aspects of the terrorist attacks. Worse, it appeared to side with the terrorist-like street gangs, not the police department. Scorsese noted in his commentary on the DVD that the early New York gangs that participated in the Five Points battle came from the lowest echelons of society. "Once you have a group of people battered to the ground, they have nothing to lose." He then universalized these rival gangs by likening them to downtrodden people in general: "They represent every group that's ever been oppressed and every group that has ever been dispossessed." In addition, Scorsese warned that these wretched masses are ready to erupt into violence. "They're the ones that are going to come out and ultimately create a day of judgment."

Scorsese's setting, the notorious Five Points neighborhood in pre–Civil War New York City, appeared "almost like a post-apocalyptic world where people had to redefine what living really is." Miramax execs worried that the film might be deemed shockingly tasteless by being perceived as a justification for downtrodden groups to engage in violence, thus eliciting reexamination of domestic terrorism. *New York Times* critic Stephen Holden noted that Scorsese's film, although begun prior to the terrorist attacks, managed to evoke the events of 9/11 "as a historical watershed."[11]

The September 11, 2001, attacks also profoundly affected the comedy genre. In 2001 Paramount seriously considered an update to *Forrest Gump,* its popular 1994 blockbuster. Eric Roth, who had scripted the original film starring Tom Hanks, met on the eve of 9/11 with Hanks and director Robert Zemeckis to finalize plans for the film, at which time Roth submitted a script for the proposed sequel. Roth recalls the dramatically altered atmosphere the day after 9/11. "Tom and [director Bob Zemeckis] and I looked at each other and said we don't think this is relevant anymore. The world had changed. Now time has obviously passed, but maybe some things should just be one thing and left as they are."[12] To Roth, Hanks, Zemeckis, and many others, the 9/11 attacks ended a long-running film era and inaugurated a radically new one. Comedies darkened, often reflecting elements of black comedy, and mainstream films suddenly seemed out of date. Pre-9/11 comedies and dramas like *Forrest Gump* (1994), *Ghostbusters* (1984), *Schindler's List* (1993), *Titanic* (1997), and *Pearl Harbor* (2001) now seemed like artifacts of an earlier, less paranoid age when few feared foreign terrorists or worried about the role of the United States in world events. For that matter, before 9/11 few films depicted government surveillance, redaction, rendition, or government-condoned torture, all of which permeate post-9/11 films.

Despite predictions that audiences could no longer stomach movie violence, violence increased noticeably in post-9/11 films. Hollywood's initial reluctance to produce violent movies quickly turned enthusiastic as audiences supported thrillers rated R for violence at an unprecedented rate. A few films have appeared that directly depicted the events of September 11—*DC 9/11: Time of Crisis* (2003), *World Trade Center* (2006), *United 93* (2006), and *Twin Towers* (2006)—but most motion pictures bearing the stamp of 9/11 reflect the attacks more obliquely. Hollywood's post-9/11 terrorists threaten cities, sports arenas, airplanes, city water supplies, and office buildings. In addition, the terrorists themselves have changed. Instead of Islamic radicals waging jihad, today's movie terrorists consist of members of secret societies, megalomaniacs, mutants, zombies, vampires, ghosts, demons, and even giant insects. They attack symbols of Western businesses and governments, but filmmakers rarely depict their hopes, fears, and aspirations. Hollywood continues to avoid showcasing the viewpoints of violent opponents of U.S. policies.

The 9/11 attacks helped generate the U.S.-led invasion of Afghanistan in 2001 and Iraq in 2003, providing two fronts in a new war on terror declared by President George W. Bush on September 20, 2001, in his address to a joint session of Congress. In addition to the military campaigns in Afghanistan and Iraq, the United States provided aid and support to Pakistan, the Philippines, Russia, and other nations facing clandestine insurgents. The term "terror" came to signify not only a violent emotion but also a military opponent (the war on terror). Fighting the war on terror was invoked against a wide assortment of groups opposed to American interests. These military actions and campaigns, launched in response to the 9/11 attacks, also elicited powerful emotional responses from audiences and producers.

CHAPTER TWO

Grief

The first images of the 9/11 disaster came from independent photographers and tourists with cameras who captured raw emotions, especially shock, in their photos and films. For weeks television audiences worldwide experienced shock as well as grief for the victims of the terrorist attacks. Soon independent filmmakers released documentaries depicting the terrorist events from their perspectives. Wary Hollywood producers placed terrorist-themed films on hold, so independents proved more assiduous in depicting the events of 9/11.

Steven Rosenbaum's *7 Days in September* (2002) became one of the first organized efforts by a filmmaker to depict the bombings. Rosenbaum's film resonates with stories documenting the heroism of rescue workers and grief for the thousands of victims of the attacks. It collects the stories and footage of "nearly 30" independent filmmakers who happened to be close enough to turn their cameras toward the Trade Center attacks. Rosenbaum interviews each filmmaker, connecting the graphic, occasionally surreal, images of the destruction of the Towers with voice-over narration by the filmmakers. More independent documentaries appeared over the years, and more than sixty 9/11 independent films may be viewed for free.[1]

The award-winning thirty-four-minute television documentary *Twin Towers* (2002), directed by Bill Guttentag and Robert David Port, pioneered the films that focused on the rescue operations. The documentary profiles the New York Police Department's Emergency Services Unit located in the South Bronx. The first segment depicts the unit's activities prior to 9/11, and the second segment looks back on the unit's actions after the World Trade Center attacks, which claimed the lives of fourteen of the unit's twenty-three personnel. The filmmakers developed backstories

13

for some of the officers who died, including two brothers, by incorporating home movie footage and interviews with family and friends. The resulting short film remains one of the genre's most interesting and memorable, winning the 2003 Academy Award for Best Short Documentary.

A culture war quickly erupted between supporters and opponents of President George W. Bush, with both sides releasing partisan documentaries that attempted to sway public opinion. Filmmakers ventured into controversial areas like rendition, redaction, and waterboarding. Brian Trenchard Smith's *DC 9/11: Time of Crisis* (2003) became the first 9/11 fiction film to appear, a made-for-TV docudrama that evoked intense controversy during the 2004 presidential race. Written by conservative scriptwriter Lionel Chetwynd, Smith's film follows the 9/11 attacks from George W. Bush's (Timothy Bottoms) perspective immediately after the attacks, as the president sat with elementary school children, and ends with his impassioned speech on September 20, 2001. In a blend of documentary, docudrama, and partisan propaganda, Smith juxtaposes actual news footage of the Twin Towers and Pentagon attacks with reenactment of Bush's dramatic flights around the country on September 11, along with the comments he made. In Smith's film, Bush emerges as a superhero instantly assessing the gravity of the situation and taking decisive actions.

The Bush of *DC 9/11* demonstrates a policy distinct from that of the Clinton administration, scornfully promising to do much more than "fire a missile into an empty camp.... I want to inflict pain." Bush wants to "bring enough damage so they understand there is a new team here, a fundamental change in our policy." When an aide attempts to persuade him to remain in hiding, Bush snaps, "Try commander-in-chief. Whose present command is: Take the president home!" Democrats observed that Smith's film delivered a well-timed partisan plug for Bush's reelection campaign, while film critics berated the film for poor-quality production values as well as a blatantly pro-Bush perspective. James Lewis "J." Hoberman of the *Village Voice* labeled it "a shameless propaganda vehicle for our superstar President."[2]

On the other side of the debate, Michael Moore's *Fahrenheit 9/11* (2004) indicts the president for stealing the 2000 election, for frittering away much of his time vacationing, for secretly siding with Saudi Arabia because of family business dealings with Saudi prince Bandar, and for waging unjust wars in Afghanistan and Iraq. Moore focuses on a mother who lost her son in the Iraq war, expressing the grief many felt in the aftermath of 9/11. Moore depicts Bush as dumbfounded and inert upon learning about the hijackings, choosing to remain in a primary school classroom reading *Stories of a Goat* instead of immediately responding to the hijackings. The documentary asserts that a weak Bush, dazed and confused by the terrorist attacks, inwardly stalled for time while outwardly focusing on the children's story. Meanwhile, the Bush White House orchestrated a secret flight out of the United States for Osama bin Laden's large and very influential family despite the national grounding of all civilian air traffic over the country.

Moore exposes Bush's policies that openly favored Saudi Arabia, explaining at one point that Saudis own between 7 and 8 percent of the entire U.S. stock market. His film presents George W. Bush as a lightweight who allowed his obsession with invading Iraq to distract him from the far more serious threats to America posed by Osama bin Laden and al Qaeda. In doing so, Bush committed too few troops and resources to the war in Afghanistan, a theory that now looks appealing in light of current events. Ultimately, Moore's film charges Bush with stupidity, incompetence, indolence, and malfeasance.

Liberals like Roger Ebert lavished praise on Moore's film for its "realistic" depiction of George W. Bush. According to Ebert, Bush comes across in Moore's film "as a shallow, inarticulate man, simplistic in speech and inauthentic in manner." Ebert further charged that "the outrage and incredulity" in Moore's film "are an exhilarating response to Bush's determined repetition of the same stubborn sound bites."[3] The popularity of Moore's film, which by 2010 had grossed over $222 million with a production budget of only $6 million, helped assure the creation of even more films focused on the government's responses to terror.[4] While Moore's film pleased liberals, it outraged conservatives and elicited angry rebuttals. Michael Wilson's *Michael Moore Hates America* (2004) not only debunks Moore's movies but also attacks the filmmaker personally. Borrowing a trope from Moore's *Roger and Me* (1989), Wilson makes repeated unsuccessful attempts to interview Moore and characterizes Moore as hypocritical, elitist, and anti-American.

Of the independent *Fahrenheit 9/11* (2004) rebuttals, Alan Peterson's *FahrenHYPE 9/11: Unraveling the Truth About Fahrenheit 9/11 and Michael Moore* (2004) reached the largest audiences. Peterson also condemns Moore's film as well as Moore personally, charging him with belittling the threat posed by terrorists. Peterson's film casts most of the blame for the 9/11 attacks on former president Bill Clinton for his allegedly weak responses to terrorism during the 1990s. Peterson marshals several prominent conservatives in support of his perspective, including Dick Morris, Ann Coulter, Ed Koch, and David Frum, who emphasize the mortal danger posed by terrorists to American security. Former New York City mayor Ed Koch explains that "these people want to kill us," and that this danger justified Bush's actions in invading Afghanistan and Iraq and in supporting the Patriot Act as well as other antiterrorist initiatives.

FahrenHYPE 9/11 presents a point-by-point rebuttal of Moore's film, crediting President George W. Bush's policies with saving America from numerous horrendous terrorist acts with intelligence gathered under the Patriot Act. Dick Morris—former pollster for President Bill Clinton, former adviser to Senator Trent Lott, and one of the leaders of the Tea Party—who scripted *FahrenHYPE 9/11,* concludes in the film that the United States is a much better country than Moore allows: "If you lose faith in yourself and your own country, the United States, you've undermined the only consistent force for good in the world." All the rebuttals to *Fahrenheit 9/11* focus on attacking Moore rather than expressing grief for the victims.

Television Films and Documentaries

William Karel's French film *The World According to Bush,* or *Le Monde Selon Bush* (2004) characterizes President George W. Bush as a compliant tool of corporate interests. The documentary received a limited distribution in the United States and Canada, primarily in film festivals and art house theaters. Karel's film resonated with liberals and progressives who denigrated President Bush and suspected that Vice President Dick Cheney and other neoconservatives had manipulated a pliable and intellectually feeble president.

Daniel Sackheim's *Homeland Security* (2004) originated as the premiere installment of a television series that went nowhere. Sackheim's film stars Scott Glenn as Joe Johansen, a CIA officer, and Tom Skerritt as Admiral Theodore McKee, appointed director of the Office of Homeland Security after the 9/11 attacks. *Homeland Security* skillfully depicts a series of missed cues and close calls in the days leading up to 9/11, including a suspicious flight instructor noticing his pupil apparently intent on learning to aim a plane at a target, not land or take off at an airport. At the National Security

Agency someone notices a theme of repeating numbers nine and eleven, and in Germany an informant tells a CIA agent that Islamic agents "plan biggest operation ever ... big American cities." All of these leads, as everyone now knows, soon fizzle as intelligence agencies fail to anticipate and prevent the terrorist attacks. Sackheim's film characterizes American intelligence agents as brave, unselfish, genuinely good human beings instead of a collection of normal people possessing flaws as well as virtues. Dan Jewell noted that "no one argues that civil liberties should be trampled in the interest of security. No one mistreats prisoners or considers using torture to get information."[5] Unfortunately, this use of flat characters transforms a potentially interesting feature into a boring propaganda piece.

On December 4, 2005, the September 11 attacks inspired a Showtime miniseries titled *Sleeper Cell: The Enemy Is Here*. Its popularity prompted a second season in 2006 titled *Sleeper Cell: American Terror*. The shows depict a virulent underground Islamic terrorist cell in Los Angeles intent on inflicting mass casualties. The characters include Daren (Michael Ealy), an FBI Islamic double agent who has infiltrated the cell. Farik (Oded Fehr), who personifies Muslim fanaticism, serves as the leader of the al Qaeda–affiliated cell. Showtime broadcast the series for two seasons.

Sharon Dymmel's *The Heroes of Flight 93* (2005), a made-for-DVD low-budget offering, glorifies some of the passengers of the ill-fated flight, particularly Tom Burnett, Todd Beamer, Jerry McGlick, and Louis Nacke. The movie delves into the lives of the passengers, discovering a large number who were athletes or former military while presenting a strong evangelical Christian perspective on the tragedy, repeatedly asking and answering, "Where was God on September 11?" Dymmel suggests, "Anybody who wants to address this question of what happened on 9/11 has to have a world view that is robust enough to be able to make sense of that. Christianity can do that." The documentary points out that airline procedures mandated that flight attendants and other flight personnel cooperate with hijackers, yet this film depicts flight attendants as well as passengers resisting the hijackers. The documentary asks how much greater would the damage have been on 9/11 if some passengers had not fought back against the hijackers, causing them to crash the plane on the ground. "Without those heroes of Flight 93 the hijackers might have completed their mission." The film claims that the passengers of Flight 93 became the first counterattack against the 9/11 hijackers.

Not all 9/11 documentaries focus on President Bush. In 2006 a documentary seemingly attacked President Bill Clinton's efforts to combat al Qaeda during his administration. David L. Cunningham's made–for–ABC TV miniseries *The Path to 9/11* (2006) became ensnared by rumors that one scene depicted President Clinton's attempts to avenge the 1993 World Trade Center bombing on Osama bin Laden and al Qaeda prior to 9/11 as feeble and ineffective. Reportedly, Clinton contacted Robert Iger, Disney CEO (ABC's parent company), and demanded that the offending scene be cut, which ultimately occurred. However, the miniseries, intended for annual broadcast on 9/11 anniversaries, was never shown again, and despite considerable interest, ABC declined to release the series on DVD.[6]

Originally made for TV, Paul Greengrass's *United 93* (2006) became the first film released in mainstream theaters chronicling the 9/11 hijackings. Greengrass's film follows the hijacked United Flight 93 alledgedly aimed at the White House. The passengers revolt against the hijackers in an attempt to retake the plane. It never reaches its intended target, crashing in an empty field outside Shanksville, Pennsylvania, about 150 miles northwest of Washington, DC. The 9/11 Commission (through testimony, tapes of passengers' phone calls, and the flight data recorders recovered from the crash) determined that crew and passengers, alerted through phone calls to loved ones about the first attack on the Twin Towers, overpowered the hijackers. The commission concluded that the hijackers crashed the plane to keep the crew and passengers from gaining control.[7] Greengrass chooses a cinema verité style for his story. To give his film a documentary quality, he avoids creating backstories for the passengers or casting known actors, instead hiring actual flight attendants and other flight officials to play themselves. He uses handheld cameras and ambient, naturalistic images and sounds, and he juxtaposes shots of the inside of the aircraft with others from the National Air Traffic Control Center, a military command center, and regional air traffic control rooms. The film begins on the morning of September 11 as the four hijackers awake in their hotel room and undertake their morning prayers before departing for their designated flight, United Flight 93 from Dulles International Airport in Washington, DC, bound for Los Angeles. During the last act, passengers begin realizing that they must act against the hijackers to prevent the plane from being used as a weapon against an undisclosed target. Some reviewers and bloggers panned the film for its depiction of the hijackers as clean, devout Muslims rather than villainous characters.[8]

However, most reviewers praised it, and the film received numerous distinctions, including two Academy Award nominations, one for editing and one for Greengrass's directing.

Oliver Stone's *World Trade Center* (2006) focuses on the grief of thousands of innocent deaths and the rescue of two Port Authority police officers trapped in wreckage at Ground Zero. John McLoughlin (Nicolas Cage) and William A. Jimeno (Michael Peña) manage to hang onto life, desperately hoping to be discovered by rescue workers. Stone's film pleased some critics, like *Variety's* Brian Lowry, who credited Stone with "attempting to convey a macro vision of Sept. 11 through a micro lens." However, Lowry pointed out that these plot elements by their very nature "result in a claustrophobic film."[9] The dramatic rescue at the end conveys a theme of persistence and heroism in the face of terrorism. Despite the claustrophobia, Stone's film serves as an answer to terrorists: "We will survive!" *World Trade Center* looks and feels like a neonoir. When rescue workers finally free the protagonists

Scene still: *World Trade Center,* 2006. New York Port Authority policeman John McLoughlin (Nicolas Cage) lies wounded in the rubble of the collapsed World Trade Center on September 11, 2001. McLoughlin here symbolizes the shock and devastation that the attacks caused, and after his rescue he becomes redeemed and ready to face new threats should they arise. (Paramount Pictures / The Kobal Collection / Duhamel, Francois)

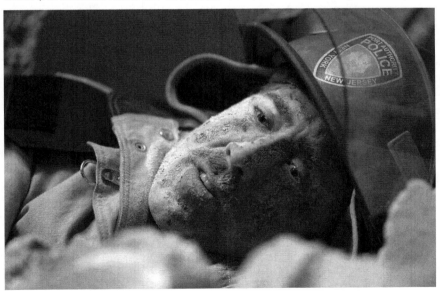

trapped under tons of steel and concrete, McLoughlin and Jimero symbolize the severe loss and helplessness felt after the 9/11 attacks. They function as nearly ideal post-9/11 protagonists, victims of domestic and foreign violence.

Conspiracy Theories

Conspiracy theories surround many dramatic events. U.S. examples include the Japanese bombing of Pearl Harbor (how much did Franklin Delano Roosevelt and his administration know about the attack in advance?), the assassination of John Fitzgerald Kennedy (was it a government operation?), and the bombing of the Alfred P. Murrah Federal Building in Oklahoma City (was it an inside job?). These events pale in comparison with 9/11, so it is no surprise that conspiracy theories about these attacks abound. Focusing on conspiracies serves as a distraction from the intense grief brought on by 9/11 and the wars that followed.

Eric Hufschmid's *Painful Deceptions* (2005) documents doubts about the official version of the events of 9/11 first recorded in his book *Painful Questions: An Analysis of the September 11 Attack,* outlining various 9/11 conspiracy theories. The film questions the account of Flight 77, the American Airlines flight that struck the Pentagon, observing, "It would take superhuman skills to fly so close to the ground at 400 MPH." In addition, it raises questions about the manner in which Tower I and Tower II of the World Trade Center collapsed into their own footprints, and even Building 7 that was never hit by a plane. Going beyond 9/11, Hufschmid produces evidence pointing to government involvement in the Oklahoma City bombing of 1995. At times, he seems to link Lee Harvey Oswald, Timothy McVeigh, and Mohammad Atta to a vast government conspiracy to dupe the public. He quotes David Porter in the *Orlando Sentinel* who states, "People are born trusting authority, so unless we discover that authorities often lie, we will believe the official sources of information. Therefore, whoever controls the official reports can control most people." He continues with an outraged tone of voice, repeatedly asking, "How can people get away with such obvious scams?" The answer, "because America is corrupt beyond your wildest dreams. There are lots of Americans willing to join these scams." As for the FBI, "They should put themselves on their Most Wanted List.'" In the end, what began with interesting theories ends with tiresome rants against a vast underground conspiracy pitting thousands of enlightened "conspiracy nuts" against the overwhelming power of the U.S. military.

Ray Nowosielski's *9/11: Press for Truth* (2006) attacks government responses to 9/11 from the perspective of the "Jersey Girls," composed of four 9/11 widows—Kristen Breitweiser, Patty Casazza, Lorie Van Auken, and Mindy Kleinberg—who become instrumental in questioning official government statements regarding 9/11. Their "press for truth," joined by many others, leads to the formation of the 9/11 Commission. With the help of Paul Thompson, author of the comprehensive *The Terror Timeline,* and an arsenal of media footage at his disposal, Nowosielski catalogs mounting frustrations with official accounts of 9/11 events and concludes that 9/11 was more than just a "failure of imagination."[10]

The majority of Indie 9/11 documentaries raise direct or indirect questions about the terrorist attacks. Some, including *Loose Change* (2005–2009) and *9/11: Press for Truth* (2006), rehash conspiracy theories involving government. *Loose Change,* a series of low-budget documentaries written and directed by Dylan Avery, charges that covert U.S. government agents bear responsibility for the September 11 attacks. He bases these claims on perceived anomalies in the collapse of Trade Center buildings and the Pentagon attack. The films received widespread attention after *Loose Change 2nd Edition* appeared on a Binghamton, New York, local television station, prompting selected theatrical releases in several cities. In 2007 Avery released yet another edition, which may be viewed in its entirety on the Internet.[11]

After the British thriller *V for Vendetta* (2006) appeared, some independent filmmakers realized that it served as a powerful yet disguised indictment of the British government's involvement in the war on terror and the Bush/Blair administrations' responses to 9/11, including unpopular wars and heightened domestic security. Several takeoffs of this film exist on YouTube, including *Vendetta 9/11; Vendetta: Past, Present, and Future; Remember, Remember, the 11th of September;* and *V for Vendetta Goes to Washington.* These shorts focus on the idea of 9/11 as a secret operation perpetrated by the Bush administration.

Conspiracy theory films reflect the views of a surprisingly large group of people. A 2006 Scripps Howard poll found that 36 percent of Americans believed the government had orchestrated the attacks, 16 percent said the World Trade Center had actually been destroyed by hidden bombs, and 12 percent said the Pentagon had been hit not by an airplane but by a missile.[12] Support of the 9/11 conspiracy theories appears to be growing. Members of Hollywood's establishment who believe the conspiracy theory include director David Lynch and actor Charlie Sheen. Lynch enraged and intrigued many during an interview in Holland in 2007 in which he questioned the official version and in a subsequent interview explained that "as far as 9/11 goes, there's things we saw that conjure questions and wondering—and something doesn't seem quite right. So it makes us wonder, and the next step is we need answers!"[13]

War on Terror

Petra Epperlein and Michael Tucker's *Gunner Palace* (2004) presented an early pro-U.S. perspective on the continuing combat operations in Iraq. The documentary follows members of the 213 Field Artillery operating out of a bombed-out palace formerly owned by Saddam Hussein. The squad goes on daily and nightly patrols around Baghdad in which it sometimes encounters combatants and bomb makers and at other times only local children or friendly neighbors. Epperlein and Tucker's film announces that the box office proceeds will be donated to families of fallen veterans of the war in Iraq. The film focuses on ten military personnel assigned to "Gunner Palace," celebrating their daily courage and focusing on them as people. The documentary pauses toward the end to remember fallen comrades like Lieutenant Ben Colgan, killed while trying to protect a bridge from a rocket-propelled grenade (RPG) attack.

Gunner Palace appeals directly to supporters of American troops in Iraq and demonizes insurrectionists as well as U.S. politicians. Roger Ebert concludes that the documentary "is not pro-war or anti-war. It is about American soldiers, mostly young, who are strangers in a strange land, trying to do their jobs and stay alive."[14] Epperlein and Tucker's documentary ends with one of the characters summarizing the film's message: "If you see any politicians be sure to let them know that while they're sitting around their dinner tables with their families talking about how hard the war is on them, we're here under attack nearly 24 hours a day, dodging RPGs and fighting not for a better Iraq, but just to stay alive."

In 2005 Joseph Costello released *The War Within,* one of the earliest feature films to depict the powerful emotions that may have motivated terrorists like the 9/11 attackers. It features Hassan (Ayad Akhtar), a brilliant young Pakistani engineer living in Paris who finds himself arrested, knocked out, and smuggled out of the country to Pakistan by American agents who falsely accuse him of membership in a terrorist cell. Hassan refuses to admit to this falsehood, subsequently enduring brutality and torture. The story picks up three years later as real terrorists smuggle a now angry and bitter Hassan to New York City as a real member of their sleeper cell. Here Hassan reunites with his best friend, Sayeed (Firdous Bamji), a successful engineer living in New Jersey with his wife and son. Still festering from his torture and wrongful imprisonment, Hassan becomes a dedicated terrorist who hates the United States, whereas Sayeed remains a loyal American citizen. The two Muslims embody the differences between extreme jihadists and mainstream secular Islamic Americans.

Hassan eventually breaks with all his former friends except for a jihadist who persuades him to create bombs with his engineering acumen and become a suicide bomber. The two jihadists set out in New York City to find an appropriate terror target, one of which is Grand Central Station. At one point when Hassan meets with the fellow terrorist in a strip club named Sinners, he objects to the sleazy surroundings. His friend explains, "It's good to taste the freedom that will kill them." Ironically, this same man displays cowardice in the final act, removing his suicide vest and leaving Hassan to sacrifice himself for the greater good of jihadism. Hassan, however, never forgot or forgave the brutal treatment given him as a prisoner by the United States and Pakistan during his abduction and torture. The onetime secular, congenial man transformed into a killer by hatred for his torturers and grief at his own suffering. Hassan's case raises serious questions about U.S. military practices and procedures during the war on terror. The film's well-crafted appearance, along with excellent performances by the principle actors, affords it a place among the better features about the war on terror.

Paul Greenwald's *Iraq for Sale: The War Profiteers* (2006) exposes the often chaotic practices of Blackwater and other private companies operating in Iraq for the U.S. military. In Greenwald's documentary, private companies avoid government oversight and the rule of law by virtue of their special exempt status. Greenwald interviews employees of companies including Halliburton, CACI, and KBR. One employee explains, "There's nothing but the money. There's no duty, honor, country among anyone at Halliburton and KBR." Greenwald shows how these corporations appoint retired senior military officers to their boards of directors to help secure lucrative government contracts. Another former employee explains that the acronym KBR stands for "Kill, Bag, and Replace people." He also exposes a "cost-plus" system by which civilian contractors receive their basic investment plus payment for their services. Whatever they spend, they receive, plus a generous profit, leaving them little incentive to save taxpayers money. This film predictably pleased progressives. Drew Tillman of the *Village Voice* opined, "For those who have let the war drift into the background noise of talking heads, *Iraq for Sale* is a much needed reminder of the criminal negligence of those who led the troops into this mess and those who have gotten rich off of it."[15]

Michael Winterbottom's *A Mighty Heart* (2007) presents a fictionalized account of events surrounding the kidnapping and murder of American journalist Daniel Pearl. Winterbottom, a celebrated English filmmaker, based his film on a book by Mariane Pearl, wife of Daniel Pearl. Angelina Jolie starred as Mariane. Brad Pitt served as producer on the project. Like the book, Winterbottom's film focuses on the search for Mariane's missing husband, *Wall Street Journal* reporter and bureau chief Daniel Pearl in Pakistan in 2002. Winterbottom focuses on the three-week interval between Pearl's disappearance and the release of a video of his grisly beheading at the hands of Khalid Sheikh Mohammad and other terrorists associated with al Qaeda. Eventually Mariane learns to cope with life, especially after the birth of her son, Adam. Winterbottom shot his film in India, Pakistan, and France, and it premiered at the Cannes Film Festival on May 21, 2007.

Francesco Lucente wrote, directed, and edited *Badland,* one of the commercially unsuccessful Iraq war films to arrive in 2007. Lucente's film seems strongly reminiscent of Terrence Malick's *Badlands,* the celebrated 1973 film about two fugitives in the North Dakota badlands. Lucente's film features Jerry (Jamie Draven), a dishonorably discharged Iraq war veteran who suffers an emotional meltdown; kills his pregnant wife, Nora (Vinessa Shaw), and their two little boys in Wyoming; and then goes on the run with his ten-year-old daughter, Celina (Grace Fulton). The pair eludes a nationwide manhunt, then settles in a small town after Jerry obtains a position as a short order cook in a local diner. Jerry endears himself to the attractive blonde owner, Ole (Chandra West), who invites him and Celina to move in with her. *Badland,* similar to *Badlands* premiered during armed conflicts, and both films resonate with wartime angst and depression. *Badlands* (1973) also features two fugitives, Kit Caruthers (Martin Sheen) and Holly Sargis (Sissy Spacek). Both couples consist of young men and underage girls, although Sargis was fifteen, whereas Celina is only ten, and Caruthers and Sargis are lovers. (Jerry and Celina, of course, are father and daughter.) However, Malick's film received outstanding reviews, whereas Lucente's opened to mixed reception. Critics faulted *Badland* for its length and other technical qualities, but *New York Times* critic Matt Zoller Seitz praised the film despite its flaws for Draven's guilt-laden performance, for the plot's unexpected twists, for the film's realism, and for "Mr. Lucente's primitivist sensibility, the likes of which hasn't been seen since Sam Fuller went to that great tabloid archive in the sky."[16] *Badland* ends after Jerry kills a cop (Glenn Jensen) who befriended him and goes on the run once again. He drives Celina to her aunt's house and orders her to leave so that he can continue his flight, but as he drives off, he turns around to take one last look and rams into a parked car. He staggers out, covered in blood and holding his pistol, and as Celina rushes toward him, she runs into the street, where a car smashes into her. Jerry rushes over to her lifeless body to the singing of the soundtrack: "You always kill the things you love." In the end, grief overwhelms all other emotions in this film. Although grief figures prominently in post-9/11 films, audiences stayed away from most of these guilt-laden movies, revealing the unpopularity of depictions of the two ongoing wars. *Badland,* produced in 2007 for an undisclosed amount, had earned only slightly more than $25,000 by 2010.[17]

In 2007 the Weinstein Company released *Grace Is Gone,* directed by James C. Strauss. The film depicts the traumatic impact of the death of a mother fighting in Iraq, Sergeant Grace Phillips (Dana Lynne Gilhooley), on her husband, Stanley (John Cusack), and their two young daughters, Heidi (Shelan O'Keefe) and Dawn (Gracie Bednarcyzk). When Stanley learns of Grace's death, he realizes he needs to tell his daughters and decides to take them on a fun-filled road trip to Enchanted Gardens, a family favorite amusement in Florida. Along the way they visit Stanley's brother John (Alessandro Nivola), who raises disturbing questions about the wars. When John learns about Grace's death, he demands that Stanley accept his wife's death and raise his family instead of running away. Eventually, Stanley comes to grips with his grief and finds the strength to tell his daughters.

Grief drives this film, as an American suburban family copes with the loss of its wife and mother. Thousands of real families whose sons, daughters, husbands, and wives never returned from the battlefields share this loss. The film touches viewers' hearts more than their minds. It makes no overt judgments about the war on terror but raises disturbing questions about wartime tragedy. Some critics objected to Stanley's long, tearful phone messages to Grace's recorded greeting on their answering machine. *New York Times* critic Stephen Holden argues that "it is perfectly plausible that Stanley would want to hear her voice now and again, but those heartfelt messages in which he vents his grief and sorrow are another matter."[18] This raises the question of the limits of sadness. At what point does grief become maudlin?

Gavin Hood's *Rendition* (2007) attacks the U.S. war on terror policy of kidnapping suspected terrorists, spiriting them to third world countries, and supervising their torture in foreign prisons. It stars Omar Metwally as Anwar El-Ibrahimi, an American citizen of Middle Eastern extraction who finds himself kidnapped while attending a conference abroad, then shipped secretly to a dismal prison in a far-off country and tortured under CIA supervision. Jake Gyllenhaal plays Douglas Freeman, the CIA station chief who supervises El-Ibrahimi's torture, until he becomes fed up with the violence and begins to suspect El-Ibrahimi's innocence. He asks a colleague, "In all the years you've been doing this, how often can you say that we've provided truly legitimate intelligence? Once? Twice? Ten times? Give me a number. Give me a pie chart. Anything, anything that outweighs the fact that if you torture one person you create ten, a hundred, a thousand new enemies."

Kimberly Pearce's *Stop-Loss* (2008) focuses on the U.S. policy of recalling soldiers against their will to serve in Afghanistan or Iraq after completing their tours of duty. Decorated Iraq veteran Sergeant Brandon King (Ryan Phillippe) returns to his hometown in Texas and attempts to adjust to civilian life. However, he discovers on the day before his enlistment ends that he must return to serve yet another tour in Iraq. When Brandon receives his orders, he confronts his commanding officer and shouts, "Fuck the President!" Arrested, he breaks away from the guards escorting him to the stockade, commandeers a jeep, and becomes a fugitive.

On the run, King inhabits a noirish world of sleazy motels and bars, until he finally accepts his fate and surrenders to authorities, resumes his military post, and accepts his redeployment in Iraq. Ultimately, his symbolic rebellion against the military's highly controversial stop-loss policy serves not as an antiwar act, because it falls short of condemning the war in Iraq, but as a protest against the stop-loss program, which remained in force until 2011, a decade after it had begun. Secretary of Defense Robert Gates finally ended the program in June 2010.[19] In 2008 Kathryn Bigelow released *The Hurt Locker,* an action/adventure film featuring three members of a U.S. bomb disposal operation in Iraq. Mark Boal, who was embedded with the unit during the early phases of the war in Iraq, wrote and coproduced this feature about a disposal unit stationed in Baghdad in 2004, a year after the U.S. war in Iraq began. Sergeant First Class Will James (Jeremy Renner), Sergeant J. T. Sanborn (Anthony Mackie), and Specialist Owen Eldridge (Brian Geraghty) face exciting and life-threatening situations on a daily basis as they defuse improvised explosive devices. James, who arrives when the company has only one month to go in its tour of duty, seems to enjoy his work, quoting Anglo-American author Christopher Hitchens's maxim that "war is a drug." He immediately rattles and perplexes his colleagues by assuming abnormal risks, including personally disarming dangerous explosive devices, tracking insurgents along back alleys, and slipping into the city after dark for some investigative work. His risk-taking behavior upsets his unit, especially after James accidentally shoots Eldridge.

Bigelow's film became the most critically acclaimed of all of the war on terror films thus far, receiving six Academy Awards nominations and winning for Best Picture. In fact, Bigelow's film tied with *Avatar,* directed by James Cameron (her ex-husband), for most Academy Award nominations, pitting wife against husband at awards time. Although it depicts violent combat as well as any action/adventure movie, Bigelow's film goes beyond the other war on terror films by focusing on the war's less attractive side—a dead Iraqi child's intestines wired into a bomb, an innocent Iraqi man forced to wear a suicide belt, and a supportive army psychologist who gets blown up. Blood and gore proliferate in this excellently crafted and acted movie. A far cry from the patriotic war films seen after World War II, *The Hurt Locker* became the most celebrated—and the grittiest—of the post-9/11 combat films focused on the war in Iraq or Afghanistan.

In 2010 Paul Greengrass released another seminal post-9/11 film, this time diving directly into the debate about the existence of weapons of mass destruction (WMDs) in Iraq after the 2003 coalition invasion. *Green Zone,* named for an area of hotels and palaces in Baghdad occupied by American forces, stars Matt Damon as Chief Warrant Officer Roy Miller, on assignment to find Saddam Hussein's hidden WMDs after the U.S.-led invasion of Iraq. Miller and his men scour site after site to find the concealed weapons but turn up empty-handed every time. Finally, he gets a break when an Iraqi called Freddy (Khalid Abdalla) informs him about a high-level meeting of Iraqi military taking place nearby. Miller and his men crash the meeting, catching a fleeting glimpse of Iraqi general Al Rawi and discovering a handwritten notebook Miller cannot translate.

Miller confides in CIA agent Martin Brown (Brendan Gleeson), who instantly realizes that the notebook contains the addresses of General Al Rawi's safehouses. At this point Special U.S. Agent Clark Poundstone (Greg Kinnear) contacts Miller and offers him a job with his military team. Miller joins with Brown to locate General Al Rawi after they discover that he knows about the WMDs. Meanwhile, Poundstone engineers a decree by Paul Bremer, appointed by American forces to administer Iraq, to disband the Iraqi army and outlaw the Baath Party that governed Iraq until the American invasion. Poundstone knew all along that the WMDs no longer existed in Iraq. According to Greengrass's film, the Bush administration also knew that WMDs did not exist but spread the rumor of their existence in order to justify the invasion of Iraq. Because of this charge, Roger Ebert predicted that Greengrass's film "will no doubt be under fire from those who are still defending the fabricated intelligence we used as an excuse to invade Iraq." Despite the political elements, or perhaps because of them, Ebert concludes that "this is one hell of a thriller."[20] Ebert's predictions about conservative backlash against the film proved well grounded. One critic blasted *Green Zone* as "an exercise in commercial cowardice masquerading as a thriller about political bravery."[21]

Another film that raised disturbing questions about the war in Iraq premiered in 2007. Brian De Palma's *Redacted* consists of a montage of short pieces that ultimately reveal the brutal rape and murder of a fourteen-year-old Iraqi girl by U.S. soldiers. De Palma's film was inspired by a real-life rape and murder by U.S. soldiers that occurred in 2003. It raises disturbing questions about the role the U.S. military plays in an occupied country such as Iraq.

The spate of thrillers set in Iraq and Afghanistan, as well as in the United States, while U.S. forces still engage with hostilities in both countries runs contrary to filmmakers' previous reticence to depict wars currently being waged. Both *Rendition* and *Redacted* performed disappointingly at the box office, as did *The Kite Runner* (2007), which happens to be set in Afghanistan but does not depict the war. Perhaps Hollywood should have adhered to the old maxim "Never depict wars still being fought."[22] Even *Green Zone,* one of the most ambitions examples of "American guilt" films about the war on terror, had barely recovered its production budget during its first few months, a disappointing return on investment compared with the massive returns earned by such films as *Spider-Man* (2002), *Twilight* (2008, 2010), and *Avatar* (2009).

Satire

Even though direct depictions of the 9/11 terrorist attacks and the wars that followed still appear taboo, these events have already inspired some notable satires. Trey Parker's *Team America: World Police* (2004) constitutes the best known of these. Parker's film satirizes U.S. geopolitical hubris in the war on terror. The film (cowritten by Matt Stone and Pam Brady) deliberately aims its satire toward the Bush/Cheney war on terror as well as political positions on terrorism taken by both left and right. The film's cast consists entirely of puppets, except for two real cats and a real cockroach. The puppetry adds to the comedic atmosphere as Arab terrorists possessing suitcase nuclear bombs attempt to destroy as much of the United States as possible in a massive attack that will be "a thousand times worse than 9/11." A team of counterterrorists recruits Gary Johnson, a Broadway actor, to infiltrate a jihadist terrorist cell. He successfully infiltrates the group, even though he speaks American English, and he convinces the jihadists that he is one of them through his acting abilities alone. Eventually, North Korean dictator Kim Jong-Il, the mastermind behind the terrorists, plans a cataclysmic worldwide attack using terrorists with suitcase nuclear bombs manufactured by North Korea, after which he expects to become world dictator. Kim Jong-Il enlists the support of the Film Actor's Guild and satirizes Hollywood personalities like Tim Robbins, Susan Sarandon, and Matt Damon. This film became a minor comedic gem.

Joshua Seftel bitingly satirizes the wars in Iraq and Afghanistan in his 2008 melodrama *War, Inc.* Seftel cast John Cusack as Brand Hauser, a high-level assassin hired by the Viceroy (Dan Aykroyd), a former U.S. vice president who administers Turaqistan, a Central Asian republic, for Tamerlane, a powerful multinational corporation apparently named after the fourteenth-century Turkic-Mongol conqueror of Central Asia. In an example of outsourcing and an indication of how much Seftel reveres U.S. corporations, the Tamerlane Company secretly controls the nation of Turaqistan through the Viceroy. Seftel's black comedy intensifies after Hauser arrives in the nation's capital, the Golden City, and meets his secret contact, Marsha Dillon (Joan Cusack). The city is awash in chaos as tanks with sponsor decals patrol streets that resonate periodically with bomb blasts and missile strikes, an obvious reference to occupied cities like Baghdad and Kabul. Hauser encounters left-wing reporter Natalie Hegalhuzen (Marisa Tomei), whom he immediately attempts to seduce over drinks and later saves from being kidnapped.

In a nod to 1960s television comedic spy spoofs like *Get Smart* and *I Spy,* Hauser receives his top-secret orders (and the obligatory attaché case full of cash) in a secret room located underneath the local Popeye Chicken restaurant. The Viceroy's words seem to come from a giant television screen playing a video of the heads of prominent people like Donald Trump, Ronald Reagan, and Arnold Schwarzenegger. The Viceroy appears to be modeled on the Wizard in *The Wizard of Oz,* and Seftel apparently resents U.S. hegemonic interests in the Islamic world. As a final and fitting blow to the Viceroy's disdain for legalities, a heat-seeking missile launches toward Hauser's fleeing aircraft. Seftel implies that Hauser and the United States will not escape unharmed after armed intervention into other nations' affairs.

In 2009 Grant Heslov released *The Men Who Stare at Goats,* another war on terror satire. The film stars George Clooney as Lyn Skip Cassady, an army officer who graduates from the army's first "New Earth Army of Jedi Knights," who learn to cultivate psychic "superpowers." Cassady embarks on his first assignment to assist in finding kidnapped officers. The mission quickly loses focus after Cassady and two associates become embroiled in the infamous Battle of Ramadi, in which two rival security organizations attacked one another in a gunfight, each blaming the other for starting it.

The government creates a secret training base called "Goat Lab" at Fort Bragg Army Base. Soon goats from Central America arrive, their vocal cords surgically removed to avoid detection on the military base. The camp trainees attempt to stop the goats' hearts through mental power alone. After many attempts Cassady finally topples a goat with his mental powers. Years later, during the Iraq war, Cassady and journalist Bob Wilton (Ewan McGregor) embark on a mission to find a secret base in Iraq. Within the base, they discover people undergoing torture by being subjected to high-pitched sounds and flashing images.

Determined to free the prisoners, the trainees spike the town's egg and water supply with LSD, which causes a riot of insanity. They release the victims of a "psyops" barracks, allowing for a massive escape from the prison. The film ends with Bob Wilton's voice saying, "Now, more than ever, we need to be all that we can be. Now, more than ever, we need the Jedi." Then he rushes across his office floor, flings himself at the wall, and slips effortlessly through the seemingly solid wall, demonstrating that he has achieved the Jedi warrior ideal of mind over matter and has become superpowerful. *The Men Who Stare at Goats* comes closest to an outright antiwar satire, but it contains enough truth to make its humor disturbing. In fact, the federal government's Star Gate Project trained personnel and researched psychic abilities for military use for many years. The project was eventually disbanded, but it provides a tantalizing clue to the connections between this comedy and real U.S. policies.[23]

* * *

Virtually all of the depictions of the war on terror appear sad, bitter, negative, or ironic and often contain criticism of U.S. foreign and military policies. They resonate with sadness, grief, anger, and rage. Few pro-war features exist. The war on terror inaugurated a new and growing cycle of films depicting military and civilian aspects of the wars in Afghanistan and Iraq. Responses to these wars, although commercially unpopular, reflect ongoing opposition and cynicism about these conflicts. As public opinion darkens about these wars, other filmmakers may be tempted to create more nuanced or outright antiwar depictions. The direct film and television responses to 9/11 and the war on terror divide between those that supported the Bush administration's war on terror and those that opposed the war. Predictably, liberals and progressives questioned and attacked the invasions of Afghanistan and Iraq, while conservatives supported those wars and the Bush administration's antiterrorism policies. President Barack Obama officially dropped the war on terror label after the 2008 election, but media still use the term, and the wars in Afghanistan and Iraq continue to vex the Obama administration. The campaign promised to gradually withdraw American troops from these troubled nations, but once in power, Obama chose not to disengage immediately. Ten years after the terrorist attacks, the war on terror continues to rage on several fronts.

Grief serves as the overarching emotion of many of these films, including grief for the victims of the World Trade Center attacks (*World Trade*

Center), for the victims of the ill-fated United Flight 93 (*United 93*), for civilian victims following the Battle of Fallujah (*Badland*), for a raped girl and murdered Iraqi family in Haditha (*Redacted*), for those abducted and tortured by American intelligence agents (*Rendition*), for those killed attempting to defuse explosives in Iraq (*The Hurt Locker*), for the families of those who died on the battlefields (*Grace Is Gone*), and for the people of Iraq (*Green Zone*). Grief for the victims of the terrorist attacks and the war on terror continue to find abundant expression in Hollywood movies.

CHAPTER THREE

Horror

Horror serves as one of the hallmarks of the post-9/11 film movement not only as a genre but also as a powerful emotion. Charles Darwin observed that if we perceive someone who offends us as "quite insignificant, we experience merely disdain or contempt. If, on the other hand, he is all-powerful, then hatred passes into terror."[1] Terror and horror both describe reactions to offensive actions, including torture and murder. Horror, according to the dictionary, means

1. An intense, painful feeling of repugnance and fear.
2. Intense dislike; abhorrence.
3. A cause of horror.
4. *Informal*: Something unpleasant, ugly, or disagreeable.[2]

Horror's "intense dislike; abhorrence" closely approaches Darwin's "distain or contempt," linking horror with fear and with repugnance and contempt, as well as with the violence and torture that constitute the hallmarks of horror films.

Although enjoying a recent surge of popularity, horror in literature dates back at least to the eleventh-century Anglo-Saxon epic poem *Beowulf*, which depicts fierce monsters and brave heroes locked in extraordinary, often horrific struggles. Like many mythological epics, *Beowulf* features a warrior hero. Beowulf encounters a dragon monster named Grendel. After Beowulf fights and finally kills Grendel, he must overcome Grendel's even more powerful mother. This plot device of having the hero slay one horrible monster only to discover an even deadlier creature yet to slay recurs in sci-fi and horror films today.

Horror serves as an integral element of tragedy. Aristotle famously defined tragedy in *Poetics* as "a form of drama exciting the emotions of pity and fear."[3] Some translations substitute "terror" for "fear." The horror in tragedy becomes apparent during the final scenes of both *Hamlet* and *Macbeth* in which the stages become littered with dead, butchered characters. Horror also permeates the Gothic literature that arose in the early nineteenth century, fueled by fears of industrialization and nostalgia for a rapidly fading rural past. Gothic fiction, epitomized in the United States by the works of Edgar Allan Poe and in Britain by the works of Mary Wollstonecraft Shelley (*Frankenstein,* 1818), Lord Byron (*The Giaouri,* 1813), John Keats ("La Belle Dame Sans Merci," 1819), and Samuel Taylor Coleridge ("Cristabel," 1791–1800), features psychological and physiological terror within gloomy castles and haunted houses, filled with an abundance of death, decay, madness, and hereditary curses. Popular Gothic fictional characters include tyrants, bandits, maniacs, femmes fatales, magicians, vampires, werewolves, monsters, and demons.

Poe (1809–1849) inspired numerous horror films, many directed by Roger Corman and starring Vincent Price. Corman directed the following Poe feature films:

- *House of Usher* (1960)
- *The Pit and the Pendulum* (1961)
- *Tales of Terror* (1962)
- *The Raven* (1963)
- *The Masque of the Red Death* (1964)
- *The Tomb of Ligeia* (1965)

Poe's writings resonate with contemporary filmmakers because of his obsession with the themes of death, decomposition, premature burial, reanimation of the dead, and mourning.[4] In the post-9/11 era, revived Poe-inspired movies include *House of Usher* (2006) and *The Pit and the Pendulum* (2009).

Horror appears throughout literature and film. As its popularity increases, critics begin to categorize and analyze this literary device. Isabela Christina Pinedo identified five characteristics of postmodern horror:

- a violent disruption of the everyday world
- transgressions and violation of boundaries

- questioning of the validity of rationality
- repudiation of narrative closure
- a bound experience of fear, which provides entertainment as long as audiences realize they are in no immediate danger

According to Pinedo, each of these characteristics changes with the genre. Modern-day horror now also includes the following:

- abandonment of a normal world
- lack of boundaries
- the irrational and nihilistic viewed as rational
- refusal of closure
- lack of comic relief
- very little insider knowledge
- dark visual tone[5]

Psychologist Susan Burggraf analyzed the elements of horror that audiences find appealing. She discovered a convergence of social theories, each of which describes part of the appeal of horror. *Relief theory* suggests that audiences enjoy horror films most at the end when they experience a profound sense of relief that the violence and pain did not occur to them personally. Because they identify with victims, audiences feel "empathic distress," which results in aesthetic pain and discomfort. Once the film ends, these feelings transform into pleasant sensations, a bit like the delicious taste of water to a severely dehydrated person. By contrast, *continuous reward theory* holds that audiences experience pleasurable feelings throughout the movies because "excitation transfer" substitutes exciting, pleasurable feelings for unpleasant, horrible ones. Finally, *arousal theory* holds that fear causes arousal, resulting in the "snuggle effect," meaning people desire greater closeness and intimacy in the face of horror, which makes horror films good "dating vehicles." Although some researchers believe that horror movies result in "catharsis" of unpleasant emotions, Burggraf did think that people possess sufficiently high levels of fright and disgust to need or desire catharsis.[6] Burggraf published her analysis in 2000, prior to the effects of 9/11 on the public. The terrorist attacks on the World Trade Center and the Pentagon and the war on terror created not only fear and disgust but also, according to some scholars, deep-seated and persistent cultural trauma.[7]

The events of 9/11 served as a perfect catalyst for horror films because of the extreme shock, violence, and nature of the attacks. The American Movie Channel's Web site explains, "Horror films effectively center on the dark side of life, the forbidden, and strange and alarming events. They deal with our most primal nature and its fears: our nightmares, our vulnerability, our alienation, our revulsions, our terror of the unknown, our fear of death and dismemberment, loss of identity, or fear of sexuality."[8] September 11, 2001, flooded media with images from "the dark side of life," creating a fertile environment for horror movies.

Early Horror Films

Horror films date back to German Expressionist classics like *The Cabinet of Dr. Caligari* (1919), *Nosferatu* (1922), and *Metropolis* (1927) and remained popular throughout the following decades. The horror genre includes such classics as

- *Frankenstein* (1931)
- *M* (1931)
- *King Kong* (1933)
- *Bride of Frankenstein* (1935)
- *The Hound of the Baskervilles* (1939)
- *Invasion of the Body Snatchers* (1956)
- *Psycho* (1960)
- *The Birds* (1963)
- *Rosemary's Baby* (1968)
- *Night of the Living Dead* (1968)
- *The Exorcist* (1973)
- *Halloween* (1978)
- *Alien* (1979)
- *The Shining* (1980)
- *Friday the 13th* (1980–2009)
- *Nightmare on Elm Street* (1984)

In 1999 Edwardo Sanchez and Daniel Myrick released *The Blair Witch Project,* a faux documentary chronicling a group of three young filmmakers: Heather (Heather Donahue), Josh (Joshua Leonard), and Mike (Michael

Williams). They embark on a hike through a dense forest to document evidence of a legendary witch, called the Blair Witch, who allegedly haunts a wilderness region in the Black Hills of Burkittsville, Maryland. They find themselves wandering in circles while someone or something torments them with strange noises and leaves primitive totems made from wood, stone, and wire. Josh disappears, leaving behind a bundle made of part of his shirt containing a bloody tongue and human teeth. Mike and Heather discover an abandoned house, where they hear Josh calling for help but fail to locate him. The two suddenly cease talking, and Heather's camera falls to the ground, still filming. They die at the end, but the killer never appears.

The Blair Witch Project became an instant hit with horror audiences, despite the film's amateurish production values. As Roger Ebert observed, Sanchez and Myrick's film appeals to audiences' most basic fears of natural phenomena like night, rain, primitive totems, and blurred sounds. It does not rely on special effects except the primitive, amateurish footage, which Ebert called "a celebration of rock-bottom production values."[9] Despite its obvious effectiveness as a horror film, audiences witness no villain or graphic violence. The film exudes vast amounts of guilt, however, especially the scene in which Heather records an apology to her parents and her friends' parents for being naïve and pigheaded. She explains contritely that "I am so sorry! Because it was my fault. I was the one who brought them here. I was the one that said 'keep going south.' I was the one who said that we were not lost. It was my fault, because it was my project. I am so scared! I don't know what's out there. We are going to die out here! I am so scared!"

The classic horror films' guilt-laden obsession with selfish or inappropriate behavior and reliance on graphic violence seem tame, however, compared to the violence and guilt found in post-9/11 horror films.

Post-9/11 Horror

The contrast between pre-9/11 and post-9/11 horror films becomes clear when one considers examples from both periods. A comparison of *The Blair Witch Project* (1999) with *The Hills Have Eyes* (2006) and *The Last House on the Left* (2009) reveals significant differences as well as similarities. All three films are set in a wilderness. But *The Blair Witch Project* features a single, slightly whimsical witch who enjoys terrorizing through construction of small piles of stones and other natural signs, whereas in the others entire gangs mutilate and kill innocent victims. Compared with the post-9/11 films, *The Blair Witch Project* appears tame and almost naïve. In all these films, death awaits those who venture into forbidden territory or travel to lonely places.

In 2003 Hollywood's reprisal of two 1980s horror classics, *Nightmare on Elm Street* and *Friday the 13th,* earned huge profits at the box office. The original version of *Nightmare on Elm Street* (1984), which cost $1.8 million to produce, earned over $25 million in the U.S. market alone.[10] *Friday the 13th* (1980) earned nearly $100 million on a budget of $550,000 in the series premiere, and by the fall of 2009 the latest episode of *Friday the 13th,* released in February 2009, surpassed all others at the box office, garnering $156 million on a budget of $19 million.[11] *Freddy vs. Jason* (2009), a repulsive but at times unintentionally humorous parody of 1980s horror icons Freddy Krueger and Jason Voorhees, garnered nearly $115 million with a production budget of $30 million, demonstrating the renewed popularity of the horror genre after 9/11.[12]

The continued fascination with the horror genre after 9/11 resulted in a proliferation of films and in many cases their promotion from B-budget into A-budget films. Instead of unknown actors and directors, horror films now command excellent directors and talented performers. Notable horror films released during the last few years include *The Texas Chainsaw Massacre* (2003, 2006), *Hostel* (2004), *The Wicker Man* (2006), *Snakes on a Plane* (2006), and *The Last House on the Left* (2009). These films are reminiscent of earlier horror classics, such as *Them!* (1954) and *Invasion of the Body Snatchers* (1956), that reflected cold war fears of atomic weapons and communism. Today's films reflect paranoia about terrorists and antiterrorists in lieu of fear about the Soviet Union and communist sympathizers, but they continue to employ fear to attract audiences.

After 9/11 filmmakers resurrected a number of horror classics from the past, including *The Ring* (2002), *The Texas Chainsaw Massacre* (2003), *The Fog* (2005), *The Wicker Man* (2006), and *The Hills Have Eyes* (2006). For the first time, notable directors like Peter Jackson, Michael Bay, and Neil LaBute contributed to this genre. In these films the shocking ravages of terrorism and war transform into microcosms of individuals and families attacked by sinister forces intent upon murder and mayhem. Critic L. Vincent Poupard observed that horror fans notice that "many of their favorite horror movies have become darker and much more brutal since 9/11," and that the causes of these changes include the powerful violent images that flooded the news media during and after 9/11 and the fact that during wars horror films become more violent and graphic.[13]

Gore Verbinski's *The Ring* (2002) became one of the first horror films released after 9/11. This plot owes a debt to David Cronenberg's *Video-drome* (1983), which features a diabolical videotape. In *The Ring* Naomi Watts plays Rachel Keller, a young newspaper reporter who receives a mysterious tape. She spends seven days desperately attempting to unlock the tape's mysteries, assisted by her former boyfriend Noah (Martin Henderson) and their young son, Aidan (David Dorfman). Daveigh Chase plays Samara Morgan, a witch child who created the tape, which executes victims supernaturally. Samara convinces Rachel and Aidan to duplicate the tape and give it to others, passing along its fatal curse to countless future victims. In 2005 Hideo Nakata released a sequel, *The Ring 2*, also starring Watts, Henderson, and Dorfman. Nakata's sequel takes up where Verbinski's left off, with Samara wreaking death and destruction after victims view the cursed tape. *The Ring* films follow a familiar pattern, with a focus on technology united with supernatural forces. Samara's "snuff tape" brims with shocking images of her own mother murdering her by suffocation. The tape's visuals show the influence of Salvador Dalí and other surrealists, which seems appropriate for the sadistic horror committed by Samara. In these films, the viral tapes may symbolize terrorist suicide tapes, suggesting that evil elements may employ technology for their own ends.

Rupert Wainwright's *The Fog* (2005), a remake of a 1980 John Carpenter classic of the same name, depicts a supernatural fog that engulfs the small Pacific Northwest island village of Antonio, killing, maiming, burning, and perpetrating chaos and mayhem. The fog contains ghosts from a nineteenth-century shipwreck and reanimates the dead. The punishing fog enacts retribution for actions perpetrated by the town's founding fathers in 1871 when they seized a floundering schooner carrying wealthy lepers and then robbed and killed them. The lepers' ghosts return to exact vengeance upon the community. Interestingly, reviewers and audiences alike panned *The Fog* for not frightening them enough. One lamented, "Wainwright fills the screen with dry ice 'till it looks like the Top Of The Pops studio circa 1977, but the effect just isn't scary."[14]

Eli Roth's *Hostel* (2005), coproduced by Quentin Tarantino, features a secret organization named Elite Hunting that recruits and delivers unwit-

Scene still: *Hostel,* 2005. The Butcher (Josef Bradna) ponders a severed hand as he prepares to torture and dismember Josh (Derek Richardson) in an abandoned warehouse in Slovakia. This client paid Elite Hunting handsomely to abuse and murder innocent victims. This movie combines sexual promiscuity with graphic torture scenes in an example of "torture porn," a genre that became popular after 9/11. (Photographer Rico Torres; Hostel LLC / Lions Gate Films / The Kobal Collection)

ting victims to clients willing to pay dearly for their torture and murder. The film begins on a hedonistic note. Three young men hitchhiking, smoking pot, and womanizing their way through Europe meet a friendly stranger named Alex (Lubomir Bukovy) in Amsterdam after a late-night visit to a local brothel winds up getting them locked out of their hostel. Alex tells them of a wonderful hostel just outside Bratislava, Slovakia, frequented by gorgeous young women eager to have sex with tourists like them. "They hear your accent and they fuck you." Because of the war in the Balkans, he explains, local men remain in short supply, so the women go crazy for foreigners. The three, Paxton (Jay Hernandez), Josh (Derek Richardson), and Oli (Eythor Gudjonsson), eagerly take the bait and journey to eastern Europe in search of the ultimate sexual adventure.

As promised, the men meet beautiful Natalya (Barbara Nedeljakova) and Svetlana (Jana Kaberabkova) at the hostel. They invite the men to join them in a sauna full of scantily clad women, then on to a local disco, where they quickly bond. The men feel as though they have been transported to paradise, but it quickly becomes a fool's paradise made especially to lure them into a hellish torture chamber, from which only Paxton escapes. In some savage acts of vengeance, Paxton kills a sadist caught in the act of gouging a young girl's eyes out, runs down and kills the accomplice women with a car, then executes the "Dutch Businessman" (Jan Vlasak), one of the Elite Hunting clients and the film's principal villain. *Hostel* serves as a cautionary tale by meting out severe punishment to youthful characters who indulge in sex and drugs. Sex, drugs, and rock and roll may appear fun, but films like *Hostel* remind youthful audiences that "the wages of sin is death." *Hostel* forms part of a post-9/11 cycle of films that critics dubbed "torture porn." David Edelstein suggested that one reason for their current popularity was that post-9/11 Americans became engaged in a national debate about the ethics and efficacy of the use of torture for prisoner interrogation.[15]

In 2005 Rob Zombie released *The Devil's Rejects,* a sequel to his 2003 *House of 1,000 Corpses.* Zombie's film features the Firefly family, a group of sadistic and venal serial killers who reputedly kill one thousand strangers, thereby instigating a massive manhunt by Texas police officers. The film opens with the Texas State Police launching a massive raid against a backwoods farm inhabited by the Firefly family. One Firefly son and several deputies die in the shootout, with the police capturing Mamma Firefly (Leslie Easterbrook) but allowing Otis (Bill Moseley) and Baby (Sheri Moon Zombie) to escape through a storm drain. Baby and Otis seek help from their mentor, Captain Spaulding (Sid Haig), a diabolical "clown" figure, and other family members, who take two innocent families hostage in a remote motel, abusing and murdering them for pleasure.

The Devil's Rejects raised the bar for horror films, inspiring positive reviews from notable critics like Roger Ebert, who both damned and praised the film, calling it "a gaudy vomitorium of a movie, violent, nauseating and really a pretty good example of its genre." Ebert further explained, "If you are a hardened horror movie fan capable of appreciating skill and wit in the service of the deliberately disgusting, *The Devil's Rejects* may exercise a certain strange charm. However, if you're the kind of fan who looks away the minute a scene … gets icky, here is a movie to see with blinders on, because it starts at icky and descends relentlessly through depraved and nauseating to the embrace of road kill."[16]

In 2005 Showtime released a one-hour film in its Masters of Horror series titled *Homecoming*. This film overtly connects horror with the war on terror. Directed by Joe Dante, the plot reanimates dead veterans of the wars in Afghanistan and Iraq. Jon Tenney stars as David Murch, a political consultant for President George W. Bush, who is running for reelection. Murch remarks on television to a Gold Star Mother for Peace (a stand-in for Cindy Sheehan, founder of an antiwar organization), "If I had one wish, I would wish that your son would come back" so that he could assure the American people about the vital importance of the war on terror. Her dead son does return, along with hundreds of other casualties, now transformed into zombies. The zombies demand to vote in the election so that they can register their disapproval of the wars. Even though they earn the right to vote, their votes fail to matter because the election is stolen by Republicans and Bush is reelected. At that point, thousands of dead vets from earlier wars return and take over the capital. The government flees into exile as dead veterans of America's wars place the country on a path for peace.

Dante included a blonde, aggressive, right-wing pundit named Jane Cleaver (Thea Gill), a stand in for Ann Coulter; a Karl Rove–like official named Kurt Rand (Robert Picardo); and assorted other conservative characters. By burlesquing conservatives, Dante's film comes closest to expressing a liberal perspective toward the war on terror, one that makes a direct antiwar statement. If anyone doubts the connection between wars and horror films, let them watch *Homecoming* (2005).

Neil LaBute's *The Wicker Man* (2006), remade from a 1973 low-budget British horror film, chronicles the exploits of a neopagan cult living on the island of Sommersile. LaBute's earlier film, *Your Friends and Neighbors* (1998), depicts not horror but conflicted, promiscuous relationships. The only horror exhibited lies in the treacherous relationships in which individuals become involved. In LaBute's 2006 film, however, horror intrudes and casts a pall on the film's events. *The Wicker Man* features Patrolman Edward Malus (Nicolas Cage), who travels to the private island in Puget Sound at the request of Willow (Kate Beahan), his former fiancée who disappeared years earlier and has now resurfaced. Malus learns from Willow, now Sister Willow, of her (their?) young daughter Rowan's (Erika-Shaye Gair) disappearance. Willow suggests that the community might be planning to sacrifice Rowan in a harvest ritual. Malus begins his investigation, hampered by the strange customs of this matriarchal community that considers males as little more than "phalluses" to be used for baby production. He eventually finds Rowan, but he, not she, becomes the intended sacrificial victim. The seemingly peaceful townspeople break his legs and then bind him inside a huge wicker statue of a man. At that point they pour honey all over him as hundreds of bees land on his face and hands. Eventually, they set fire to the structure, finally killing the tortured Malus.

In LaBute's film pagans symbolize Islamic militants, but their zealousness proves no less pernicious. James Rocchi in his review asked, "What's the difference between a murder to appease the harvest gods, a suicide bombing in the name of Allah, and shooting a doctor who performs abortions in the name of Jesus? How can rational civilizations best set themselves against irrational ones?"[17] The notion of religious zealots willing to murder innocent victims for religious purposes evokes 9/11 terrorism.

In 2006 Jonathan Liebesman updated the 1974 classic *The Texas Chainsaw Massacre.* Liebesman's film takes place in a lonely and foreboding desert location in 1969, the height of the Vietnam War. The film begins with the closing of the local slaughterhouse, the last remaining business in the tiny hamlet. Thomas "Leatherface" Hewett (Andrew Bryniarski), a deranged and disfigured employee, bludgeons the foreman to death with a large mallet upon learning about the business closure. Next, his deranged uncle Charley Hewett (R. Lee Ermey) murders the sheriff, who was about to arrest Leatherface. Uncle Charley then assumes the identity of the murdered Sheriff Hoyt. At that point a jeep crashes nearby, delivering up four young victims: two brothers, Dean (Taylor Handley) and Bailey (Diora Baird), and their girlfriends. One of the brothers intended to ship out to the Vietnam War, while the other planned to flee to Mexico. First, a biker woman attacks them, and then Charley kills her. Charley then captures and imprisons the four, and he and Leatherface commence torturing and cannibalizing their victims. Although driven to heroism by their desperate circumstances, none of the characters escapes the cannibals alive. The film's epilogue provides a historical context for the violence by explaining that "from 1969 to 1973 the Hewett family murdered 33 people across the state of Texas. To this day their killing spree is universally regarded as one of the most notorious and sadistic crimes in the annals of American history." This film amply qualifies as torture porn, a popular new genre in the United States since 9/11.

Alexandre Aja's *The Hills Have Eyes* (2006) epitomizes the remade 1970s horror films. Aja remade Wes Craven's 1977 classic with post-9/11 sensibilities. Here zombielike mutants, spawned by decades of atomic testing, attack the naïve Carter family vacationing in a remote New Mexico desert. Surrounded by images of decay and chaos, audiences witness the rape and murder of women, kidnapping of an infant, and burning to death of the family's patriarch, Papa Bob (Dan Boyd). The film never rises above cliché, however, as weird noises accompany the Carters with each exposure to the camera. Bobby, Bob's youngest son, repeatedly charges through the desert following one of the family's two German shepherd dogs, who run off barking uncontrollably. Eventually, the family discovers the dogs' bodies.

The Carter family functions, in the words of one critic, as "a microcosm of post-9/11 Yanks."[18] The Carters serve as ideal victims of the mutants. Symbolic of the typical American family, they appear incredibly naïve in the face of danger. First, they stop at a sleazy gas station and accept some improbable shortcut when there is only one highway. Next, they display disunity, making additional serious mistakes. Divided, they become easy victims of the mutants, who attack and kill most of them. Doug Bukowski (Aaron Stanford), not an original Carter but one who married into the Carter family, finally destroys the nasty villains after shedding his liberal ideology and accepting the role of ruthless warrior by "killing every one" of them. The message for post-9/11 audiences suggests that only raw military power, ruthlessly executed, can save America from chaos and violence. Peace can arrive only after every mutant (terrorist) dies.

In post-9/11 Hollywood, threats to security appear from a variety of fronts. Stephen Hopkins's *The Reaping* (2007) exemplifies the genre of post-9/11 apocalyptic thrillers in his film, which stars Hilary Swank as Katherine Winter, a university professor and debunker of the supernatural. She soon finds herself investigating strange events including a river that turns blood-red, frogs falling from the sky, and animals acting strangely, similar to the Egyptian plagues described in the Book of Exodus. This film represents an Evangelical apocalyptic perspective referencing the end of days as depicted in the Book of Revelation.

In 2007 noted director Robert Zemeckis turned to the oldest of English epic poems, *Beowulf.* The unknown author wrote this poem sometime between the seventh and eleventh century and created the prototype for medieval dragon-slaying myths, possibly inspired by legendary King Arthur. Zemeckis's *Beowulf* stars Ray Winstone as the Anglo-Saxon hero Beowulf, Anthony Hopkins plays King Hrothgar, and Angelina Jolie plays a dazzling shape-shifting dragon. Like the medieval epic, Zemeckis's film relates a struggle between forces of darkness and living heroes and delivers a subtle yet distinct post-9/11 message. Beowulf slays three monsters of the same family, analogous to the Axis of Evil. One reviewer, Alexander Zaitchik, maintained that the three slain dragons represent Iraq, North Korea, and Iran. Zaitchik noted that Beowulf slays the first dragon, Grendel, fairly easily, coinciding with the U.S. occupation of Iraq. However, "he loses his soul in the process and becomes prisoner to the battle's legacy." The second monster, Grendel's beautiful shape-shifting mother (Jolie), is too powerful to slay, so Beowulf instead accepts a night's lovemaking with the monster's human persona, a beautiful, golden-colored young woman. She corresponds to North Korea's provocations and the staunch U.S. refusal to invade that country. The third and biggest monster, symbolizing Iran, turns out to be Beowulf's own son from his encounter with Grendel's mother. In order to slay this monster, Beowulf must pay with his life.[19]

Matt Reeves's *Cloverfield* (2008) combines elements of horror with science fiction, chronicling events experienced by young New York City professionals celebrating their friend's promotion and reassignment to Japan. An earthquake and blackout force them into the city's streets, where they watch several distant explosions and see the Statue of Liberty's severed head crash onto the street in front of them. Eventually, they catch glimpses of a huge reptilian monster over three hundred feet tall that appears to be furiously destroying city landmarks, including one of the Woolworth towers. Rob Hawkins (Michael Stahl-David), Hudson "Hud" Platt (T. J. Miller), Marlena Diamond (Lizzy Caplan), and Beth McIntyre (Odette Yustman) attempt to flee the city after Rob and Hud rescue Beth from underneath fallen roofing supports. Eventually, the military, unable to faze the resilient monster, evacuates the city and plans to incinerate it with a nuclear warhead.

Cloverfield functions as a 9/11 allegory, with the monster substituting neatly for the 9/11 hijackers. The damage to quintessential New York icons, including the Statue of Liberty, the Woolworth Building tower, and the Brooklyn Bridge, obviously evokes the 9/11 attacks, complete with trapped civilians buried in building ruble. The threat from the unnamed monster never abates, even after several direct hits by U.S. fighter planes and tanks. The film's final comment tells viewers that the monster still lives. Reeves's film emphasizes the impotence of the U.S. military as it contemplates use of nuclear weapons to destroy the creature, even though that would totally annihilate New York City.

Fox News blasted this film for shamelessly evoking sympathy for 9/11 victims. After reminding readers of Hollywood's reluctance to use images of New York being destroyed by anyone, Fox's Roger Friedman chided *Cloverfield*'s filmmakers for depicting New York City "being pulverized. Very quickly and without warning, downtown New York is destroyed. The first bit of damage is depicted by a World Trade Center–like structure exploding and collapsing downward, sending off a cloud not unlike those my friends ran from that day."[20] However, Reeves's film joins a long list of Hollywood movies featuring monsters destroying New York City, like *King Kong* (1933) and Eugene Loure's *The Beast from 20,000 Fathoms* (1953). Similar to the 9/11 attackers, the *Cloverfield* monster arises from nowhere, attacks without warning, and appears impossible to stop. Even the nuclear solution for wiping out the monster is not presented as necessarily the correct one, and its success is not guaranteed.

In 2009 Marcus Nispel released an updated, post-9/11 version of *Friday the 13th*. In it, Nispel resurrects Jason Voorhees (Derek Mears), one of the most bankable horror villains of all time. Nispel's film became the third out of twelve post-9/11 adaptations of the *Friday the 13th* franchise. In the latest remake a group of teenagers manage to find the original slasher site referenced in the 1980 movie while on an adventure to find and harvest some valuable marijuana growing in the nearby woods. Like many horror victims, the youthful characters then proceed to take drugs, listen to rock and roll, and have sex, including one character without a partner masturbating. In the midst of this moral chaos Jason returns from the dead like an avenging demon, wreaking savage vengeance on them for disturbing his peace and for engaging in hedonism.

Dennis Iliadis's *The Last House on the Left* (2009) punishes the villains by allowing the victims to eventually triumph over their attackers. The Collingwood family consists of seventeen-year-old Mari (Sara Paxton); her father, Dr. John Collingwood (Tony Goldwyn); and her mother, Emma (Monica Potter). They play the "good family" in Iliadis's film. They encounter a thuggish gang led by Krug (Garrett Dillahunt), an escaped criminal, and his brother, crazed girlfriend, and teenage son, Justin (Spencer Treat Clark). Krug and his "evil family" assault two young women, including Mari, who not so innocently accepted an invitation from Justin to smoke marijuana and fool around in a rural motel room until Krug and his gang return. They then abuse, rape, and murder one girl, but Mari manages to escape.

John and Emma Collingwood attack the Krug gang. After a series of fiercely violent battles using knives, a fireplace poker, a gun, a monkey wrench, a rock hammer, and assorted other deadly implements, the Collingwoods manage to torture and kill the Krug gang, with the exception of Justin, who, repelled by his father's violence, joins the "good family" and helps kill his own father. John and Emma arrange for Krug's head to explode in a faulty microwave oven. Like *The Hills Have Eyes* and *Hostel,* the villains die at the hands of the victims. These films enact cinematic vengeance against powerful and dangerous terrorists, and in the post-9/11 world audiences find these emotions very appealing.

In July 2009 Phillippe Martinez released *The Chaos Experiment* (British), part global warming thriller and part post-9/11 horror film. In Martinez's film, crazed university professor Jimmy Pettis (Val Kilmer) traps six people in a steam room and starts turning up the heat. He demands that a local newspaper publish a front-page story about earth's impending doom from global warming. When the temperature in the steam room reaches 130 degrees, the same temperature that will arrive on earth in 2012 via global warming, the captives will die of seared lungs, collapsing eyeballs, and general physical deterioration. In true horror film style, Martinez's camera zooms in on the sweaty captives, including the partly clad women, and depicts their physical, emotional, and spiritual destruction in excruciating detail.

Another subplot revolves around Pettis's interrogation by a Miami police detective, played by Armand Assante, who then incarcerates Pettis. Pettis's accomplices strafe one of the female captives with a nail gun, and another becomes electrocuted while trying to escape before renewed violence erupts. The global warming metaphor of rising temperatures and growing chaos makes the choice of title seem apt. Martinez's film echoes the chilling dystopias depicted by other post-9/11 horror movies.

Vampires

Stories of vampires and other blood-sucking demons appear in nearly every human culture and date to the dawn of human history. Ancient Greeks sometimes referred to them as Lamia, Empusa, or Stirge, mythological creatures that fed on human blood and sometimes engaged in sexual relations with humans. In ancient Assyria and Babylon, *Ekimmu,* the souls of the dead who had violated rigid taboos while alive, roamed the earth tormenting the living and sometimes sucking away their lives. Ancient Romans believed in *Lemures,* spirits of departed humans who engaged in draining their victims' life forces. Bloodsuckers and similar demons also populated Druid and Indian mythologies.[21] Eastern Europe possesses an especially rich vampire tradition, much of it brought back from the Far East by travelers on the Silk Road. Slavic peoples believed that the mysterious deaths of farm animals and people signaled the presence of vampires, who possessed powers of shape-shifting and hypnosis. By the eighteenth century, vampire myths had become popular in England and western Europe.

Today vampire films enjoy a greater popularity than ever before. Bram Stoker's 1897 novel *Dracula,* long a mainstay of Hollywood and foreign horror movies, continues to inspire contemporary vampire characters. Joel Schumacher's *The Lost Boys* (1987) epitomizes pre-9/11 vampire films by appealing to rebellious youth. Schumacher's vampires strongly resemble biker gangs of the 1980s, except they are blood-sucking immortals. Movies associate Satan, hell, and assorted demons with vampires. Lycans, or werewolves, may play pivotal roles in vampire films or may serve as the chief antagonist in other films. Given the post-9/11 bleak realities, it should come as no surprise that these immortal and superpowerful beings enjoy widespread popularity.

Vampire films form a subgenre combining elements of science fiction, horror, and superhero movies. They hearken back to F. W. Murnau's 1922 German Expressionist classic *Nosferatu,* starring Max Schreck as Count Orlok, a Transylvanian nobleman suffering from the disease of vampirism, a condition that causes him to shun sunlight and drives him to feast on human blood. Orlok's image began the tradition of sinister-looking movie vampires that followed, including characters played by Bella Lugosi and Christopher Lee. However, a transformation in the vampire role began around the time of 9/11 when filmmakers began emphasizing more attractive characteristics of the vampires, including immortality and superpowers. Just prior to 9/11, vampires began to undergo a literary makeover, morphing into likeable superheroes capable of ensuring human safety and well-being, a transformation that accelerated after the 9/11 attacks.

Michael Oblowitz's *The Breed* (2001) appeared just two months before 9/11, giving it the distinction of being the last major pre-9/11 vampire movie. Oblowitz sets his film in a future-retro setting in which protagonists drive vintage 1950s cars and the U.S. government appears socialist despite many Nazi icons. Oblowitz's film evokes the Warsaw ghetto uprising and the Holocaust, and he chose actual Jewish ghettos from the World War II era in eastern Europe to obtain the desired noirish ghetto effect. His vampires fall into two groups: good or evil. Good vampires include Aaron Gray (Adrian Paul), who is Jewish, and Lucy Westenra (Bai Ling), who is Chinese. Evil vampires include rogue individuals unwilling to give up killing humans for blood. Aaron Gray, a vampire working with a Nazi-like National Security Administration (NSA), teams up with FBI officer Steve Grant, an African American, played by Bokeem Woodbine, to track and arrest a rogue vampire accused of murdering half a dozen young women and drinking their blood. Many vampires recently came out of the casket and admitted their condition in an effort to attain "peaceful coexistence" with humans. But some human scientists working in secret NSA labs invent a virus that will infect and kill all vampires and finally rid the earth of this ancient menace to humans. In a plot twist, the inventor of the virus emerges as a vampire disguised as a human scientist, who creates a second lethal virus that will infect all humans and transform them into vampires or kill those whose blood contains the antivampire antigen. This film, situating vampires as symbolic Jews, raises some interesting issues involving contemporary majority/minority conflicts. Oblowitz's film associates vampires not only with Jews but also with African Americans and Native Americans.

The Breed's underlying conflict consists of a racial war between two separate but related species: humans and vampires. Both groups attempt to exterminate the other, and Oblowitz evokes the Jewish Holocaust and the genocidal nineteenth-century wars against Native Americans. But elements of Nazism emanate from humans as well as vampires, and ultimately their identities merge into one species divided racially and culturally. The good vampires in *The Breed* assist and serve their human counterparts, as human Grant falls in love with vampire Westenra, who vows to stay with him throughout his life, even though she will never age. Gray, an NSA agent, saves his partner Grant's life more than once, proving his loyalty to humans, not vampires.

In 2003 the first installment of the Underworld series appeared, inaugurating the post-9/11 vampire cycle and launching a new trend in vampire films pitting "good" against "evil" vampires. Len Wiseman directed the first in the series about a vampire named Selene (Kate Beckinsale), who falls in love with a human named Michael Covin (Scott Speedman). Michael possesses a blood antibody that might allow the creation of a hybrid race of immortals—part vampire, part human. The other installments include *Underworld Evolution* (2006) and *Underworld: Rise of the Lycans* (2009), a prequel. These films chronicle a war between vampires and Lycans (werewolves) that rages over many centuries, culminating in a contemporary war. Apparently these superpowerful species harbor animosities toward each other dating back to the dawn of time, much like the clash between Islamic and Christian civilizations that lies at the root of the 9/11 events. These films scored impressive box office returns. *Underworld Evolution,* with a $45 million budget, earned $111 million worldwide by 2009, and *Underworld: Rise of the Lycans,* released in early 2009 with an unspecified production budget, had earned $89 million by the summer of 2009. The fourth *Underworld* is already in production and is slated for release in 2012.[22] The success of *Underworld* emboldened other producers eager to invest in vampire movies, many relying on Bram Stoker's classic tropes as well as more modern models penned by Stephanie Meyer and Anne Rice. Steven Sommers's *Van Helsing* appeared in 2004, which Sommers wrote and directed, starring Hugh Jackman as the legendary vampire hunter Van Helsing and Kate Beckinsale as Anna Valerious, a gypsy princess who bears a hereditary grudge against Count Vladislaus Dracula (Richard Roxburgh) for four hundred years of oppression. She and Van Helsing form an alliance to kill Dracula, aided by a bond of love that grows between them.

Sharon Waxman noted in her review of *Underworld* that "vanquishing evil, battling for freedom and dying for honor will be Hollywood's preoccupations this summer, as big movies gestated in the insecure post-Sept. 11 world finally make their way onto screens." Waxman also noted that post-9/11 films like *Van Helsing* possess little moral ambiguity. Audiences never doubt that, in the worlds of the film's tagline, "evil has one name to fear,

Van Helsing."[23] *Van Helsing* proved very successful at the box office, doubling its $120 million production costs by 2009.[24] Its success tempted other filmmakers to capitalize on the emerging trend.

David Roodt released *Dracula 3000* in 2004, a poorly made reprise of the venerable Count Dracula, here called Count Orlock (Langley Kirkwood) after the vampire in *Nosferatu*. In this blend of sci-fi and horror, a spacecraft on a routine mission in the year 3000 spots a long-lost transporter spacecraft that appears uninhabited. It lands on the ship and discovers that it serves as home to none other than Count Dracula/Orlock, taken aboard along with fifty coffins in the remote space station Transylvania. Despite hundreds of years of fashion development, Orlock still wears a medieval hooded cape (black, of course). With Dracula/Orlock around, vampire slayer Van Helsing must be close behind. He surfaces as young starship commander Captain Abraham Van Helsing (Casper Van Dien), who just happens to be distantly related to the original vampire slayer. Orlock promptly bites one of Van Helsing's assistants, a drug addict named 187, who transforms into a superpowerful and deadly vampire commanded by Orlock.

In typical post-9/11 fashion, Roodt's film combines horror with science fiction, providing Dracula with a new setting in deep space that affords additional opportunities for blood and gore. Roodt's film goes even further than most vampire offerings by including pain, torture, and dismemberment. Even Orlock himself becomes a victim when Van Helsing successfully prevents him from entering his crew's room aboard the spacecraft and in the process severs the vampire's arm at the elbow. This graphic rending of flesh surprisingly causes Orlock to writhe in agony, yet the film never reveals how this superpowerful character could face defeat in a contest of strength with humans. In earlier Hollywood movies, Count Dracula was never so vulnerable.

Dracula's inclusion in a future setting failed to resonate with critics, who condemned *Dracula 3000* as a poorly written amalgam of horror/sci-fi. Nevertheless, the film still managed to attract a few loyal fans. Orlock and his vampires certainly lack the panache of classic Dracula films, but they do function as part of a typical post-9/11 supervillain plot to destroy all life on earth, leaving everything "dark, dark." Unfortunately, this supervillain lacks depth, and so does the hero who ultimately kills him. The film ends enigmatically by having the deceased captain of the starship execute a self-destruction order from beyond the grave.

Jonathan Dueck's *The Last Sect* (2006) adds a modern twist to the vampire genre. In this film, an online dating service provides fresh victims for vampires. The vampires follow a mysterious yet attractive woman (actually an ancient vampire) named Anna/Anastasia (Deborah Odell), who presides over the dating service, as well as a vampire cult called Artemis. According to this film, vampires require long periods of sleep, during which they must find special persons/vampires to serve as caretakers during their decades-long coma. Anna/Anastasia becomes severely sleep-deprived. She meets Sydney (Natalie Brown), a journalist assigned to research a feature article about the dating service, and decides she has found the person to assume the caretaker role. Dr. Van Helsing (David Carradine) and his colleague Karpov (Julian Ritchings), vampire hunters, attempt to stop Anna from turning Sydney into a vampire. Despite the professionalism with which they attempt to execute the vampires (in self-defense), they ultimately fail, and Sydney becomes the vampire caretaker who will help unleash the cult.

As in most vampire films, sex plays a huge role in *The Last Sect*. The dating service entices young men to meet the female vampires, who then bind them and feast upon their blood. Anna seduces Sydney sexually and romantically before she bites her and transforms her into a vampire. Similarly, Sydney's photographer friend Sam (Sebastien Roberts), who goes through the first part of the film making lewd remarks and semiserious sexual advances toward Sydney, transforms into a vampire and ends up dead at Van Helsing's hands. Van Helsing and Karpov personally dispatch several vampires and ghouls they encounter during the movie, but they ultimately fail to destroy the cult because they allow Sydney to go free, not realizing her transition to vampire. The final scene depicts Van Helsing and his assistant sitting up late at night when a knock suddenly reverberates from the door. The two men exchange concerned glances before the curtain falls, leaving audiences to speculate that Sydney or another vampire waits just outside. Audiences enjoy being titillated, and this film presents plenty of nearly bare female breasts and sexual banter to entertain the most jaded viewer.

Catherine Hardwicke's *Twilight* (2008) epitomizes the post-9/11 "good vampire" film. Capitalizing on the commercial success of Stephenie Meyer's 2005 novel by the same name, Hardwicke's film stars attractive Kristin Stewart as Bella Swan, a high school student who moves to the small town of Forks, Washington, to be with her father. While attending the local high school, she falls in love with handsome senior Edward Cullen (Robert Pattinson), a vampire. Cullen possesses the same physical appearance as when he became a vampire in 1918, but as a vampire he possesses extremely potent superpowers, including immortality, superstrength, mind reading, the ability to move at blinding speeds, and the ability to climb vertical walls and make huge leaps. He soon charms Bella with his wit, intelligence, and quiet demeanor. Despite being physically a teenager for ninety years, Cullen attends high school, though at this point he knows all the answers to all the exam questions his teachers could possibly ask. In the novel, Cullen garners some college degrees in the evening, but the film omits this fact. Consequently, one question that emerges from the film is how could a being possessed of high intelligence withstand high school for so many years? Does he not get bored at some point?

Cullen lives in an opulent home with other vampires in a "family." As fully mature vampires, they adopt a "vegetarian" diet consisting solely of the blood of animals they track down and capture in the nearby forest, and they refrain at all times from drinking human blood. Their lifestyle becomes threatened by the presence of Bella, who possesses a singularly attractive blood scent. Ultimately, Bella and Edward become romantically attracted to each other, and one day Cullen invites her to join his adopted family for a game of baseball. The baseball scene in which two teams of Cullen members compete using their superpowers proves pivotal after a band of nomadic vampires joins the game.

Hardwicke's film focuses on the dynamics between the "good vampires" in the Cullen family and the "bad vampires" led by James (Cam Gigandet), a gifted tracker possessing unparalleled strength, accompanied by vampire Victoria (Rachelle Lefevere), his mate. After James senses Bella's true nature at the Cullen family baseball game, he threatens to attack her and drink her blood, but the Cullens, who respect Bella because of Edward's attraction to her, resist these bloodthirsty impulses. Subsequently, James becomes obsessed with Bella, causing a rift between the two vampire groups. In the film's climax Edward proves unable to defeat James by himself, but with the Cullen family's help, their combined superstrength overpowers James, allowing them to tear him apart and burn him to death.

In 2008, P. J. Peace released a long-awaited sequel to Joel Schumacher's 1987 cult classic *The Lost Boys*. Peace's sequel, titled *Lost Boys: The Tribe*, features Tad Hilgenbrink and Autumn Reeser as Chris and Nicole Emerson, two orphan siblings who visit an aunt in Luna Bay, a seaside town with a large number of surfers and other unruly young people. Angus Sutherland plays Shane, the head of a cult of vampires who inhabit the local community, often attacking and killing other youthful residents. After Shane forms an attraction to Nicole Emerson, Chris bloodies his nose and warns him to keep away from his sister. For her part, Nicole finds Shane irresistible. At this point Chris encounters the local vampire killer, Edgar Frog (Corey Feldman), who informs him that Nicole has already become infected with Shane's blood and currently hovers in a hybrid state of existence halfway between vampire and human. Chris must kill Shane before Nicole kills to feed on human blood, or she will become a full-fledged vampire.

The vampire band in *Lost Boys: The Tribe* first appear as attractive characters, playfully riding their motorcycles around the local sheriff's department in order to lure the deputies to chase them, but the deputies fail to outmaneuver the superhuman bikers and end up crashing their cars into each other. Later, Shane's "family" members murder some young women they've lured to a remote beach, and then they attack Chris. From this point on an all-out war ensues between the "good vampires," namely Chris (who has transformed into a quasi vampire) and Nicole, and Shane and his "lost boys" gang. Basically, the story reverts to the modern convention of good vampires with superpowers battling evil vampires who also possess superpowers. In the end, good triumphs over evil.

In 2008 HBO launched a very successful vampire television series titled *True Blood,* directed by Alan Ball and based on characters and situations from Charlaine Harris's Southern Vampire book series. The third season began in 2010, and the fourth season launched in 2011. The first two episodes chronicle the exploits of Sookie Stackhouse (Anna Paquin), a Louisiana barmaid possessed with mind-reading powers. Her life turns around dramatically after a vampire named Bill Compton (Stephen Moyer) walks into her bar two years after vampires came "out of the closet" on national television and began consuming synthetic blood called "true blood." Stackhouse, excited at the prospect of meeting a vampire, finds herself attracted to Bill, despite the fact that she and all of the patrons in her bar know instinctively what he is as well as the dangers involved with relationships between vampires and humans. *True Blood* contains abundant plot tropes of sex and violence, two dramatic ingredients highly successful with post-9/11 audiences. Critics praised this series from the beginning, and its continued success provides additional evidence, as if any were needed, of the popularity of the vampire genre. One reviewer opined, "Ball is having a ball with the tone. It's all over the map—part scary, part funny, dramatically intense and yet kind of silly. Audaciously sex-filled but also violent and bloody."[25]

The rising popularity of vampire films transformed *Twilight* into a popular franchise. *The Twilight Saga: New Moon*, directed by Chris Weitz, appeared in November 2009. It continues along the narrative path begun in Hardwicke's installment. In Weitz's film Bella (Kristin Stewart) becomes injured and bleeds as she celebrates her birthday with Edward, and the resulting barely suppressed blood passion convinces the Cullen family to leave the town of Forks, Washington, for Edward's and Bella's sake. Bella, originally heartbroken, tries to forget everything through heedless living. Of course, danger lurks everywhere for her, echoing the audience's deep-seated fears and insecurity.

The Twilight Saga: Eclipse dominated ticket sales when it arrived in the summer of 2010. In this episode the Cullen vampire clan, headed by Dr. Carlisle Cullen (Peter Facinelli), unites with the nearby werewolf tribe, led by Sam Uley (Chaske Spencer), against Victoria (Bryce Dallas Howard) and her army of Newbies, humans recently transformed into vampires. Despite this alliance, Edward and Jacob actively compete for Bella's affection. In the meantime, Victoria vows to kill Bella, now Edward's fiancée, to avenge Edward's killing of her boyfriend, James, in the first episode of the saga.

In this film, director David Slade joins powerful myths into a unified force of vampires and werewolves combating the small "army" of revenge-crazed superhuman vampires. Edward and Jacob represent two mythological traditions. In religion, vampire myths reference the Blood of Christ as well as the Holy Grail and other sacred traditions. In psychological terms, they may evoke taboo sexual relationships. Currently, vampire films suggest a return to Victorian morality. As Roger Ebert observed, "The 'Twilight' movies are chaste eroticism to fuel adolescent dreams, and are really about Bella being attracted and titillated and aroused and tempted up to the ... very ... brink! ... of surrender, and then, well, no, no, she shouldn't."[26]

After 9/11 vampires transformed from supervillain terrorists intent on world domination into attractive mates and humane protectors struggling against evil monsters or tormented souls striving desperately to retrieve their humanity. This vampire role reversal first appears in *Underworld*, later in *Twilight*, one of the most popular vampire films of all time. *Twilight*, which cost $37 million to produce, had earned over $383 million by 2009, a return on investment of more than ten to one.[27] With profits like these who wouldn't want to invest in vampire films? No wonder vampire films now constitute one of Hollywood's most popular genres.

The post-9/11 world—fraught with terrorism, war, disease, financial meltdowns, and global climate change—proves an extremely fertile ground for vampire films. Post-9/11 vampire films remain popular, according to Indiana University's Michael Dylan Foster, because they "personify real-world anxieties." According to Foster, "During these post-9/11 times of increased vigilance, representations like the 'Twilight' series reflect a kind of conspiracy-theory mentality, a fear that there is something secret and dangerous going on in our own community, right under our noses."[28] In the post-9/11 world, conspiracy theories proliferate, including those involving President Barack Obama as a Muslim and former president Bill Clinton as the Antichrist. In fact, belief in vampires and belief in the Antichrist share remarkable similarities because both include belief in the supernatural, belief in a global conspiracy, and belief in a coming apocalypse.

The message contained in many post-9/11 vampire movies translates into this: In order to conquer hostile, terroristic vampires, humans must become monsters themselves, if only for enough time to defeat the evil vampires. After that, humans may revert to their normal form. This message is especially clear and pronounced in *Lost Boys: The Tribe* (2008). Of course, this maxim also reflects political realities. Translated into sociopolitical terms, it means that in order to defeat al Qaeda–type terrorists, the United States must adopt—possibly temporarily—some of their tactics. In other words, suspend the Bill of Rights and the Geneva Convention's prohibition against mistreatment of prisoners of war and the UN Convention Against Torture in order to defeat terrorists.

Horror at the Box Office

Not only vampire films but also all post-9/11 horror films capitalize on the era's fears, anxieties, and overall paranoia. Far from satiating public demand for violent entertainment, the events of September 11 only whetted audience appetites for more torture, murder, and mayhem. These three elements appear in horror films and in thrillers, sci-fi, and war films. Horror films prosper at the box office like never before, driven by waves of younger fans. Today blood fests prove especially lucrative. *The Hills Have Eyes* (2006), for instance, cost $14 million and cleared more than $40 million domestically. Financial success like this continues to tempt filmmakers into making horror films.[29] The main difference between Wes Craven's original and the remake, apart from replacing the 1970s hillbillies in the original with post-9/11 nuclear-test mutants, is an increased amount of blood and gore. The new version inspired a sequel in 2007, *The Hills Have Eyes II,* which cost $15 million and earned more than $37 million by 2009.[30]

Other reasons beside economics account for horror's growing popularity in the post-9/11 era. In Hollywood, terrorist violence begets movie violence. Films simply became more violent after 9/11, and horror films, among the most violent anyway, became even bloodier. Today the link between social violence and movie violence appears stronger than ever. Movie violence continues to accelerate even as the 2001 attacks slowly recede from memory. Are viewers simply acting out their innermost fears and desires for revenge?

In contemporary horror films victims cannot survive by themselves—they must band together in order to defeat the powerful chaotic forces deployed against them. When one of the victims of *The Texas Chainsaw Massacre* asks the head of the villains why he kills and mutilates victims, he answers, "You've all got to pay for your sins!" Their guilt means that only through violence and renunciation of their last vestiges of security can characters in horror films find redemption. The victims must symbolically descend into hell, pursued by monstrous human and supernatural antagonists. Only then can they face the shocking insecurities of the current age. Like the pacifistic young men and women of the classic Westerns who ended up using a six-shooter out of sheer necessity, today's movie victims must embrace their dark sides and symbolically merge with their attackers in order to survive. Like the military's plan to nuke Manhattan in order to destroy the *Cloverfield* monster, only by resorting to extreme violence can today's victims of movie horror hope to survive the world in which they find themselves.

Guilt for indulging in hedonistic pleasures also helps explain the public fascination with horror films. Slasher films like *Freddy vs. Jason* and the latest versions of 1970s and 1980s horror classics systematically punish youthful victims immediately after they've had sex, smoked pot, drunk too much, and engaged in other crimes and misdemeanors. In movies like *The Fog,* guilt stems from ancestral crimes akin to original sin. As Elizabeth Williams (Maggie Grace) observes at the film's denouement, "Something did come back from the sea. Sooner or later, everything does." Although the robberies and murders perpetrated by the founders of Antonio Bay are ficti-tious, in fact all the United States originally belonged to Natives, and some of the ancestors of the whites who now live in the United States may have been involved in the destruction of Native peoples. Other sources of guilt include the Vietnam War in *The Texas Chainsaw Massacre* (2003), media addiction in *The Ring* (2005), and the excesses of the postmodern blended family in *The Hills Have Eyes* (2006). Guilt-saturated post-9/11 films come complete with abundant free-floating anxiety. The characters, the situations, and the dialogue paint a portrait of an entire decade of movies seemingly under the grip of powerful symbols and burdensome guilt. But where does all this guilt originate? Perhaps post-9/11 guilt stems from guilt about past and present neocolonialism as exemplified in the war on terror.

Today's horror genre obsesses over depictions of pain, violence, and sex. The resounding national and international debate occasioned by the U.S. policy of torturing suspected terrorists despite the prohibitions of the Geneva Convention now provides filmmakers with powerful plot devices. As the wars in Iraq and Afghanistan drag on, already the longest in U.S. history, news media provide new headlines about terrorist bombings and other violent acts. The violence never ceases, feeding audiences' anxieties and traumas. As a result, many turn to horror films, which provide symbolic reflections of today's unpleasant realities.

CHAPTER FOUR

Rage

Charles Darwin identified anger as one of the primary emotions and noted that anger and hatred eventually turn into rage. Darwin believed that few people "can long reflect about a hated person, without feeling and exhibiting signs of indignation or rage."[1] Rage best expresses the responses of the Bush administration to 9/11. In a speech delivered immediately after 9/11, President George W. Bush branded the attacks as "evil, despicable acts of terror."[2] Secretary of Defense Donald Rumsfeld, speaking in 2007, outlined important questions raised by the 9/11 attacks: "With the growing lethality and the increasing availability of weapons, can we truly afford to believe that somehow, some way, vicious extremists can be appeased?"[3] For Rumsfeld, the answer lay in waging war against terrorists. From the beginning, the Bush administration focused on outrage and evoked warfare as the only reasonable and proper response to the "despicable acts" that had occurred on 9/11. Warfare calls for rage to motivate the troops. While the Bush administration fomented outrage against the terrorists and anyone who sided with their grievances, Hollywood audiences began frequenting combat movies that also expressed outrage, setting the emotional stage for the wars in Afghanistan and Iraq.

After the 9/11 attacks unfolded, and wars erupted in Afghanistan in 2001 and Iraq in 2003, filmmakers focused on movies about distant wars, depicting atrocities and bloody battles in faraway places while resonating with post-9/11 anger. Later, even as the wars in Afghanistan and Iraq became unpopular, audiences continued to watch films depicting and often glorifying combat, experiencing the clash of arms, the sounds of explosions, and the adrenaline rush felt by men playing with "boy toys." Under an informal "code," no film would negatively depict any war in which the United States was currently engaged.[4] Early anti–Vietnam War films *Catch 22* (1970) and *M.A.S.H.* (1970) depicted World War II and the Korean War and implied a critical perspective on the Vietnam conflict. It was not until after hostilities ceased in 1974 that openly antiwar films of the actual war appeared, such as *Coming Home* (1978), *The Deer Hunter* (1978), and *Apocalypse Now* (1979). Similar rules apply to the conflicts in Afghanistan and Iraq.

World War II: The Good War

World War II functions as the quintessential "good war" in American culture, the greatest U.S. victory since the War for Independence. In countless films World War II achieved a semisacred status as the finest American war, a fascination that still continues. Michael Bay's *Pearl Harbor* (2001), crafted prior to 9/11, depicts American heroism in the Battle of Pearl Harbor. Bay's film follows the actions of two airmen, Rafe McCawley (Ben Affleck) and Danny Walker (Josh Hartnett), as they launch an air defense of the island of Oahu during the Japanese air raid. Although, the film contains a large number of historical inaccuracies about the Japanese attack, from Franklin Roosevelt's actions to those of the American commanders, it resonates with feelings of patriotism.

Jean-Jacques Annaud's *Enemy at the Gates* (2001) celebrates the USSR's victory over Nazi Germany in the Battle of Stalingrad in 1942. This battle bears heavy symbolism for Russians, equivalent to the Battle of Pearl Harbor, D-Day Europe, and the Doolittle raid on Tokyo for Americans. Annaud's film depicts the marksmanship of Russian supersniper Vassili Zaitsev (Jude Law), who engages in a deadly duel with German supersniper Major Erwin Konig (Ed Harris). The chilling science of sharpshooting forms the backdrop of the plot, which centers on the skills and mental agility of Zaitsev, who eventually becomes a Soviet hero after defeating Konig in the final showdown.

Those films were pre-9/11. The mood of war films darkened significantly after the attacks. Clint Eastwood's *Flags of Our Fathers* (2006) examines the lives of the three flag-raisers at Iwo Jima and explores the long-range effects of combat on soldiers. Eastwood recreates the Battle of Iwo Jima in bloody detail, illustrating a "war is hell" theme. In true "good war" fashion, the film showcases traditional military values of bravery and camaraderie, evoking a patriotic spirit during a time when real wars rage in Afghanistan and Iraq.

However, it also depicts war's brutality and debunks the notion of World War II as a "good war."

In December 2006, Eastwood released a companion piece, also set in Iwo Jima, titled *Letters from Iwo Jima*. This time Eastwood organized the film around the buried letters of some of the Japanese defenders of the island. Like *Flags of Our Fathers,* it depicts the Battle of Iwo Jima, but Eastwood focuses on the Japanese side of the conflict, even shooting it almost entirely in Japanese with English subtitles. Ken Watanabi stars as Army Lieutenant General Tadamichi Kurabayashi, the island's commanding officer, along with Kazunari Ninomiya as Army Private First Class Saigo and Tsuyoshi Ihara as Army Lieutenant Colonel/Baron Takeichi Nishi. In the film, Eastwood includes traditional World War II guts and glory action, but American audiences struggled to sympathize with the Japanese characters who were America's enemies during World War II.

Steven Soderbergh's *The Good German* (2006) depicts postwar military operations in Germany on the eve of the 1945 Potsdam Conference, which divided Europe among the Allies. Far from showcasing military virtues, Soderbergh's film presents Americans as rife with corruption, ignoring and condoning Nazi atrocities at an underground missile plant (Camp Dora). The entire atmosphere reeks of greed, duplicity, and nationalism. Patrick Tully (Tobey Maguire) explains wartime greed this way: "You can say what you want about the war ... but, the war was the best thing that ever happened to me. Because when you have money, then, for the first time in your life, you *understand* it, what money does for you." Soderbergh shot the film in black and white, using vintage lenses, newsreel footage, and natural lighting to provide a "film noir" look, and included the necessary femme fatale, Lena Brandt (Cate Blanchett), a part-time prostitute who conceals her Jewish identity. Moral conditions become so confused that protagonist Jake Geismer (George Clooney), an American military journalist, reminisces about how World War II resembles "the good old days when you could tell who the bad guys were by who was shooting at you." The film implies that these facile distinctions no longer exist as "good" and "evil" morph into each other.

Eastwood's and Soderbergh's films exemplify opposite poles in depictions of World War II. Eastwood's *Flags of Our Fathers* and *Letters from Iwo Jima* showcase American and Japanese bravery and tenacity, although both depict outrageous behavior and a "war is hell" perspective. Soderbergh's film undermines the high moral ground held by most World War II films by depicting American greed and corruption. The usual American outrage over Japanese and German imperialism globalizes to foreign governments, militant movements, multinational corporations, and, surprisingly, the United States. These post-9/11 World War II films carry coded messages about the current wars by propagandizing battlefield valor while exposing corrupt, behind-the-scenes political dealings in postwar Europe. Just as Vietnam-era films resonate with undercurrents of antiwar sentiment (when Captain John Yossarian [Alan Arkin] in *Catch-22* [1970] attempts to be certified "insane" so that he cannot continue to fly World War II combat missions and the Korean War army doctors in *M.A.S.H.* [1970] illustrate war's chaos and contradictions), current combat films expose glaring gaps between America's official self-perception as a bastion of democracy and the often sordid reality of U.S. foreign policy. Post-9/11 war films highlight deep suspicions about U.S. policy while affirming the values of courage, heroism, and tenacity during wartime. They also rely on long-established film noir icons, including ominous settings, shadowy duplicitous characters, and retro cinematography.

Vietnam: The Bad War

No war in U.S. history evoked such dissension and controversy as the Vietnam War (1959–1975), which became the first full-fledged U.S. military defeat, eclipsing the Korean War, which had ended in stalemate. Cinematic responses to the war ranged from a few early patriotic films like *To the Shores of Hell* (1966) and *The Green Berets* (1968) to later more nuanced features like *Coming Home* (1978), *Apocalypse Now* (1979), *Full Metal Jacket* (1987), *Casualties of War* (1989), and *Born on the Fourth of July* (1989). The first two films contain patriotic plot elements (the Viet Cong capture an American doctor to minister to their wounded in *To the Shores of Hell*, and Green Beret colonel Mike Kirby [John Wayne] instructs an antiwar journalist about Viet Cong brutality in *The Green Berets*), whereas each of the later films contains significant antiwar elements. The war in Vietnam proved popular during John F. Kennedy's term but turned increasingly negative during Lyndon Johnson's and Richard Nixon's administrations as U.S. strategies failed to gain widespread support among the Vietnamese people. After 1975, as U.S. troops completed their hasty withdrawal from Vietnam, filmmaker after filmmaker weighed in, each with a personal interpretation, including Stanley Kubrick, Francis Ford Coppola, Oliver Stone, Hal Ashby, and Brian De Palma (*Full Metal Jacket, Apocalypse Now, Born on the Fourth of July, Coming Home,* and *Casualties of War,* respectively).

Post-9/11 Vietnam

Vietnam War films enjoyed a revival during 2001 and 2002 with two feature films that explored yet again the agonizing defeat amid heavy casualties that characterized the war for many Americans. Sidney J. Furie's *Under Heavy Fire* (2001–2002), in production prior to 9/11, relates a tragic story of courageous but very human warriors fighting against overwhelming odds. The story begins as marines from Echo Company confront a deadly enemy deeply entrenched in underground tunnels and largely supported by local peasant farmers. Rookie Captain Ramsey (Casper Van Dien) struggles to gain the respect and obedience of his men, some of whom crack and mutiny during a particularly devastating battle. Suddenly, withering friendly fire engulfs them from an attack helicopter, killing several marines. At that point, Furie's film jumps ahead more than three decades as surviving members of the company return to the scene of the battle, this time as tourists on a healing journey. Documentarian Kathleen Martin (Carre Otis) accompanies the veterans with her cameraman to record their return to the scene of the friendly fire airstrike. Most blame Captain Ramsey for ordering the strike on his own mutinous men. Through flashbacks to the original battle, the men gradually learn more about it, their comrades, and themselves. In the end, their battle-forged intimacy proves stronger than their individual grudges, and they depart hugging one another. The film strongly implies that although the U.S. military suffered defeat at the hands of Vietnamese forces, the courage and dedication of individual fighters were never to blame. American forces emerge victorious if only for their renewed personal bonds and, for many, long-repressed healing.

Randal Wallace's *We Were Soldiers* (2002), also begun prior to 9/11 and released later, paints a positive portrait of U.S. military performance during the Vietnam War, even though Wallace set the film during the Battle of Drang Valley, known as the Valley of Death, which became the first major land battle of the war and the first American military defeat. In this battle

2,000 Viet Cong ambush and defeat a much smaller force of 400 from the First Battalion of the U.S. Army's Seventh Cavalry, Custer's old regiment. Mel Gibson plays Lieutenant Colonel Hal Moore, a seasoned veteran and skillful commander, and Sam Elliott plays Sergeant Major Basil Plumley, Moore's battle-hardened aid. The soldiers who take the hill face a deeply entrenched enemy with strong local connections that refuses to surrender. Roger Ebert summarized the film's political message in his review: "It is not a victory; it's more the curtain-raiser of a war in which American troops were better trained and better equipped, but outnumbered, out maneuvered and finally outlasted."[5] Wallace presents a somber backdrop to his narrative about epic courage under fire despite overwhelming odds. This rather realistic depiction of war's horrors and defeats sounds a softly antiwar note in an otherwise patriotic vehicle.

Phillip Noyce's *The Quiet American* (2002), adapted from Graham Greene's novel, depicts some very disturbing events in Vietnam prior to the war. Thomas Fowler (Michael Caine), a middle-aged British journalist living in Saigon, encounters Alden Pyle (Brendan Fraser), a young aid worker from the United States. The two compete for the affections of Fowler's beautiful Vietnamese girlfriend, Phuong (Do Thei Hai Yen). Their triangular romantic relationship symbolizes the three-way conflict among Britain, the United States, and the Vietnamese people over the eventual fate of Vietnam. Pyle turns out to be a CIA operative working to destabilize the French colonial government and defeat the Vietnamese communists. He engineers the rise of General The (Quang Hai), an anticommunist guerrilla leader who terrorizes the countryside through massacres and bombings blamed on the communist Viet Minh. Noyce based General The on actual Vietnamese rebel leader Trinh Minh The. Eventually, a Vietnamese fighter kills Pyle, presaging the coming U.S. defeat in the Vietnam War. Noyce clearly intends his film, released after the U.S.-led invasion of Afghanistan, as a cautionary tale against U.S. interventionism. The result of U.S. covert actions, as Fowler explains at the end, is that "people are dying every day."

With unresolved wars raging in Iraq and Afghanistan, filmmakers avoid dramatic depictions of the failed Vietnam War. Comedic ones, however, seem more acceptable to audiences. Comedian Ben Stiller directed and starred in *Tropic Thunder* (2008), a satire of serious Vietnam War films. Stiller uses as plot device a movie company shooting a documentary film. The film crew works with Four Leaf Tayback (Nick Nolte), the author of the combat memoir being adapted, who eventually confesses that he was never in the Vietnam War and spent the entire conflict in the Coast Guard stationed in the United States. As real-life events spin out of control, the crew learns that it's involved in a film based on a faked book. The film's comedic, ironic tone safely distances the American defeat, and the personal victory over an opium gang places the film in "good war" territory.

Afghanistan

After the U.S.-led invasion of Afghanistan on October 7, 2001, a few film-makers began depicting successful instances of U.S. clandestine involvement in the Soviet-Afghan war (1979–1989). U.S. media depict this war as a conflict between mujahideen "freedom fighters" and Soviet occupiers and credit the CIA's clandestine aid to the mujahideen as the decisive factor forcing Soviet withdrawal. With direct U.S. military involvement in Afghanistan currently stretching nearly a decade, it was only a matter of time before Hollywood began revisiting the earlier conflict. Mike Nichols's *Charlie Wilson's War* (2007) depicts the Soviet-Afghan war from the perspective of Charlie Wilson (Tom Hanks), a U.S. congressman who sits on two strategic committees responsible for funding covert operations. At first Wilson comes across as a hedonistic lightweight who spends his free time womanizing and snorting cocaine at hot tub parties. However, his friendship with wealthy conservative Joanne Herring (Julia Roberts), who adopts the cause of the Afghan mujahideen, and CIA operative Gust Avrakotos (Phillip Seymour Hoffman), also dedicated to a Soviet defeat in Afghanistan, persuades Wilson to approve increasingly larger sums of money to support the Afghan fighters. Eventually, Wilson helps Avrakatos arm the fighters with powerful U.S.-built Stinger handheld missiles. Armed with improved weaponry, these "freedom fighters" gradually defeat the more numerous and better-armed Soviet army. After the Soviets leave Afghanistan, a CIA official presents Wilson with a special award for his role in arming the mujahideen and says:

> The defeat and break up of the Soviet empire, culminating in the crumbling of the Berlin Wall, is one of the great events of world history. There were many heroes in this battle, but to Charlie Wilson must go this special recognition. Just thirteen years ago the Soviet army appeared to be invincible. But Charlie, undeterred, engineered a lethal

body blow that weakened the communist empire. Without Charlie, history would be hugely, and sadly different. And so for the first time a civilian is being given our highest recognition that of honored colleague. Ladies and gentlemen of the clandestine services, congressman Charles Wilson.

This speech exemplifies a central problem with the "Charlie Wilson's war" myth as promulgated by Nichols's film, namely that it minimizes the contributions of the Afghan people in their ultimate victory. In fact, the refusal by the Afghan people to support the USSR's occupation, the subversion of their religion, and the domination of their resources constitutes the real force behind the USSR's defeat. Wilson showed remarkable prescience in arming them, but he did not foresee the rise of the Taliban from within their ranks. Nor did he foresee the role that one of the mujahideen, Osama bin Laden, would play in future years. Nichols's film, by focusing on one man's contribution to the war effort, slights the heroic efforts of the Afghan people. An even more disturbing issue arises regarding the historical treatment of the war's aftermath. In the movie Wilson tries but fails to convince Congress to support a $1 million bill to build schools in Afghanistan. According to the film, that failure doomed the new Afghan government and allowed it to be taken over by elements of the very forces that Wilson and the CIA supplied. As Wilson himself admits in the movie, "We bear responsibility because we didn't try to rebuild Afghanistan. We left a vacuum and the vacuum was filled by the Taliban and Al Qaeda."[6] Charlie Wilson and his friends notwithstanding, the Soviet-Afghan war set the stage for a larger conflict that eventually led to the 9/11 attacks.

After 9/11 the handheld FIM-92 Stinger missiles, made possible by Wilson's funding for the Soviet defeat, suddenly became liabilities. Al Qaeda's presence in Afghanistan increased the danger of Stinger missiles falling into terrorists' hands. In fact, because the CIA supplied the mujahideen with hundreds of them, each capable of downing a combat helicopter, Afghanistan contains the world's largest arsenal of Stinger missiles. Many wondered what would happen if any fell into the hands of terrorists. Now we know. In July 2010 when more than 90,000 top-secret documents pertaining to the U.S.-Afghan war were released, the world became aware of the continued use of these Stinger missiles against forces from the North Atlantic Treaty Organization (NATO).

Charlie Wilson's long-term legacy ultimately depends on Afghanistan's future stability, a very uncertain proposition. The Soviet-Afghan war presaged the U.S.-led invasion of Afghanistan. Like the Soviets, U.S. forces concentrated initially in Kabul, leaving remote provinces unprotected against rising Taliban influence. In addition, the cozy relationship between the Pakistan military and the mujahideen, forged during the Soviet-Afghan war, continues. Instead of the staunch ally against Islamic extremism that *Charlie Wilson's War* imagines, Pakistan presents many faces to the United States and NATO, including that of covert Taliban supporter.

In many ways Nichols's film endorses the policies of the Bush and Obama administrations toward Afghanistan. If the public believes that a Texas congressman can win the cold war for the United States, then the public might believe just about anything regarding the current wars. The United States could have many reasons for invading Afghanistan. The country possesses many strategic benefits and was identified as a safe location for a vast oil pipeline from Central Asia to the Caspian Sea, an enticement to oil companies. And recent U.S. estimates value Afghanistan's untapped mineral resources at $1 trillion.[7] The suggestion that a single congressman affected a distant war through military resources alone oversimplifies complex issues.

Distant Wars

In 2008, twenty-six years after the premiere of the original *Rambo: First Blood* (1982), Sylvester Stallone directed, starred, and coscripted the fourth installment of the franchise, this time titled *Rambo 4* or simply *Rambo*. The film's tagline reads, "Heroes never die.... They just reload." (This tagline may have inspired former Alaska governor Sarah Palin in her Tea Party appearances and talk show comments in which she exhorted supporters, "Don't retreat—reload!") In this installment John Rambo (Stallone) plays a semiretired curmudgeon in Thailand, dividing his time between capturing dangerous snakes for entertainers and ferrying others in his primitive jungle boat. A group of Christian missionaries led by Michael Burnett (Paul Schulze) and Sarah Miller (Julie Benz) asks Rambo to ferry them up the river to the war-torn Karen region of Burma (Myanmar), where they plan to minister to the Karen people, whom the film depicts as Christians (in fact, the Karen divide religiously among Buddhism, Christianity, and animism).

Initially Rambo refuses to help, and when he learns from Sarah that the missionaries carry no weapons, he scornfully comments, "You won't change anything." Predictably attracted by pretty Sarah, he relents. Rambo joins a small team of mercenaries who defeat the Burmese forces. Images of violence in the Rambo series incrementally climbed, with one critic counting 83 "bad guys" killed by Rambo in the 2008 sequel, 40 bad guys killed by accomplices of Rambo, and 113 good guys killed by villains, for a total of 236 people killed, almost doubling the 132 people killed in *Rambo III* (1988) and more than tripling the amount killed in *Rambo II* (1985).[8] In the post-9/11 movie world diplomacy appears weak and ineffective and only forceful, military-type actions succeed.

Andrew Niccol's *Lord of War* (2005) chronicles the rise and fall of shadowy Ukrainian munitions dealer Yuri Orlov (Nicolas Cage), who becomes involved in wars in Liberia and Sierra Leone as a successful gunrunner for all sides. The brutality of Liberian president Andre Baptiste (Eamonn Walker) and his thuggish son and followers, coupled with the squalor of poverty-stricken Liberia, adds realistic elements to this movie. Ultimately, the chief villain in Niccol's film turns out to be the international arms trade. The movie depicts this industry and its carnage through Yuri's artfully deceitful career. In the end, each faction commits atrocities against its antagonists. As Yuri explains, "They say 'evil prevails when good men fail to act.' What they ought to say is 'evil prevails.'" He states, "I do rub shoulders with some of the most vile, sadistic men calling themselves leaders today" and then claims that "the President of the United States ... ships more arms in a day than I do in a year. Sometimes it's embarrassing to have his fingerprints on the guns. Sometimes he needs a freelancer like me to supply forces he can't be seen to supply. You call me evil, but unfortunately for you I'm a necessary evil." He concludes cynically, "You know who's going to inherit the earth? Arms dealers, because everyone else is too busy killing each other. That's the secret of survival—never go to war, especially with yourself." To make the points even more explicit, a postscript proclaims, "This film is based on actual events. While private gunrunners continue to thrive, the world's biggest arms dealers are the U.S., the U.K., Russia, France, and China. They are the also the five permanent members of the U.N. Security Council." The film exudes an aura of pessimism as audiences realize that the United States and its allies constitute the chief architects of international arms races and the carnage of regional warfare.

Edward Zwick's *Blood Diamond* (2006) focuses on a forgotten civil war on Africa's west coast in 1999, yet it reminds audiences of current wars. Zwick stars Leonardo DiCaprio as Danny Archer, a white Rhodesian outwardly functioning as a diamond smuggler but secretly working for the CIA. He learns that a local fisherman named Solomon Vandy (Djimon Hounsou), forced by a rebel group to work in a diamond mine, discovered an extremely valuable huge pink stone. Archer negotiates 50 percent in exchange for coordinating its sale and teams up with journalist Maddy Bowen (Jennifer Connelly). Archer ultimately sustains injuries and passes the mission on to Vandy and Bowen. Zwick's film indirectly condemns U.S. corporate greed, apathy, and corruption, lessons that could easily apply to American military missteps in the war on terror. In the last act, American ambassador Walker makes Zwick's points explicit: "The Third World is not a world apart ... and the witness you will hear today speaks on its behalf. Let us hear the voice of that world. Let us learn from that voice ... and let us ignore it no more. Ladies and gentlemen, Mr. Solomon Vandy." Vandy transforms into a symbol of African nationalism, while Archer symbolizes colonialism and commercial exploitation, but he dies before accomplishing his mission, signaling the end of the era of colonialism and CIA covert support. The blood diamond of the movie's title symbolizes the pain and suffering caused by oil and mineral industries in the developing nations. The film's support for American business interests reminds viewers of special "sweetheart" military contracts awarded to American corporations Halliburton and Blackwater.

Antipathy toward the U.S. relationship with developing countries also forms the backdrop for Don E. FauntLeRoy's *Mercenary for Justice* (2006), which stars a corpulent Steven Seagal as CIA special ops agent John Seeger. A rogue CIA section led by "dirty deeds" man John Dresham (Luke Goss) coerces Seeger into rescuing a billionaire's son from an "escape proof" prison outside of Cape Town, South Africa. The bulk of the film consists of military and quasi-military operations, with Seeger outshooting and outfighting the prison guards. He finally confronts and defeats Dresham and "Black Ops" CIA officer Anthony Chapel (Roger Guenveur Smith). In the final scene Chapel attempts to escape in a car wired with a bomb. As Chapel confidently speeds away, Seeger activates the bomb, obliterating the car and the operative. In the end, Dresham and Chapel pay for their roguish behavior in a fiery explosion as Seeger (and the United States by extension) rights the wrongs and punishes the guilty. *Mercenary for Justice* epitomizes the profound distrust of the country's intelligence agencies witnessed in many recent thrillers (the Bourne series) after their failure to prevent or predict the 9/11 attacks and their equally disappointing failure to realize that Iraq possessed no weapons of mass destruction at the time of the U.S. invasion.

Ancient Rage

Filmmakers need not focus on remote civil wars in order to showcase warfare. Wolfgang Peterson's *Troy* (2004) reaches back in history to the twelfth-century BC Trojan War as depicted in Homer's epic *The Iliad*. Peterson's film stars Brad Pitt in the role of Achilles, a Greek warrior-hero; Eric Bana plays Trojan hero Hector; and Diane Kruger stars as Helen. Rated R for graphic violence, Peterson's film fairly wallows in bloody combat scenes, presenting a "good war" theme emphasizing battlefield courage and valor. Peterson's film, like most combat movies, fits in the "action adventure" genre as well as the war combat genre. The clash of ancient Greek and Trojan civilizations in Peterson's movie reminds viewers of the clash between Christian and Islamic civilizations in the war on terror.

Zack Snyder's *300* (2006) sets scenes of carnage in the Battle of Thermopylae. Spartan king Leonidas and an elite band of three hundred warriors fight to the death against Xerxes and his invading Persian army in the fifth century BC, providing crucial time for other Greek forces to regroup and ultimately repulse the invasion. The trope of dedicated warriors defeating large armies reappears in other films, like *Charlie Wilson's War* and *Rambo*. This pattern recurs in many war films, showcasing "good war" themes of patriotism, courage, valor, and sacrifice and providing indirect support for the military campaigns of the war on terror.

Return of the Good War

After 9/11, filmmakers ceased to make paeans to the American military of World War II owing to the darkening of the national mood. Finally, seven years after the attacks, Hollywood returned to that good war era with Edward Zwick's *Defiance* (2008). Zwick chose to depict not American forces but Polish resistance fighters battling the Nazi invasion of Belarus. Survivors of Nazi attacks in 1941 band together, led by tough-looking Zus

(Liev Schreiber) and Tuvia (Daniel Craig). They hide deep in the forests to wage a clandestine war of resistance, building a mountain redoubt and establishing an intelligence network on German activities. As a Russian commander encounters the Bielski brothers, he exclaims, "Jews don't fight." The Bielski brothers prove him wrong as they join their "Bielski Brigade," a highly motivated, well-organized group of 1,200 Jewish refugees, with their Russian compatriots. They recruit more from the Jewish ghettoes of Minsk, where the inhabitants face the prospect of slavery in German factories.

The situation deteriorates after Tuvia, the eldest Bielski brother, assumes command of the Bielski Brigade. Acts of violence occur as the war rages on, including the killing of a captured German soldier by the Bielski community. Their Russian allies suddenly withdraw upon discovering an impending German attack, leaving the Jewish comrades to their own fate. This true-to-life depiction of the Bielski Brigade contradicts the charge that Europe's Jews were too docile to resist the Holocaust.

In 2009 Quentin Tarantino contributed to the genre with *Inglourious Basterds,* casting Brad Pitt as Lieutenant Aldo Raine, who heads a commando team of Jewish Americans in 1941 Germany, affectionately called the Basterds. Once they arrive in Nazi-occupied France, Raine and the Basterds are assigned to Operation Keno, a plot to kill Adolf Hitler and other top Third Reich officials at the opening of *Pride of the Nation,* the new film by Minister of Propaganda Joseph Goebbels. The film flashes back to four years earlier when S.S. Colonel Hans "Jew Hunter" Landa (Christoph Waltz) murders an entire Jewish family in a French dairy, except for the young daughter Shoshanna (Melanie Laurent), who escaped. Now, four years later Shoshanna owns the Parisian movie theater where the Nazis congregate for the premiere of Goebbel's film. As an act of revenge she plans to lock the theater doors and set fire to the auditorium. Meanwhile, members of the Bastards plant dynamite under the Führer's and Goebbel's seats.

In a bold act of historical revisionism Tarantino allows the killing to take place, strongly implying that the death of Hitler and other top Nazis at the theater brought the war to an abrupt halt. Tarantino's plot resonates with post-9/11 elements by glorifying insurgents, as have *Charlie Wilson's War* (2004), *Defiance* (2008), and *Avatar* (2009). Insurgents constitute the chief antagonists in the wars in Afghanistan and Iraq, and Pakistani insurgents threaten the stability of the national government. Tarantino's and Zwick's portrayals of Jewish resistance fighters contrast with Steven

Spielberg's *Schindler's List* (1993). Spielberg's pre-9/11 film depicts "good Germans"—Oskar Schindler and his Jewish employees—and bad Germans like Amon Goeth (Ralph Fiennes). Zwick's post-9/11 movie honors the Jews themselves, not their German benefactors, and as such seems a more powerful statement about Holocaust resistance. Tarantino's film also honors American Jewish fighters. And in both films Jews successfully stand up to Nazis. In post-9/11 Hollywood, Islamic terrorists bear striking similarities to Nazis. The return of World War II films evokes patriotism, noticeably absent in a number of contemporary films containing antiwar and anticorporate themes, like *Syriana* (2005), *Rendition* (2007), *Badland* (2007), and *Redacted* (2007). Victims of Nazi atrocities remind viewers of the victims of the 9/11 attacks. Native insurgents become glorified. However, audiences that cheer the mujahideen in *Charlie Wilson's War* may experience some unease if they contemplate the rapid transformation of Wilson's freedom fighters into the Taliban. Rage fairly shouts from these contemporary combat films, but the brunt of the rage becomes focused on repressive elements in third world countries, big corporations' interference in regional governments, and corrupt intelligence officers.

CHAPTER FIVE

Vengeance

The shock, grief, and rage that Americans experienced in response to 9/11 fueled a desire for revenge against al Qaeda, the Taliban, Osama bin Laden, and even Saddam Hussein. With this feeling came an embrace of violence. Gun sales spiked, immigrants came under attack by homegrown "vigilantes," and the general public supported war. These traits lasted for more than a year, and vestiges still remain.[1] Meanwhile, audiences flocked to superhero films, often adapted from popular comic books created during the "golden age" of comic-book heroes in the 1940s and 1950s. Why the sudden popularity of superheroes, and how did these superheroes change after the terrorist attacks?

Lois Gresh and Robert Weinberg observed that superheroes typically arise from either the science fiction or fantasy genres.[2] Science-based protagonists include Superman, X-Men, the Flash, Iron Man, and the Hulk; fantasy superheroes arise from myth, mysticism, and magic. Humanity's earliest mythology includes superheroes. These powerful characters, often perceived as gods and goddesses, played extensive roles in mythology's account of earth's creation, its dramatic wars, its climatic disasters, and other traumatic events. Greek gods like Apollo, Zeus, and even Herakles (Hercules), a human promoted to the rank of god, performed countless miraculous deeds that qualify them as superheroes. Zeus wielded lightning bolts to strike down his enemies, whereas Herakles employed his courage, superstrength, and warrior skills to perform amazing feats. Ancient gods and goddesses exist in many cultures and include the following:

- Shiva, a major deity in Hinduism
- Isis, the Egyptian mother goddess

- Osiris, Egyptian god of the underworld
- Quetzalcoatl, Mesoamerican feathered serpent deity
- Hare, Native American trickster god
- Thor, Scandinavian fire god

In mythology, gods often work closely with mortal heroes, sometimes beginning as mortals themselves (Herakles) and gaining god status after overcoming difficult obstacles. These ancient characters possessed humanity's most important powers, including intelligence, strength, perception, and courage, the same qualities possessed by today's superheroes. The ancient gods and goddesses served as behavioral models for people of all ages and their followers exhibited aspects of modern religious congregations.

Richard Corliss observed that today's superhero characters function like supernatural beings, "comic-book heroes are the Greek gods of a modern kid's mythology. At once superhuman and all too human, they rise from meager surroundings to an Olympus of grandeur."[3] Early comic-book superheroes of the 1930s and 1940s possessed single superpowers: speed (the Flash and Johnny Quick), flight (Hawkman and Black Condor), and superstrength (Captain America, Popeye the Sailor). Creators of these characters drew inspiration from the science and technology of the period, such as evolutionary biology, physics, chemistry, and even new food preservation technology. Popeye the Sailor, first appearing in 1929, received superhuman strength only after eating a can of spinach, a reference to nutritional studies involving fruits and vegetables of the period. The Flash (created in 1940) acquired his superpower after accidentally ingesting hard water (deuterium), a reference to contemporary experiments in nuclear physics. Hour-Man (1940) possessed a special pill that provided superpowers for only sixty minutes, referencing experiments with anabolic steroids during the 1930s and 1940s. Captain America, making his first appearance in 1941, achieved superstrength after receiving injections of "supersoldier" serum from the army, a reference to contemporary military experiments with anabolic steroids.[4] The 1962 comic-book hero Spider-Man received his arachnid-like powers after being bitten by a radioactive spider, a reference to the budding science of genetics.[5]

Early Superheroes

Superman, one of the first comic-book characters possessing superpowers, appeared in 1938, during a period dominated by the Great Depression. Before he waged war against the Axis powers, Superman battled corrupt slumlords and greedy munitions monopolists back home, unpopular characters in Depression-era America. After the Japanese attack on Pearl Harbor, Superman and other pioneer superheroes (Batman, 1939; Captain Avenger, 1940; Captain America, 1941) enlisted in the war effort and began battling the Third Reich and Imperial Japan. Other popular comic-book superheroes appeared as movies, starting with *Adventures of Captain Marvel* (1941), *Batman* (1943), *The Phantom* (1943), *Captain America* (1944), and *Superman* (1948), amid the emotional upheavals of World War II. Early superheroes appealed not only to children but also to adults, especially American soldiers. The popularity of early superhero movies presaged the surge of popularity in the ones released during the post-9/11 period, reflecting both eras' traumas and issues.

The early Superman was "faster than a speeding bullet, more powerful than a locomotive," and "able to leap tall buildings in a single bound." These amazing powers appear weak when compared with the Superman who has evolved. In 1938 he had not mastered flight, having journeyed to earth originally aboard a small rocket ship from the planet Krypton. He developed his powers after being adopted by human parents, the Kents, in the town of Smallville. Relatively powerless though he was, the original Superman became one of the world's most popular characters.[6] After the Japanese attack on Pearl Harbor, Superman's powers increased exponentially in response to the wartime threats posed by Imperial Japan and by Nazi Germany, and he began to mete out vengeance against Nazi and Japanese agents. He gained the ability to fly through the atmosphere (and later through space) solely by exercising his will. Eventually, he acquired heat vision, X-ray vision, superhearing, breath more powerful than tornadoes, and the ability to hypnotize instantly.[7] Superman's powers expanded further during the cold war when he combated criminal masterminds bent on domination of the universe (symbolizing the often assumed Soviet goal of world domination).

Superhero films proved popular in the late 1970s and 1980s, perhaps the result of the U.S. withdrawal and defeat in the Vietnam War. The Superman franchise, which now includes the post-9/11 era, originally consisted of five films: *Superman* (1978), *Superman II* (1980), *Superman III* (1983), *Supergirl* (1984), and *Superman IV: The Quest for Peace* (1987). Superman (Christopher Reeve) conceals his true identity behind the persona of Clark Kent, a mild-mannered newspaper reporter working for a large newspaper, the Metropolis *Daily Planet.* He battles supervillains from Krypton as well as a notorious human criminal, Lex Luthor.

Another popular series, the Batman series, first came to the screen in a 1966 movie titled *Batman: The Movie,* followed by *Batman* (1989) directed by Tim Burton, *Batman Triumphant* (1997), and *Batman: Dark Knight* (1998). Each installment features further adventures of the "Caped Crusader," who exhibits a marked fascination with bats, including his secret residence in an underground "Bat-Cave." Batman actually possesses no superhuman powers, only an enormous fortune, a dedication to fighting criminals, and a wealth of technologically advanced accessories, like his Batcar and Batcape. He represents law and order, military science, and technology.

Superhero films appearing just prior to 9/11 feature protagonists very different from those after 9/11. One of the more memorable pre-9/11 films, M. Night Shyamalan's *Unbreakable* (2000), features David Dunn (Bruce Willis) and Elijah Price (Samuel L. Jackson), two seemingly ordinary citizens, who turn out to be superheroes. Dunn, a security guard at a sports stadium, possesses superstrength and can be hurt only by water. Price, also known as "Mr. Glass," serves as his supervillain nemesis. These two characters seem much more human than the superheroes after 9/11.

The comic-book industry responded quickly to the September 11 attacks. Marvel Comics commissioned a special 9/11 edition called *Marvel's Heroes* in December 2001, which featured an image of an angry Captain America towering above Manhattan, his massive legs arising from the location of the destroyed Twin Towers. In February 2002 a special memorial edition of the *Spider-Man* comic (#36) appeared in which 9/11 survivors ask Spider-Man why superheroes did nothing to stop the hijackers. The shocked Spider-Man replies that "we couldn't imagine. [Events like the 9/11 attacks] are beyond words" and "beyond comprehension."[8] Rudiger Heinze observed that, although many of the images in the comic memorials contain elements of a "still standing proud" sentiment, the superheroes in the comic-book tributes to the victims also appear battered, dispirited, shocked. Even the purportedly unbreakable shield of Captain America appears frayed and damaged.[9] Transformations also occurred in the film industry, but in this case the superheroes exhibit anger in response to society's fears and anxieties.

Some superheroes qualify as "mutants," or radically altered humans with extranormal powers "arising or resulting from mutation."[10] Wilmar H. Shiras introduced us to mutants in the popular science fiction novel titled *Children of the Atom* (1953), in which children of factory workers who experience an atomic munitions explosion develop superintelligence and other advanced abilities. When they become teenagers, they form a special school for gifted "mutants." The plot of Shiras's widely popular novel forms the basis for the X-Men comic-book series and post-9/11 X-Men movies. Early mutant characters in films often appeared as villains, monsters, or aliens wielding superpowers that threatened the United States or even the entire earth. In 1972 giant mutant rabbits terrorize citizens in William F. Claxton's *Night of the Lepus,* and in John Cardos's *Mutants* (1984) the citizens of a small midwestern town mutate into murderous zombies after a local plant releases toxic chemicals into the environment, in a Love Canal analogy. Post-9/11 mutants experience accelerated rates of genetic mutation when compared with the teenage protagonists of *Children of the Atom.* Contemporary mutant characters owe their superpowers not just to atomic radiation but also to the more intense bombardment from gamma rays, cosmic rays, exposure to toxic chemicals, abuse of steroid drugs, or advanced chemical formulas able to transform ordinary human beings into powerful machines.

Bryan Singer's first installment, *X-Men* (2000), exemplifies pre-9/11 "scientific" superheroes. Planning for the film adaptation of the popular Marvel Comics characters surfaced as early as 1969, but after lengthy negotiations Twentieth Century Fox hired Singer to direct the film thirty years later, in 1999. Singer initially planned a sci-fi film after the success of his neonoir *The Usual Suspects* (1995), but he turned down Fox's first offer to direct the adaptation because he believed that comics represented a backward medium. Singer changed his mind after reading the X-Men comics and decided that his experience directing an ensemble film like *The Usual Suspects* would prove valuable in the new film.[11]

The film features a collection of powerful yet kinky characters, both men and women, created in a rare instance of accelerated evolution. A corrupt human government attempts to suppress and neutralize mutants through congressional legislation called the Mutant Registration Act, similar to contemporary legislation aimed at illegal immigrants. The newly evolved X-Men find themselves pitted against a militant mutant group, called the Brotherhood of Mutants, commanded by the most powerful mutant, Eric Lehnsherr/Magneto (Ian McKellen). The Brotherhood abducts Senator Robert Kelly (Bruce Davison), the bill's leading advocate, and induces mutations in him, but they soon encounter strong opposition to the militant agenda. Professor Charles Xavier (Patrick Stewart) and his "friendly" X-Men group, Logan/Wolverine (Hugh Jackman), Marie/Rogue (Anna Paquin), Dr. Jean Gray (Famke Janssen), and Ororo Munroe/Storm (Halle Berry) resist the villainous mutants and defeat armed police and military units. Professor Xavier explains the existence of mutant powers in his narration: "Mutation: it is the key to our evolution. It has enabled us to evolve from a single-celled organism into the dominant species on the planet. This process is slow, normally taking thousands and thousands of years. But every few hundred millennia, evolution leaps forward." This appeal to the theory of evolution, albeit radically altered from Charles Darwin's nineteenth-century ideas, provides a glib explanation of mutant powers. Could the process of mutation, which normally unfolds over many generations, result in the power to move vast amounts of physical matter through willpower? Could such a transformation scientifically account for the widespread mutant power to heal damaged body tissues in seconds, even mortal wounds? Could it result in the ability to fly? Movie mutants accomplish all of that with little scientific basis.

Post-9/11 Superheroes

Dramatic changes in the X-Men franchise reveal volumes about the impact of 9/11 on Hollywood genres. Bryan Singer reprised this popular film in 2003 with many of the original characters. However, the heroes of *X-Men 2* appear more conflicted than those in the original, and the villains in Singer's sequel seem far more brutal and menacing. Early in the film, a mutant named Nightcrawler (Alan Cumming) attempts to assassinate the U.S. president, who barely escapes. A scientist named General William

Stryker (Brian Cox) searches for the location of the mutant school and the power chamber Cerebro to identify and kill all the mutants. Soon a full-fledged war breaks out between American humans, led by Stryker and the "good" mutants led by Professor Charles Xavier (Patrick Stewart), and ter-roristlike mutants led by Magneto (Ian McKellen). Eventually, Magneto's mutants unite with the X-Men to defeat Stryker's powerful forces. The dramatic changes seen in *X-Men 2* testify to the remarkable potency of the 9/11 trauma.

The surprising popularity of *X-Men 2* assured the creation of another sequel, called *X-Men: The Last Stand* (2006). In this installment the clash between mutants and humans grows even darker and more violent. Scientists discover an "antidote" to mutant powers, possibly even killing them in the process. In this sequel, the mutants tire of facing human discrimination and even seem willing to trade their superpowers for a normal human existence. The X-Men mutants may represent U.S. minorities of any type. Meanwhile, the film's humans appear discriminatory. *X-Men: First Class,* a prequel, appeared in 2011. The X-Men wield their superpowers to cleanse the earth of chaotic forces and to avenge atrocities.

Sam Raimi's *Spider-Man* (2002) went into production as a major film featuring teenage geek Peter Parker (Tobey Maguire). A radioactive spider bites Parker, and he mutates into Spider-Man, a superhero sporting a mus-cled physique and new ability to crawl up walls, shoot webs from his wrists, and travel through the air as if possessing the gift of flight. At first Parker functions as a classic reluctant hero but eventually learns that he must fight crime and become a police vigilante. Kanti C. Kotecha and James L. Walker described police vigilantism as "acts or threats by police which are intended to protect the established socio-political order from subversion but which violate some generally perceived norms for police behavior."[12] Spider-Man qualifies as such, battling crime as a private citizen with no official author-ity. But his superpowers provide a personal arsenal against criminals, who function as symbolic stand-ins for Islamic terrorists. Raimi casts billionaire Norman Osborn (Willem Dafoe) as the villain, who ingests a performance-altering potion and transforms into a ruthless supervillain called the Green Goblin.

To highlight Spider-Man's crime-fighting powers, advance trailers for the film featured gunmen robbing a Manhattan bank and making a getaway in a helicopter that runs into Spider-Man's web spun between the Twin

Scene still: *Spider-Man 3,* 2007. Peter Parker (Spider-Man) transforms into a darker version of himself in order to defeat the potent villains who threaten New York City. (Marvel / Sony Pictures / The Kobal Collection)

Towers. After 9/11 Sony deleted this trailer. When the film finally arrived in theaters in May 2002, *Spider-Man* resonated with post-9/11 audiences, who applauded Parker as he defeats the Green Goblin and reestablishes order in New York City. Raimi's film immediately dominated the box office, earning $118 million in its opening weekend, nearly recapturing its production budget of $139 million. After only sixty-four release days, the film's earnings topped $400 million, placing it among Hollywood's top-grossing films. Only *Titanic; Star Wars; E.T., the Extraterrestrial;* and *Star Wars: Episode 1, the Phantom Menace* had earned more box office revenues than *Spider-Man.*[13] *Spider-Man* sequels proved even more popular and profitable, with *Spider-Man 2* (2004) grossing over $783 million with a $200 million budget and *Spider-Man 3* (2007) with a budget of $258 million grossing over $890 million.[14]

   In *Spider-Man 2,* also directed by Raimi, an older Peter Parker (Tobey Maguire) enrolls in college, where he continues to struggle in his relationships. Raimi opts for the same plot devices employed in *Spider-Man,* unmasking the hero to his girlfriend, then having him renounce his super-powers in an attempt to become "normal." Dr. Otto Octavius (Alfred Molina), the supervillain of *Spider-Man 2,* adds to the film's appeal and almost steals the show from Spider-Man, with his hybridized arms and octopus fixation. As a reluctant hero, Spider-Man eventually uses his superpowers to fight Dr. Octavius. September 11 created audiences that welcomed powerful superheroes fighting domestic terrorists.

The phenomenal success of *Spider-Man* launched numerous new films designed to capitalize on the superhero market. Mark Steven Johnson released *Daredevil* in 2003, featuring another mutant superhero, this time based on a popular Marvel Comics character of the same name. Ben Affleck stars as Matt Murdock, a Hell's Kitchen lawyer who as a child accidentally witnesses his father, a washed-up boxer, ruthlessly beating a man at the behest of a local gang leader named Fallon. Shame and anger cause Matt to run away, heedless of a nearby container of toxic waste. The waste spurts into his eyes, blinding him but in the process somehow endowing him with superpowers. Murdock trains his body to sense his environment with the help of special sonar powers that allow him to "see" as clearly as a sighted person. In addition, he develops abilities to dive from the top of skyscrapers and escape death with deft acrobatic moves, leading to his nickname, "Daredevil."

Daredevil confronts Bullseye (Colin Farrell), an assassin possessing the power to throw projectiles with 100 percent accuracy as well as the usual superpowers of flight and might. Along the way Daredevil meets Elektra (Jennifer Garner), a martial artist who also possesses the ability to jump to ledges high above her head and to swing from and virtually fly along skyscrapers like Daredevil and Bullseye. Elektra becomes angered at Daredevil after Bullseye murders her father and makes it appear to be the work of Daredevil. After nearly killing Daredevil in the final scene, Elektra herself seemingly dies at the hands of Bullseye. However, Daredevil eventually defeats and kills Bullseye, and Elektra sends him a sign that she is still alive (in case of a sequel). Daredevil follows in the post-9/11 pattern of masked superheroes/vigilante crime fighters popularized by Spider-Man.

Ang Lee's *Hulk* (2003) brings to the screen a fairly complex Marvel Comics figure with an Oedipal backstory. The protagonist, Bruce Banner (Eric Bana), a young biochemist accidentally exposed to intense radiation, discovers that when he is angered, his body transforms into a green giant with superhuman powers. During the presidential elections of 2004 and 2008, a Web site hosted mock elections pitting the Incredible Hulk against Kerry/Edwards and Bush/Cheney in 2004 and Obama/Biden and McCain/Palin in 2008. The results are hardly startling—the Hulk came in third behind the major political candidates. However, the comic-book character polled strongly because of his superhuman strength. After the 2004 election this Web site noted that Bush/Cheney focused on the search for weapons of mass destruction in Iraq, whereas the Hulk "is a weapon of mass destruction." In times of national trauma, film audiences find superheroes like the Incredible Hulk especially attractive.[15] This character serves as a perfect post-9/11 superhero because his superpowers flow from his anger.

Jonathan Mostow's *Terminator 3* (2003) features a robotic "cyborg" from the future, the Terminator (Arnold Schwarzenegger). The Terminator battles valiantly to save humanity from a plot engineered by a new strategic defense computer system called Skynet, which is actually attempting to dominate earth. The Terminator facilitates a human rebellion that defeats Skynet's control. Mostow's film, along with others like *I, Robot* (2004) and *Transformers* (2007), expresses ambivalence about technology, especially military weaponry and Internet technology. However, futuristic technology empowers superheroes like Iron Man, Batman, and the Terminator as well as their nemeses.

Guillermo Del Toro's *Hellboy* (2004) introduces a mutant character, Hellboy (Ron Perlman), a human-demon hybrid conjured up by the Nazis during World War II but raised and tamed by Professor Trevor "Broom" Bruttenholm (John Hurt) on a U.S. military base. Hellboy, a huge, red, horned, but very human demon, becomes an essential tool in secret U.S. efforts to combat monsters that seem to appear with increasing frequency. Finally, the Bureau of Paranormal Research, headed by Professor Bruttenholm, enlists two assistants for Hellboy, Sapien (Doug Jones), an aquatic mutant possessing psychic powers, and Liz Sherman (Selma Blair), a mutant with pyro-telekenetic superpowers. Armed with these superallies, Hellboy defeats the monsters threatening to unleash Armageddon. Hellboy's human assistant, Agent John Meyers (Rupert Evans), articulates the film's philosophy in a final statement asking, "What makes a man a man?" The answer is, "The choices he makes, not how he starts things, but how he decides to end them." Clearly, the combined forces of the superhero crime fighters must be brought to bear against the supervillains they face. This Manichean perspective of good versus evil reflects Bush administration policies in its war on terror.

It was only a matter of time before a studio created a full-length animated superhero movie. Pixar released its own animated version in 2004 titled *The Incredibles*. Written and directed by Brad Bird, the film features the Parr family of superheroes, headed by Bob Parr (Craig T. Nelson), nicknamed "Mr. Incredible" for his superstrength and athletic abilities. Bob marries "Elastigirl" (Holly Hunter), who possesses an ability to stretch her pliable body around corners and flatten and elongate arms, legs, hands, and fingers in order to fight crime. After a public backlash, similar to the *X-Men* plot, Congress enacts antisuperhero legislation, and the Parrs retreat into suburbia, where Bob takes a job as an insurance agent. The couple produces three children, each possessing superpowers: Dash (Spencer Fox) possesses superspeed, Violet (Sarah Vowell) can become invisible and produce a powerful force field, and Jack-Jack (Eli Fucile and Maeve Andrews) is a shapeshifter with the ability to turn himself into anything, including the ability to burst into flames, transform into metal, and turn into a powerful monster. After fifteen years spent in suburbia, in which the family refrains from superhuman activities, Bob "comes out of the closet" and resumes his role as Mr. Incredible. Eventually, the family reunites as a powerful team of crime fighters. Joined by other out-of-work superheroes, the Parr family defeats powerful robots controlled by a supervillain named Syndrome (Jason Lee). Returning to suburban anonymity, the Parrs soon become recruited to combat another supermenace, called the Underminer (John Ratzenberger), and so the cycle repeats.

The Incredibles, like *X-Men 2* (2003) and *Watchmen* (2009), feature superheroes harassed by federal legislation. These laws restricting superheroes evoke events such as the withdrawal of U.S. military forces from Vietnam at the conclusion of the Vietnam War and the curtailment of CIA covert operations toward the end of the cold war. Conservatives often charge that the legislative branch hamstrings covert operations by insisting they abide by the U.S. Constitution, analogous to the fictional legislative acts. The "legislation" in these movies eventually lead to civil war between rival factions of mutants and/or superheroes. In addition, restrictive legislation in superhero films evokes repressive policies against illegal immigrants in real life.

Rob Bowman's *Elektra* (2005) is spun from *Daredevil* (2003). Jennifer Garner plays Elektra Natchios, the daughter of a Greek billionaire and a carefully trained superhero crime fighter. The story takes up where *Dare-devil* leaves off, with Stick (Terence Stamp), a martial artist, bringing Elektra back to life and teaching her a new form of martial art. This form, Kimagure, endows its possessors with the ability to foresee the future and control life and death. Elektra and other Kimagure students confront an evil band of assassins known as the Hand. After Elektra graduates as a full-fledged Kimagure assassin, she receives an assignment to kill Mark Miller (Goran Visnjic) and his thirteen-year-old daughter, Abby (Kirstin Prout), on a remote island. After befriending Abby and her father, Elektra decides not to assassinate them. But before she leaves the island, she observes two other assassins arriving to replace her. She stays behind to kill the assassins, then flees with Mark and Abby back to the mainland.

At this point the Hand retaliates by sending Kirigi (Will Yun Lee), along with Stone (Bob Sapp), Tattoo (Chris Ackerman), and Typhoid (Natassia Malthe), to penalize Elektra and to capture Mark and Abby. Now desperate, Elektra seeks Stick's help. Only then does she realize that Abby is actually "the Treasure," a powerful young mutant/assassin in her own right. Together with the Treasure and Stick's followers, Elektra defeats the Hand supervillains and saves the lives of Mark and Abby. This story reinforces the maxim that enlisting allies results in victory, whereas independence results in defeat. Superheroes defeat the supervillains by taking cooperative action in which their strengths become magnified. *Elektra* was one of the first superhero films to emphasize the theme of strength through community.

In 2006 Bryan Singer, flush with *X-Men* success, reprised the Superman franchise and released *Superman Returns.* The venerable Man of Steel dominates, played this time by Brandon Routh, who bears a strong resemblance to Christopher Reeve, star of *Superman* (1978) and *Superman II* (1980). In this post-9/11 sequel, Superman returns from a five-year private journey to view the remains of his home planet, Krypton. Upon his return to earth, he encounters a greatly altered Metropolis. Lois Lane (Kate Bosworth), angered and frustrated by his unexplained absence, has moved on to a relationship with Richard White (Frank Marsden), son of Perry White (Frank Langella), editor of the *Daily Planet,* and also now has a son.

Kevin Spacey plays Lex Luthor, the film's villainous ex-con who threatens humanity by creating a new, virulent continent in the Atlantic. Acting as a mad agent of chaos, Luthor enacts a plot to destroy most of humanity while terrorizing and extorting those remaining, who he believes will flock to the new continent to be ruled by Luthor or face extinction. Luthor has already managed to amass kryptonite rocks, which emerge from the Atlantic and may remind viewers of global climate change. Superman steps in to confront Luthor but finds himself powerless in the presence of kryptonite. Superman undergoes a brutal and humiliating beating at the hands of Luthor and his henchmen. Finally, Luthor stabs Superman in the back with a green kryptonite knife, and the Man of Steel plunges from a precipice into the ocean.

Superman nearly dies after expending his strength uprooting Luthor's kryptonite continent. With Lane's help, he ultimately recovers, and Luthor ends up stranded, with little food, on a desert island. In the finale, like a proverbial outlaw hero, Superman flies off into the sunset after promising Lane that he will remain earth's savior: "I'm always around." Singer's Superman qualifies as the most pessimistic and postmodern of the Superman characters. Compared to the original, Singer's Superman appears much more vulnerable and introspective, brooding away on Krypton, and leaving Lois to become involved with a rival. Like classic Western heroes, Superman must retreat periodically from public awareness, yet he supposedly remains a watchful presence. Singer plans to reboot the Superman series with *Superman: Man of Steel*, slated for release in 2012, also starring Brandon Routh. The new version will venture even further along the dark trajectory of its most recent predecessor and cast Superman as an "angry god."[16]

Critic Lowell Goodman compared Superman to President George W. Bush. Both characters have "mission impossible" events, both retreat into secret hideaways during times of crisis, and both allow messy situations to develop on their watches. In Goodman's view, "*Superman Returns,* which was the number one movie in America on its opening weekend in June 2006, is a listless, wilted, drawn-out film in which incompetence and distraction are celebrated ahead of focus and achievement—in short, it's the perfect metaphor for the George W. Bush presidency."[17] The events of 9/11 reinvigorated Superman. Gregory McNeill, writing in the Superman homepage, noted that after 9/11 "living with the fear of future terrorist attacks and uncertainty has made us ask 'Where is Superman'? In fact," wrote McNeill, "the truth is he does exist" in powerful, positive imagery. The story of Superman has become a story of antiterrorist Americanism in which the Man of Steel still serves an important social role.[18]

In addition to Elektra, the superhero phenomenon included other females endowed with superpowers. Films depicting female superheroes include *Catwoman* (2004), *Ultraviolet* (2006), *My Super Ex-Girlfriend* (2006), *Wonderwoman* (2009 animated film), and *Wonderwoman* (2011 feature film). From Halle Berry's depiction of Catwoman to the animated Amazon Wonderwoman, female superheroes provide some surprising insights into recent gender wars. These films depict superfemales who survive and triumph in violent settings. Jean-Christophe "Pitof" Comar's *Catwoman* (2004) failed to impress critics, although it performed reasonably well at the box office. Halle Berry's depiction of Patience (a significantly named graphics designer) and her magical mutation into Catwoman, capable of almost unlimited feats of strength, become a bit difficult for many viewers to accept, but the raw animal magnetism of her simulation of a human-cat hybrid appears impressive at times, a bit tedious at others. Berry's acting abilities provide the film with sexy movements and seductive gestures and glances, but critics and audiences alike were less than enthusiastic. Pitof's film, which cost $100 million to produce, grossed only $82 million by 2011.[19]

Kurt Wimmer's *Ultraviolet* (2006), set in the late twenty-first century, presents Violet (Milla Jovovich), a young woman afflicted by a blood disease that provides her with superpowers. Violet derives powers both from her enhanced fighting abilities and from advanced technology. She possesses an arsenal of weapons hidden in another dimension and an antigravity machine allowing her and her motorcycle to traverse walls and walk upside down on ceilings. She belongs to a population of other "hemophages." After a successful fight against armed warriors intent on killing or capturing Six (Cameron Bright), a very special young boy, Violet befriends the boy. He supposedly carries a deadly pathogen in his blood that would annihilate all hemophages, but she refuses to turn him over to the Arch Ministry, an evil dictatorship. Soon a war erupts between hemophage superheroes and humans, with corruption visible on both sides. Ultimately, Violet defeats all antagonists and even returns to life after being murdered.

Ivan Reitman's comedy *My Super Ex-Girlfriend* (2006) depicts superhero G-Girl (Uma Thurman), whose powers arose after she touched a glowing meteorite while in high school. She instantly acquired superstrength, superhearing, laser vision, and flight. Like most superheroes, G-Girl hides behind an alternate identity, Jenny Johnson, a young art gallery employee. Jenny sheds her business attire and even changes her hair color to become

G-Girl, who fights crime, extinguishes a high-rise fire, saves an airliner, and even deflects an errant guided missile. She becomes enraged when her ordinary human boyfriend, Matt Saunders (Luke Wilson), falls in love with his coworker Hannah Lewis (Anna Faris); G-Girl decides to use her powers to wreck the romance and revenge herself against Saunders. Eventually, Hannah, the "other woman," touches another glowing meteor and acquires similar superpowers. She battles G-Girl to protect Saunders. No doubt the spectacle of two beautiful superheroines fighting over a mortal man fanned many male fantasies, and Reitman's light comedy excelled at the box office, bringing in nearly $61 million with a budget of $20 million while earning a nomination as MTV's "best fight" film (between G-Girl and Hannah).[20]

Christopher Nolan's *Batman Begins* (2005) presents a new Batman in which Bruce Wayne (Christian Bale) combats domestic terrorists who threaten to overrun Gotham City. Initially, eight-year-old Wayne (Gus Lewis) watches helplessly as his wealthy parents die at the hands of thugs. He travels to Asia, where he joins a Ninja-like cult of martial artists. Eventually, he returns to Gotham to direct his family business, Wayne Industries. After he discovers a huge cavern beneath his mansion, Wayne decides to adopt the persona of a superbat, a powerful masked avenger striking fear into the hearts of evildoers. One such person, Mafia don Carmine Falcone (Tom Wilkinson), controls Gotham City and threatens to take over Wayne Industries. Wayne explains his motives this way: "They told me there was nothing out there, nothing to fear. But the night my parents were murdered I caught a glimpse of something. I've looked for it ever since. I went around the world, searched in all the shadows. And there is something out there in the darkness, something terrifying, and something that will not stop until it gets revenge ... Me." As a child helplessly watching his parents' brutal murder, Wayne experiences a rage common to the post-9/11 American culture.

Christopher Nolan's *The Dark Knight* (2008) updates the Batman franchise with another post-9/11 rendition of the popular superhero. Christian Bale again stars as Batman/Bruce Wayne, the dualistic superhero whom many call the most human of the current crop of superheroes. Nolan presents a dark, inglorious, flawed human being, yet leaves Batman with considerable charisma and high-tech weaponry. The Joker (Heath Ledger) represents terrorism and chaos. At the start of the film, we discover that Batman has been strangely absent from Gotham, but the Joker's arrival prompts Batman's return to the public arena. His faithful assistant, Alfred

Scene still: *The Dark Knight,* 2008. Batman (Christian Bale) and the Joker (Heath Ledger) appear in the darkest *Batman* film to date. The superhero and supervillain lock in mortal combat, with the fate of Gotham City's entire population hanging in the balance. Although Batman possesses no superpowers, he compensates with technology and personal training. (Warner Bros / DC Comics / The Kobal Collection)

Pennyworth (Michael Caine), explains that Batman must function above and outside of the law. "He can be the outlaw. He can make the choice that no one else can." Although public acclaim proves fickle, Pennyworth explains that "even if everyone hates him for it, that's the sacrifice. He's not being a hero, he's something more than that."

Eventually the Joker destroys a hospital in a series of explosions reminiscent of 9/11. Manohla Dargis explained that references to 9/11, including firefighters battling a fire raging in a collapsed building, come at a time when larger numbers of mainstream thrillers contain oblique references to the events of September 11. "Like any number of small- and big-screen thrillers, the film's engagement with 9/11 is diffuse, more a matter of inference and ideas (chaos, fear, death) than of direct assertion." Dargis concluded by observing that "a spectacle like this one confirms that American movies have entered a new era of ambivalence when it comes to their heroes."[21] This ambivalence toward heroes involves the perceived need for some extraordinary beings to serve not only as stand-ins for military power but also as compensation for our inadequacies in combating random acts of terrorism. The avengers and protectors eventually transcend law and order. Like the gunslingers of classic Westerns who ride off into the sunset in the finale, today's superheroes fade into the background once they accomplish their missions, to reappear like saviors of the social order when needed.

The Dark Knight resonates with film noir and neonoir icons, from the darkness and venality of Batman to the noirish look of Gotham City, transformed in this film into a seedy urban jungle. Despite its superhero trappings, as Steve Biodrowski remarked, Nolan's film "is more a piece of film noir, a style that typically uses hard-boiled plot lines laced with machismo.... It's the old story of 'a man's gotta do what a man's gotta do,' but in hard-boiled plot, unlike the Western, what a man's gotta do is often not nearly enough."[22]

Tim Story's *Fantastic Four* (2005) features an ensemble of four superpowerful characters. Doctor Victor Von Doom (Julian McMahon) finances a space voyage for himself, along with Reed Richards (Ioan Gruffudd), Sue Storm (Jessica Alba), Johnny Storm (Chris Evans), and Ben Grimm (Michael Chiklis) for a scientific study of DNA. Once in space, the voyagers encounter a violent storm emitting cosmic waves that affect each traveler differently. Von Doom becomes a nearly invincible warrior, whereas Richards becomes Mr. Fantastic, with the ability to flatten his body and stretch his limbs into any shape he desires. Storm gains the ability to make herself invisible and transforms into Invisible Woman. She must first strip naked and stow her clothes to prevent normal people from noticing clothes walking around on their own. Her brother, Johnny, the "Human Torch," possesses the ability to raise his internal temperature to hundreds of degrees and shoot fire from his fingers. In addition, he learns to fly. Grimm grows to become the Thing, a Hulklike being with massive scales covering his body. His hands and feet mutate into enormous, blunt appendages, and he possesses superstrength.

The Storm siblings, Richards, and Grimm unite in group actions, becoming the Fantastic Four. The supervillain Von Doom, known as "Dr. Doom," possesses almost limitless destructive powers but loses the struggle to the Fantastic Four. Similar to previously mentioned films, *The Fantastic Four* clearly demonstrates the benefit of a group approach to facing adversity, a sentiment popular in the post-9/11 era. Interestingly, after the summer 2005 London Tube terrorist attacks that claimed fifty-two lives, the bomber's leader, Omar Baki Mohammed, in a videotape in which a top al Qaeda operative also appeared, referred to the four bombers, who also blew themselves up in the attacks, as the "Fantastic 4." Clearly, this message of unity also appeals to terrorists.[23]

Fantastic Four: Rise of the Silver Surfer (2007) serves as a continuation of the exploits of the Fantastic Four. They square off against the Silver Surfer (Doug Jones), a supervillain working for Galactus, an enormous energy cloud that devours planets. Eventually, the Fantastic Four unite with the Silver Surfer, but not before the supervillain zaps Johnny with a strange energy that nearly kills him and results in all of the Fantastic Four swapping superpowers with each other. Things resolve as the superheroes reunite to defeat a newly empowered Dr. Doom and ultimately Galactus itself. The message reiterates the lessons heavily drawn from the first film—no strength without unity. Not surprisingly, both *Fantastic Four* movies proved extremely popular with audiences. *Fantastic Four,* with a budget of over $87 million, grossed more than $154 million by July 2009. *Fantastic Four: Rise of the Silver Surfer* grossed more than $143 million by July 2009 on a studio investment of $120 million.[24]

Jon Favreau's *Iron Man* (2008) brings yet another Marvel Comics superhero to the silver screen. Favreau's film stars Robert Downey Jr. as Tony Stark (aka Iron Man), a billionaire weapons manufacturer and inventor.

In the first act Stark journeys to Afghanistan to attend a demonstration of Stark Industries' latest weaponry—the Jericho cluster missile system. His convoy comes under attack by the Ten Rings, a terrorist group led by Raza (Faran Tahir). Raza takes Stark prisoner, and Stark awakens in a cave, where he discovers a special electromagnetic device implanted in his heart by fellow captive Dr. Yinsen (Shaun Toub) to reject shrapnel. Stark teams up with Yinsen to formulate an escape plan. In the meantime, Raza demands that Stark build a Jericho cluster missile system for him, and Stark agrees. He appears to work on the missile system but actually invents an "arc reactor" armor suit. The suit, a large metallic exoskeleton, not only shields the wearer from bullet attacks but also functions as a weapons system and personal rocket that allows Stark to escape his captors by flying.

When Stark returns home after his three-month captivity, he announces that his company will no longer invent and manufacture weapons systems, and he spends his time creating an improved version of the power suit, complete with a more powerful arc reactor. During trials of the suit, media pundits label Stark "Iron Man." Stark's second in command, Obadiah Stane (Jeff Bridges), informs him that the board of directors opposes getting out of the weaponry business, and later Stark learns that Stane secretly supplied the Ten Rings insurgents with Stark Industries weapons. Stark and his personal assistant, Virginia "Pepper" Potts (Gwyneth Paltrow), encounter Agent Coulson (Clark Gregg) of Strategic Homeland Invention, Enforcement, and Logistics Division (SHIELD), a military counterterrorism organization, who has been investigating Stark Industries. Stark and Potts learn of Stane's intention to have the Ten Rings kill Stark, clearing the way for Stane to succeed him as CEO of Stark Industries. Stark and Potts inform Agent Coulson, who sets out to arrest Stane, but before he does, Stane paralyzes Stark, then removes the arc reactor from his chest to energize his own power suit, which he built by reengineering Stark's original suit recovered from Afghanistan.

In the end Stark dons his Iron Man exoskeleton and fights with Stane in his suit, dubbed "Iron Monger," a larger, more powerful version. The two duke it out over downtown Los Angeles, with Iron Monger's more powerful suit affording him the advantage. Stane tells Stark, "How ironic, Tony! Trying to rid the world of weapons, you gave it its best one ever! And now, I'm going to kill you with it." Just as Stane is about to destroy Stark, however, Stark flies off to a high altitude in his suit because he knows that Stane's suit is not equipped to deal with ice formation. When Iron Monger finally catches up with Iron Man, Stark asks him, "How'd you solve the icing problem?" Stane's suit promptly ices up and plunges to the ground thousands of feet below. Iron Man has survived to fight again, which appears likely after he encounters Nick Fury (Samuel L. Jackson), director of SHIELD, who informs Iron Man about an upcoming project known only as the "Avenger Initiative." This refers to a Marvel Comics team of superheroes that includes Iron Man, Ant Man, and the Incredible Hulk.

Iron Man differs in several respects from other superhero movies. In the first place, Iron Man is not a mutant. His power, like Batman's, springs exclusively from technology, especially robotics, computer science, metallurgy, and personal flight technology. Mutant superheroes reference technology, too, but their hybrid status focuses attention more on evolution than on technology. Iron Man and Batman rely completely on technological innovations.

The commercial success of *Iron Man* made a sequel all but inevitable, and *Iron Man 2* emerged in 2010, directed, like *Iron Man,* by Jon Favreau. Favreau updated his earlier film by having Tony Stark (Robert Downey Jr.) dying because his heart machine is running out of nuclear fuel. As in the first episode, Stark faces competition from a rival "iron" suit, this time manufactured by archrival Justin Hammer (Sam Rockwell). The two ultimately battle it out for supremacy, and of course Iron Man wins the fight. Roger Ebert raised the question of how anyone could survive in the Iron Man suits unharmed. "Sure, the suits are armored, but their bodies aren't. How many dizzying falls and brutal blows and sneaky explosions can you survive without breaking every bone in your body?"[25] Physics aside, *Iron Man* provides a perfect post-9/11 hero—a billionaire inventor with a conscience.

Doug Liman's *Jumper* (2008) narrates the story of David Rice (Hayden Christiansen), a powerful mutant possessing the ability to teleport himself through willpower instantaneously to any part of the globe, including bank vaults, thereby allowing him to amass great material wealth without much effort. His hedonistic lifestyle comes to a grinding halt, however, after Roland (Samuel L. Jackson) arrives as a professional "jumper" policeman assigned to apprehend or kill jumpers like Rice. *New York Times* critic Manohla Dargis pointed out that *Jumper* parallels the theme of the lone hero stalked and persecuted by a shadowy government agency, the same theme that Liman addresses in his 2002 thriller *The Bourne Identity*, but in *Jumper* the results are very different. Dargis described *Jumper* as "a barely coherent mishmash about a guy who transports himself across the globe at will."[26] The film lacks depth and fine acting, but it does raise once again the question of what exactly is going on regarding mutants and movies. Guys who can go anywhere instantaneously merely by willing it seem especially postmodern, embodying the speed of the Internet with near instantaneous satellite communications.

Gavin Hood's *X-Men Origins: Wolverine* (2009) further develops the X-Men series. Hood focuses on the origin of James Logan/Wolverine (Hugh Jackman). After fighting in numerous wars, from the Civil War through World War II, superhero Logan/Wolverine decides to retire to the Canadian woods and work as a lumberjack. His retirement ends abruptly after his girlfriend dies, apparently at the hands of Victor Creed/Sabertooth (Liev Schreiber), his biological brother but longtime nemesis. Wolverine vows revenge and enrolls in a government program designed to enhance superpowers. His body's weaponry becomes lethal when his horny talons (claws that extend when he is angry or threatened) are replaced with long curved knives made of a hard meteorite metal that slices through any surface with ease.

Wolverine gradually uncovers a clandestine program headquartered at Three Mile Island and led by archvillain William Stryker (Danny Huston). Stryker hopes to achieve nothing short of world domination with his latest mutant creation, Weapon XI, a superhero combining all known superpowers in a single being. Weapon XI fights Wolverine, who finally teams up with Sabertooth to defeat XI and save earth. Critics tended to dislike *X-Men Origins*. *New York Times* critic A. O. Scott complained that *Wolverine* seemed badly flawed. Scott found it "almost programmatically unmemorable, a hodge-podge of loose ends, wild inconsistencies and stale genre conventions."[27] In 2011, *X-Men: First Class,* a prequel, appeared as a new installment to the series.

Zack Snyder's *Watchmen* (2009) is set in a retro yet futuristic 1985 in which masked superheroes' appearances are normal. It features the Watchmen, a set of aging superheroes, only one of which, Dr. Manhattan (Billy Crudup), possesses true superpowers. He maintains the "balance of power" with his immortality and formidable firepower. When someone murders one of the retired Watchmen, Walter "Roschach" Kovacs (Jackie

Earle Haley) launches an investigation that leads to a mysterious conspiracy to rid the earth of superheroes. Richard Nixon, still president in 1985, enlists Dr. Manhattan to assist in the Vietnam War, which results in a U.S. victory. However, the world appears at the brink of a cold war–style nuclear Armageddon, and riots erupt in the streets after a massive police strike in New York City. The Watchmen fill the power vacuum and restore order, while Dr. Manhattan works feverishly to invent a free source of energy to replace the worldwide competition for oil and gas resources. These heroes represent the possibilities—and limits—of technology to solve the world's problems. The original novel contained a bloody scene at the end, but Snider decided against it in the movie version because he empathized with the post-9/11 audience. In an interview, screenwriter David Hayter explained that the ending of the book "shows just piles of corpses, bloody corpses in the middle of Times Square, people hanging out of windows just slaughtered on a massive scale." He explained, "To do that in a comic book, and release it in 1985, is different from doing it real life, in a movie, and seeing all of these people brutally massacred in the middle of Times Square post 2001. That's a legitimate concern, and one that I shared."[28]

Paul McGuigan's *Push* (2009) chronicles the exploits of paranormal superheroes in Hong Kong. A shadowy quasi-governmental agency called the Division recruits and genetically transforms mutants possessing paranormal abilities into superwarriors. Nick Grant (Chris Evans), who possesses the ability to move objects and people telekinetically (labeled a "mover"), hides in Hong Kong until he receives a visit from Division personnel searching for Kira Hudson (Camilla Belle) a powerful "pusher," someone with the ability to control people by planting thoughts into their minds. Soon thirteen-year-old mover Cassie Holmes (Dakota Fanning) enlists Nick to help her find Kira.

Nick, Cassie, and Kira possess psychic powers, some of which parallel those of the X-Men and the Fantastic Four. Although the *Push* superheroes lack the ability to fly or to shoot flames from their bodies, their psychic powers prove extremely potent. For example, in order to escape from Division officers, Kira plants thoughts in one agent's head that compel him to shoot his partner, allowing Kira to escape. They also encounter supervillains with extreme superpowers. One villain possesses the ability to scream at a pitch powerful enough to shatter plate glass and cause internal bleeding, whereas another pusher lifts Nick off the ground mentally and smashes him against the ceiling, then lets him drop to the ground. Somehow Nick survives without any suffering—not a broken back, neck, or ribs.

Is telekinesis real? The phrase "mind over matter" conjures up strange and potent mental abilities that may affect the material world. Many telekinesis artists of the past proved to be charlatans. That no scientific evidence supports this superpower fails to stop comic-book writers and filmmakers from creating characters with this ability. Science now reveals that minds can be trained to move computer cursors and control robotic arms. According to Assistant Professor Jose Carmena of the University of California, Berkeley, "The brain can form a motor memory to control a disembodied device." Dr. Carmena reported in 2009 that for the first time experimental subjects, in this case monkeys, could be trained to operate game joysticks and other mechanical devices solely with their minds, assisted by electrodes implanted in their brains.[29] Although this experiment used brain implants, it may be possible in the future to train individuals to control matter telekinetically. That continues to be remote from the powerful movers in *Push*. For now, telekinesis serves as a weapon only for comic-book writers and filmmakers, not the military.

Post-9/11 audiences gravitate to superheroes who save humanity. In an age of uncertainty these powerful characters make audiences feel less vulnerable to unexpected, violent acts of aggression against U.S. targets. At the same time, the superheroes themselves have darkened and grown more vulnerable. These new characters, as potent as their predecessors but vulnerable and more attuned with contemporary styles, make audiences feel secure. "There was that thing of 'Why didn't Superman save us? Why didn't he come along and stop the planes?' There was a brief debate about whether superheroes were relevant any more. In a strange way, though, they've become more relevant."[30] A. O. Scott believed that "this decade has been a somewhat golden age for large scale action movies featuring guys in high-tech body suits battling garishly costumed, ruthless criminal masterminds."[31] In the post-9/11 period superheroes enjoy greater popularity with motion picture audiences than ever before in film history.

Supervillains

Superheroes arise during periods of extreme national danger, including World War II, the cold war, and the post-9/11 era, to combat potent antagonists like Adolf Hitler, Hideki Tojo, and Benito Mussolini. Comic-book heroes battle these antagonists, but their creators realize the necessity of creating villainous characters that serve as appropriate antagonists. Similar to the fate of the heroes, previously threatening villains seem weak compared with those after 9/11.[32] Post-9/11 superheroes require supervillains, characters who threaten to destroy social order and stability. These include the 1940s and 1950s comic-book villains Lex Luthor, Superman's nemesis, and the Joker, Batman's antagonist. But in the post-9/11 period these characters morph into urban terrorists intent not only on killing or maiming the superheroes but also on annihilating everyone else along with them. In *Superman Returns,* archvillain Lex Luthor hatches a plot to destroy the entire North American continent using crystals of kryptonite, which also weaken Superman. The Man of Steel must defeat Luthor to save the lives of millions, if not billions. And the Joker's nefarious plans for Gotham City include murder on a mass scale. Clearly, these villains have become more dangerous over the past few years.

Kristoffer Tabori's *Fireball* (2009), a made-for-TV movie, features Tyler Draven (Aleks Paunovic) as a former NFL linebacker turned convicted wife beater and steroid abuser who undergoes a genetic mutation caused by an overabundance of designer steroids. He becomes a human torch, bursting into flame when angered. At one point Draven takes his anger out on his prison, burning the place down and escaping. Fire inspector Ava Williams (Lexa Doig) goes into hot pursuit, especially after she realizes that Draven's fire-filled rage appears likely to vent on a nuclear power plant and will kill many people. This irascible supervillain morphs into a mindless killing machine who is eventually stopped and killed, but only after having burned and killed innocent people. Fireball's pyrotechnical superpower affords some interesting scenes, but this movie falls short on character and plot development. Nevertheless, it is one of the few examples of a film based on a supervillain without a superhero nemesis and only normal human investigators, who eventually defeat this villainous character.

Science and Technology

The science fiction genre of the 1950s and 1960s owed much of its scientific (and pseudoscientific) underpinning to popular scientific advancements of the post–World War II era, including aerospace engineering ("rocket science") and nuclear physics. These sciences played important roles in the postwar era as the USSR and the United States faced off in what became the cold war. Each side deployed increasingly sophisticated missile and warplane technology and kept peace through a "balance of terror" under constant danger of mutual nuclear annihilation. Cold war technology also included advanced surveillance devices and, during the later phase, increasingly sophisticated computer technology. Post-9/11 superheroes reflect the sciences of genetics, bioengineering, electronics, and astrophysics.

This technology includes tiny performance-enhancing microprocessors; metallurgy; nanotube fabrics; state-of-the-art automobiles, motorcycles, and aircraft; and performance-stimulating drugs and potions. Today's superheroes act as superpowerful soldiers and police officers able to establish and maintain order in a world perceived as increasingly violent and chaotic. Potent supervillains threaten New York City, the United States, and the earth itself, a cinematic reflection of the real dangers facing contemporary citizens, including the constant threat of terrorist attacks; the closely related threat of invasive, dictatorial, corrupt governments; and the threat of global climate change or other ecological or geological disasters. Finally, the threat of economic depression has arisen since November 2008.

The protagonists of contemporary superhero films may be genetic mutations (X-Men, Spider Man, Fireball, Daredevil), labeled "mutants" in comic books and Hollywood movies. Such mutants owe their fictional existence to Darwin's theory of evolution, one of the most productive and controversial theories in the history of science. Even today Darwin's theory provokes ire in groups as disparate as Christian Fundamentalists and scientific skeptics (the latter group including Harvard biologist Stephen J. Gould, now deceased). Darwin proposed that genetic mutations on the cellular level might result in changes in an organism's morphology. Because of cellular complexity, mutations might be helpful, harmful, or neutral.[33] Most of the changes would have little or no effect on an organism, but occasionally a mutation might result in an organism having greater chances to survive, mate, and, possibly, replicate the mutated gene in his or her progeny. It is through this process that species "evolve" over millennia.

Iron Man helped popularize the notion of a personalized rocket-powered suit that renders its wearer almost invulnerable. Of course, the suit consists of exotic metals, not iron. After Iron Man flies to the edge of space, Jarvis the robot suggests to Tony Stark, the inventor of the flying exoskeleton, that he might need to reinforce the mechanism's exterior if Stark intends to visit other planets in his suit. Stark tells Jarvis to order the automated construction system to reconfigure the metal alloys used. "Have it reconfigure the shell metals," he instructs. "Use the gold titanium alloy from the seraphim tactical satellite. That should ensure fuselage integrity while maintaining power-to-weight ratio. Got it?"

Dreams of personal flying machines have resonated in Hollywood for many decades, harkening back to the Commando Cody series of the 1950s. James Bond borrowed Cody's famous jetpack for one episode, but Bond's car occasionally doubles as a boat or plane. Of course, Batman's Batmobile also doubles as a personal aircraft. To date, aside from ultralight airplanes, no personal flying system exists commercially, although the military no doubt experiments with such systems fairly often. No flying suit exists to date, but a Japanese company plans to market the leg sections of an exoskeleton soon. The leg exoskeletons reduce the weight of backpacks by 80 percent owing to weight transference through the exoskeleton legs to the ground. Project Solo Trek tested an entire flying exoskeleton that was reportedly capable of flying 125 miles, but the project was canceled after a crash in 2002. Finally, Stark's high-tech computer-imaging system already exists in the 3-D Tactile Interface programs.[34] Although Iron Man's name implies an older technology, the movie actually makes use of existing cutting-edge technology.

Much of Batman's appeal results from advanced technology. Bruce Wayne possesses no superpowers, except for his superabundant finances, but that doesn't stop this character from performing feats worthy of true superpowers. Batman's technology includes his Batmobile (aka "the Tumbler"), a cross between a military Humvee and a Lamborghini sports car. This vehicle has become Batman's signature, evolving through the decades in comic books and movies to look like every teenager's dream car. In *The Dark Knight*, however, the Batmobile becomes disabled and Batman must pursue the Joker in his two-wheel Bat-Pod. Its designers borrowed heavily from the Dodge Tomahawk concept vehicle that comes equipped with a V-10 500-horsepower engine. The Bat-Pod also bears a resemblance to two-wheelers now under development in which the engines lie inside of the massive wheels.

Batman's costume, or Batsuit, consists of hundreds of interlocking armor plates that move easily when Batman goes into action. This suit references advances in body armor, yet it resembles ancient samurai armor worn in feudal Japan. Batman's cowl moves more easily than in previous Batman costumes owing to its resemblance to motorcycle racing helmets. Although constructed of the most modern materials, like titanium and Kevlar, the Batsuit also makes Batman more mysterious and seem more powerful. Finally, Batman employs a 3-D sonar system reminiscent of contemporary Lidar sonar systems employed by the military. For personal mobility, of course, Batman uses a system of powered grapples and ropes to defy gravity and fly to the top of buildings. His Batcape functions as a gliding device allowing him to float around Gotham City skyscrapers with ease.[35]

Batman's technology blends high-tech military equipment with trendy fashion. It references history along with the latest. Batman appears as fantastical as a contemporary soldier in full battle array, yet his black clothing and Art Deco retro appearance definitely provide a fashion edge over real-life soldiers. In fact, the Caped Avenger functions as a glamorous crime fighter who could just as easily be battling insurgents in Iraq or Afghanistan as patrolling Gotham City's rooftops.

Iron Man, a superhero powered not by superbiology but by supertechnology, joins Batman as a "made" superhero, and the post-9/11 adaptations of the Batman franchise continue their emphasis on state-of-the-art technology. Bruce Wayne created and paid for his Batgear with his personal fortune, supposedly worth billions of dollars. His Batmobile surely ranks as one of the chief allures of both *Batman Returns* and *The Dark Knight*. According to physicist Adam Weiner, Batman's most recent car, the Tumbler, actually consists of several vehicles, each with a specific purpose. "These are high performance vehicles capable of accelerating to 60 mph in 5 seconds." Weiner pointed out that each Batman vehicle comes equipped with a special suspension system similar to those found in Baja racing trucks. He noted that "in order to help the car negotiate high speed turns, each rear wheel is equipped with extra brakes that can be activated separately with hand levers. Engaging the supplemental brakes on only one side provides a greater net torque on the car and a tighter turning radius compared to normal braking." The prototype for the current Batmobile possesses "a rugged steel frame, which, with the aid of the suspension, allows the car to execute 30-foot jumps without crumpling on impact. And it attains a top speed over 100 mph."[36]

"Watchers," or mutants possessing the ability to perceive distant events through extrasensory perception, may well reference "remote viewing" training used by the U.S. military. During the 1990s, the U.S. government operated the Star Gate Project, a secret intelligence agency that gathered intelligence on antagonists through remote viewing. This project seems a likely referent for the U.S. intelligence agency relying on "mutants" in *Jumpers,* and it also relates to secret government agencies depicted in *Watchmen* and *Wolverine.*[37]

Cyborgs

Wolverine, armed with surgically implanted metal talons and other advanced mechanisms, joins Iron Man and other superheroes with technologically enhanced bodies. Although real "cyborg" technology lags far behind these superheroes, recent scientific advance have already created such cyborgs in the insect kingdom. In 2008 Cornell University researchers successfully implanted electronic circuits into tobacco hornworms in the early pupae stage of development. The hornworms then progress through the chrysalis stage and mature into adult moths whose muscles can be controlled with the electronic implants. The resulting micro-system-controlled insects possess great potential value to the military and homeland security. These large moths can be outfitted with tiny cameras to serve as stealth surveillance devices or remote-controlled microbombs.[38]

Shape-Shifters

Werewolves, those dark creatures from science fiction, have long possessed the ability to radically alter their bodies, adopting one shape after another. Count Dracula, too, possessed the ability to morph into a bat, and other vampires of fiction and film also shape-shift. Mystique (Rebecca Romijn), one of the X-Men characters depicted in the X-Men movies, possesses this ability. Although no scientific evidence exists for actual shape-shifting, the Indo-Malayan octopus ("mimic octopus") possesses the ability to camouflage its identity by mimicking sea snakes, banded sole, shellfish, lionfish, and even rock formations. The creature's unusual shape-shifting abilities received publicity in 2001 in an article published by the Royal Society.[39] It may have served as the model for some current shape-shifter characters.

Psychics

Psychics, those possessing the paranormal ability to foresee the future or project their minds over great distances, enjoy great popularity in science fiction and superhero movies. *Push* (2009) includes "watchers," individuals able to "see" over great distances using only their psychic powers. Of course, history reveals numerous individuals claiming to possess the power to see into the far distance, including the future. Seers and oracles populated the ancient world, and renowned psychics like Jean Dixon make predictions regarding future events. The U.S. government's National Security Agency reportedly developed a top-secret program known as Star Gate during the 1990s that enlisted and trained individuals with paranormal abilities who were reputably capable of gathering intelligence on potential foes. During the cold war the Star Gate and other top-secret programs attempted to gather intelligence about the USSR and its allies. According to government sources, Congress transferred the Star Gate program from the National Security Agency to the CIA, where it was subsequently killed.[40]

Echolocation

Matt Murdock, aka Daredevil, adapted a technology from the world of bats and dolphins in order to replace his lost vision after being blinded by some caustic chemicals in his youth. Daredevil learns to "watch" with his ears alone, finding a driving rainstorm the best source of the tiny sounds he learned to decode in order to regain "vision." His vision replacement allows Daredevil to navigate through New York City's labyrinthine skyline while diving and soaring up and down skyscrapers. However, is echolocation actually possible for humans? According to some, anyone can learn how to echolocate by focusing on sound produced by tongue clicks for two hours per day over a period of a few weeks. An article posted in *Wired Science* reports that a person can actually learn to "see" objects in the dark using echolocation the same way dolphins and bats do.[41]

Supervigilantes

Since September 11, 2001, superheroes have applied their powers for domestic law enforcement or warfare, functioning as virtual military forces capable of maiming or killing any antagonist they encounter. For example, Wolverine, one of the modern X-Men, possesses retractable metal claws and the ability to heal almost instantly whenever his body sustains injury. Professor Xavier, who administers a special school for the gifted mutants known as X-Men, is the most powerful telepath in the world, able to control people through his telepathic powers. Archangel, another X-Man, sprouts wings in order to fly, whereas Cyclops possesses a powerful ray that shoots through his eyes at will. Storm, a regal black woman, controls the weather. Each of these characters is a "mutant" in the sense that the term appears in science fiction, not in its usual scientific meaning.

In fact, these characters stretch the theory of evolution almost to the breaking point. At the DNA level, individual mutations occur in every species, but these tiny changes result in slow, gradual evolutionary changes in species. None to date has occurred in a living individual that resulted in his or her immediate transformation, and none has resulted in superpowers. In Darwin's theory animals gradually developed flight, but only through countless generations of progressive mutations that eventually resulted in wings. Many species emanate various forms of light, but none thus far possesses the ability to focus deadly beams of radiation. Cats and other felines possess retractable claws, but these consist of bony tissue, not metal. No one has ever documented a human with retractable talons. If such a mutation occurred, it would most likely manifest itself over generations, not in a single evolutionary moment. In films, the evolution of contemporary mutant characters conflates the usual evolutionary process into a single lifetime and even a single moment.

Not only Iron Man and Batman but also a number of other post-9/11 movie mutants undergo technological enhancements. The Fantastic Four receive cosmic ray treatments that dramatically transform and in some instances enhance their superpowers. *Push* superheroes experience enhanced psychic powers after receiving powerful enhancement drugs administered by a quasi-government agency. And Wolverine and other X-Men superheroes experience enhanced powers after undergoing extensive treatments in government laboratories. Wolverine receives grafts of a superhard metal retrieved from a meteor, transforming his formerly horn-like claws into metallic blades able to slice through any substance with ease.

In the post-9/11 era superheroes populate motion pictures like never before, a testimony to widespread feelings of disempowerment, vulnerability, anger, and revenge released by the events of September 11, 2001, and the violent wars that followed. Ultimately, superheroes evoke technology, particularly military, with characters' superpowers standing in for weapons of mass destruction. Iron Man's flying exoskeleton proves invulnerable when he attacks Islamic extremists in Afghanistan, and Batman's exotic crime-fighting paraphernalia are reminiscent of recent developments in military and civilian technology.

Crime-fighting superheroes act essentially as vigilantes, superior to federal, state, and local authorities. They mete out stern vengeance to criminals and assassins. In essence, they form a group of "police vigilantes," a term coined by Kanti C. Kotecha and James L. Walker.[42] Comic-book superheroes who fight crime and assist local, state, and federal agencies in keeping order function as superpowerful police adjuncts, resented by their human supporters for their immense power, yet useful to those charged with enforcing the law and maintaining social stability. In this sense superhero vigilantes act as conservative agents fighting to maintain the status quo.

Since September 11, 2001, superpowerful movie characters like Superman, Batman, Spider-Man, X-Men, the Fantastic Four, Iron Man, the Hulk, Daredevil, and the Watchmen continue to enjoy great popularity with movie audiences. These superheroes, far from social change agents, work to maintain society as it currently exists, wreaking vengeance upon all evildoers. They act in consort with other post-9/11 films and genres featuring revenge. In fact, all post-9/11 genres reek with revenge, and who better to dole it out than superheroes?

The rising popularity of superheroes comes as the expense of respect and approval of government agencies, including the military, the police, and, especially, the intelligence community. After all, neither the CIA nor the FBI proved able to predict or stop the 9/11 attacks, so why trust them now? In the aftermath of the Patriot Act and the Department of Homeland Security, government power over civic freedoms and civil rights expanded exponentially. All of the traumas and disappointments about government's role as protector of liberties are reflected in today's superhero movies. They reveal a society deeply afraid of violence and terror, especially coming from foreign or alien sources.

Contemporary superhero films owe a huge debt to science, even while most of them distort scientific theories and studies. Science in superhero movies chiefly serves as inspiration, not true background. Many superpowers contain a hint of real science, but usually they turn out to be scientifically unlikely, even preposterous, and, above all, impossible to duplicate in the real world. Some, like mutants with superpowers, badly distort scientific theories like the theory of evolution. For most contemporary science fiction, the science presented turns out to be bogus and useful only as a plot device that may or may not be believable.

Nevertheless, a few superpowers turn out to be more believable and possible to create in the real world. For example, the powers of psychic intelligence, shape-shifting, and echovision resemble contemporary scientific discoveries adequately enough to render them as real possibilities for future scientific endeavors. Flying saucers and other spacecraft that currently populate science fiction may have been inspired by top-secret experiments on advanced aircraft conducted on earth by the United States, Nazi Germany, or the USSR.

Satire

Spoofs have always played a role in the later development of a genre. They emerge after the public begins growing weary of the standard genre conventions. Mel Brooks's *Blazing Saddles* (1974) and Robert Aldrich's *The Frisco Kid* (1979) spoofed classic Westerns, treating venerable Western icons like shootouts, cattle drives, steam train rides, and wagon trains humorously. Films like Brooks's and Aldrich's arise long after the popularity of their genre peaks, and their appearance implies that a segment of the audiences has tired of the conventional.

Peter Berg's *Hancock* (2008) satirizes the superhero John Hancock (Will Smith) by casting him as a drunk who hangs out on park benches and makes unwelcome passes at women. When he swings into action as a crime fighter, he causes so much destruction and collateral damage that citizens actually boo him. *Hancock*'s taglines refer to him by stating, "Meet the superhero everybody loves to hate," and "He is saving the world whether we like it or not." Although he possesses almost unlimited powers, including the ability to fly at supersonic speeds, pick up moving trains with his bare hands, and paint a heart-shaped logo on the moon, Hancock's battling of crime and cataclysmic accidents in Los Angeles occurs in rare spurts of activity. He usually creates more chaos than he prevents. For example, he saves a man whose car stalls on a train track from an oncoming train by derailing and destroying the train, wreaking complete havoc at the scene.

Hancock saves the life of Ray (Jason Bateman), a public relations executive who decides to repay the favor by rejuvenating Hancock's public image. The plot spirals out of control after Hancock meets Ray's wife, Mary (Charlize Theron), who instantly dislikes him. Soon it becomes apparent why. She, too, possesses superhuman powers. In fact, they existed as a married couple many centuries before the present. Yes, the powerful superheroes existed for thousands of years, regarded as gods, angels, and devils by early humans. Although they were created as duos, pairing with a mate sapped their powers, and they became easy marks for ruthless criminals. To prevent this dire consequence from recurring, Mary vows to distance herself from Hancock by forcing him to leave the area. The two struggle, with Mary heaving a large semitruck at Hancock, but eventually reunite, resulting in a more focused Hancock. Together, they save the earth from evil supervillains.

Craig Mazin's *Superhero Movie* (2008) stars Drake Bell as Dragonfly, a high school student who develops superpowers after being bitten by a genetically modified dragonfly. Like most superheroes, Dragonfly exists in order to fight crime, as he explains during the film's conclusion: "I'm the Dragonfly, and as long as there's crime and injustice I will forever be a superhero." However, before Dragonfly can fight crime, he must learn to harness and focus his powers. First, he must conquer his high school nemesis, an evil bully also possessing superpowers. Even high school superheroes find supervillains among their classmates. Even the comedic superheroes like Dragonfly symbolize the world's dominant countries, especially the United States, and serve as superpolice and super military.

Revenge

Vengeance forms the central motivation in superhero films. Just as Captain America stared glaringly at the wreckage of the World Trade Center towers in the special 9/11 tribute comic book, heroes with superpowers provide powerful payback to criminals and terrorists. Batman demands vengeance against the Joker, just as Superman extracts vengeance from Lex Luthor. X-Men superheroes like Wolverine struggle against evil supervillains like Magneto and ultimately extract vengeance from them. Superpowerful characters enact painful retribution against evildoers, just as the U.S. military attempted to punish the Taliban and al Qaeda. After 9/11, vengeance quickly became the most important thematic element in superhero movies, thrillers, and other science fiction films. In fact, revenge plays a major role in a surprisingly large number of post-9/11 movies.

The current popularity of movie superheroes demonstrates once again the traumatic emotions that find expression in post-9/11 films. Like dreams, they reflect social and political realities through symbol, metaphor, and innuendo. Superheroes function as powerful symbols of American military power. Their superstrong bodies and other superpowers ultimately succeed in eradicating a wide array of insidious elements bent on destroying society. They embody reaction to widespread feelings of distrust, powerlessness, and growing paranoia about government surveillance, interference, and control. In many post-9/11 superhero films like *Watchmen* (2009), *X-Men: Origins* (2009), and *Push* (2009), the government itself sponsors secret, illegal assassination squads; creates monstrous killing machines; abrogates civil and human rights; and resorts to torture and murder to obtain its goals.

The X-Men may not resemble true mutants as defined by biologists, but everything remains possible in movies. Even more interesting than narrators' pseudoscientific explanations is the symbolic question, what do superpowers represent? On one level superpowerful characters personify the United States. Captain America serves as a prime example of this identification. Superman also reflects U.S. self-images during the cold war, World War II, and the post-9/11 world. On another level superheroes may represent advanced American technology, which in essence provides American workers with powerful production tools and American consumers with abundant electronic and mechanical gadgetry. Superheroes may also reveal unconscious perceptions of the U.S. military, multinational corporations, or perceived character strengths of U.S. citizens. Whatever the reference, however, cinematic superheroes represent potent forces battling social disorganization from a variety of sources, including domestic terrorists, organized crime syndicates, and government malfeasance. When dangers appear on the horizon and times look especially bleak, as in the post-9/11 era, audiences turn to superheroes as never before.

CHAPTER SIX

Terror

Terrorism, long a popular theme in Hollywood movies, became even more fashionable after 9/11 as violent "terrorists" appeared with increasing frequency in many genres, including thrillers. Charles Darwin observed that the more powerful an antagonist appears to be, the more our anger transforms into terror.[1] Darwin also commented upon terror's relationship with surprise. "Attention," he wrote, "if sudden and close, graduates into surprise; and this into astonishment; and this into stupefied amazement. The latter frame of mind approximates terror."[2] The dictionary defines "terror" as

1. Intense, overpowering fear.
2. One that instills intense fear: *a rabid dog that became the terror of the neighborhood.*
3. The ability to instill intense fear: *the terror of jackboots pounding down the street.*
4. Violence committed or threatened by a group to intimidate or coerce a population, as for military or political purposes.
5. *Informal:* An annoying or intolerable pest: *that little terror of a child.*[3]

September 11 produced a variety of emotional responses, including intense fear, which for many transformed into full-blown terror and panic. Those feelings helped inspire the post-9/11 cycle of terror-themed films.

After 9/11 the definition of "terrorism" quickly became controversial and remains so today. Can U.S. citizens commit acts of terrorism without belonging to jihadist groups? That question arose on August 18, 2010, after Joseph Andrew Stack flew his single-engine airplane into the side of an Austin, Texas, high-rise office building containing offices of the Internal Revenue Service to protest an ongoing tax dispute he had with the IRS. In a rambling note published on the Internet discovered after the crash, Stack wrote, "Well, Mr. Big Brother IRS man, let's try something different; take my pound of flesh and sleep well."[4] Does this act constitute terrorism? The word "terrorist" means

1. The use of violence and threats to intimidate or coerce, esp. for political purposes.
2. The state of fear and submission produced by terrorism or terrorization.
3. A terroristic method of governing or of resisting a government.[5]

A spokesperson for the Department of Homeland Security explained that "at this time, we have no reason to believe there is a nexus to criminal or terrorist activity," so the agency refused to label Stack's actions "terrorism."[6] However, Stack's crash certainly seems an act of violence designed to make a political statement, so many asked, "Why is this not terrorism?" This study assumes a broad definition for "terrorism" that includes domestic acts like Stack's.

Thrillers

Hollywood's most popular genre reacted dramatically to the September 11, 2001, terrorist attacks as a new round of films appeared depicting an array of foreign, domestic, and corporate "terrorists," though few film villains resemble the 9/11 attackers or possess Middle Eastern heritage and culture. Thrillers attempt to deliver shocks to their audiences. The word itself means "a person or thing that thrills."[7] Martin Rubin defined thrillers as a "mega-genre" that "gathers several other genres under its umbrella," like spy thrillers, detective thrillers, and horror thrillers.[8] The new wave of violent thrillers increasingly vilifies domestic and foreign terrorists, depicting rogue agents working for the CIA, the National Security Agency, and other branches of the government or globalized corporations engaged in neocolonial mayhem. Contemporary thriller heroes often spring from social margins: loners, outlaws, and corporate bandits.

Pre-9/11 Terrorists

Hollywood's war on terrorism began much earlier than the 2001 attacks. As early as World War I, films depicting foreign terrorists appeared, including *I Want to Forget* (1918). Alfred Hitchcock later pioneered the British terrorist-related thriller in the 1930s with *The Man Who Knew Too Much* (1934) and *The 39 Steps* (1935). *Saboteur* (1942) emerged as the most memorable of the World War II terrorist films. Hitchcock's protagonist, Barry (Robert Cummings), a factory worker, encounters a Nazi terrorist cell run by Charles Tobin (Otto Kruger). Like more recent filmmakers, Hitchcock chose his subject from the headlines, depicting a group of homegrown Nazis called America Firsters and a group of Nazi saboteurs who landed near New York City in 1942 armed with a boatload of explosives and intent on blowing up a war-production plant. It includes actual shots of the *SS Normandie* lying on its side, a victim of sabotage.[9]

The 1960s brought a new cycle of cold war melodramas—the James Bond thrillers—depicting clandestine terrorists preying on American interests and subjecting the United States and the rest of the world to nuclear blackmail. Examples include *Dr. No* (1962), *Goldfinger* (1964), *Thunderball* (1965), and *You Only Live Twice* (1967). The villains in these films, including the infamous Spectre organization, posed cold war–style threats. Unlike today's terrorist films, James Bond and British intelligence agents of the 1960s inevitably defeat the terrorist villains, who are motivated either by greed or megalomania. Spectrum and Dr. No stand in stark contrast to real-life 9/11 terrorists like Mohammad Atta, Osama bin Laden, and Khalid Sheikh Mohammad, who appear motivated by ideology, not personal greed. Prior to 9/11 the idea that terrorists might be ideologically motivated attained little currency, and even today depictions of dedicated Islamic terrorists rarely appear in Hollywood movies.

John McTiernan's *Die Hard* (1988) served as a model for many pre-9/11 films about terrorism. McTiernan's film features John McClain (Bruce Willis), an overworked New York policeman who stumbles upon a group of German terrorists who have commandeered an office building and taken hostages. McClain defeats the terrorists through a combination of martial arts, creative thinking, and the seeming inability of any of the terrorist gunmen to hit him. Post-9/11 thriller heroes often lack this element of luck.

A few years later the first bombing of the World Trade Center in 1993, the Oklahoma City bombings of 1995, and other terroristic acts inspired films focusing on such diverse subjects as the Irish Republican Army (IRA) in films like *Patriot Games* (1992) and *The Devil's Own* (1997), attacks on commercial airliners as in *Passenger 57* (1992), hijacked city buses in *Speed* (1994) and *The Siege* (1998), nuclear blackmail in *True Lies* (1994) and *Broken Arrow* (1996), blackmail using conventional explosives as in *Die Hard with a Vengeance* (1995), chemical attacks from terrorists as in *Executive Decision* (1996) and *The Rock* (1996), the capture of the president's aircraft in *Air Force One* (1997), and homegrown terrorists in *Arlington Road* (1999).

Philip Noyce's *Patriot Games* (1992) provides an excellent example of pre-9/11 terrorist thrillers. Noyce's film highlights the terrorism of an off-shoot of the IRA and features former CIA agent Jack Ryan (Harrison Ford) as an innocent tourist in London who accidently encounters a group called the Provisional IRA attempting to assassinate a member of the British royal family. Instinctively, Ryan attacks the terrorists, killing one and disarming another. As it turns out, Ryan disarmed the rebel leader, Sean Miller (Sean Bean), and killed his younger brother. Miller escapes from police custody and targets Ryan, his wife, and their daughter to avenge his brother's death. Typical of pre-9/11 films, Noyce's equates terrorism with motivations other than political ideology. Miller fights for Irish freedom, but revenge exerts the most powerful motivation and distracts him from his ultimate ends. This thirst for vengeance undoes Miller, and Ryan eventually kills him. The message of this film clearly reads, "Don't tangle with the CIA."

Kevin Hooks's *Passenger 57* (1992) foreshadowed the 9/11 hijackings of civilian airliners. Hooks's film stars Wesley Snipes as John Cutter, a terrorism expert who becomes vice president for antiterrorism with a major airline. Shortly thereafter, terrorist Charles Rane (Bruce Payne) hijacks an airliner bound for Los Angeles on which Cutter is a passenger. Cutter battles Rane and his terrorist gang, eventually defeating the famed terrorist responsible for hijacking and holding for ransom scores of aircraft. *Passenger 57* was scheduled to air on a Starz Entertainment Group channel the night of the September 11, 2001, attacks, but owing to the similarities between Hooks's film and the 9/11 hijackings, the channel quickly canceled the broadcast.

Philip Noyce's *Clear and Present Danger* (1994) continues along the path blazed by his 1992 *Patriot Games* and also features superspy Dr. Jack Ryan (Harrison Ford). Shortly after Ryan's promotion to deputy CIA director

(Intelligence), President Bennett (Donald Moffat) seeks vengeance for a terrorist killing of a prominent U.S. businessman, his wife, and their daughter aboard their yacht. The culprits turn out to be pirates tied to Colombian drug lord Ernesto Escobedo (Miguel Sandoval). President Bennett decides that the drug cartel constitutes "a clear and present danger" to the United States and orders an illegal special ops attack on the cartel's home base in Colombia. The film raises some interesting questions about covert U.S. operations and evokes the Iran-contra scandals, among other Washington missteps. As in the other pre-9/11 terrorism film examples, Noyce depicts terrorists motivated by money and power rather than by political or religious ideology.

Edward Zwick's *The Siege* (1998) seemed to anticipate some of the events of 9/11, although on a much smaller scale. Zwick's film stars Denzel Washington as FBI agent Anthony Hubbard and Annette Bening as CIA agent Elise Kraft. They launch an investigation in New York City after an Islamic sect sets off a series of explosions. The United States empowers the military in the person of Major General William Devereaux (Bruce Willis) to establish order. Devereaux declares martial law and attempts to round up the city's Arab American population and place them in detention centers, triggering a struggle between the military and civilian intelligence agencies. Zwick's film explores anti-Arab racism and overzealous politicians willing to suspend civil liberties in response to terrorist bombings, themes that became more popular in film after 9/11.

Bob Misiorowski's *Air Panic* (2001) came uncomfortably close to the actual events of September 11, 2001, in its depiction of airliners as missiles. Misiorowski's plot covers familiar ground by featuring a rogue computer programmer named Cain (Alexander Enberg) as the film's evil but largely unbelievable villain, who hatches plans to control airliners from his home computer and then send them off to their destruction. The first jetliner he commandeers crashes into the Pacific Ocean, killing all on board. He sends another crashing into a mountain, and the next one, in an eerie foreshadowing of the 9/11 attacks on the World Trade Center, crashes into a Denver skyscraper and transforms the entire downtown area into a blazing inferno. Finally, Cain takes over the controls of a jetliner and sends it on a collision course with a giant nuclear power plant, threatening to engulf the entire Eastern seaboard in an apocalyptical conflagration. Cain acts partly out of anger over a lab accident in which he received severe burns but mostly to demonstrate to the world his awesome computer skills. Again, like most pre-9/11 movie terrorists, Cain acts from personal, though twisted, motives.

Phil Alden Robinson's *The Sum of All Fears* (2002), created before 9/11 and put on hold after the attacks, eventually appeared in 2002, when it seemed to receive a box office boost. The film returns to the threat of nuclear terrorism but goes far beyond older spy thrillers like *Thunderball* (1965). Robinson's film depicts an Austrian neo-Nazi named Richard Dressler (Alan Bates) who plots to ignite a nuclear war between Russia and the United States, thereby eliminating the two superpowers and allowing for neo-Nazi domination. Dressler sends the bomb to Baltimore, arriving just in time to bomb the Superbowl. President Robert "Bob" Fowler (James Cromwell), in attendance at the game, escapes, but other American officials are killed. The terrorists also plan a false attack on U.S. forces in Berlin by East Germans disguised as Russian soldiers, thereby provoking nuclear war between the United States and Russia. Robinson's film seems a throwback to the cold war (fears of Russia) and World War II (Nazis). But despite these anomalies, Robinson's film became the third top-grossing terrorist film in history, ranking behind only *Air Force One* (1997) and *True Lies* (1994). Its success points to a surge in audience interest in terrorism after 9/11.[10]

Post-9/11 Terrorists

As these examples reveal, terrorism-themed thrillers served as a Hollywood mainstay prior to 9/11, but after the terrorist attacks their popularity increased and their plots became far darker. The terrorists themselves grew more dangerous and sinister and their attacks more devastating. The danger in today's terrorist thrillers no longer arises from Colombian drug cartels, neo-Nazis, rogue Russian generals, or demented Americans. Post-9/11 thriller villains include such diverse groups as jihadists at war with the United States, greedy corporate executives, ruthless Wall Street traders, serial killers, and rogue intelligence agents who plot assassinations, detonate bombs, torture victims, and carry out hijackings.

Although foreign and domestic terrorists remained popular subjects after 9/11, few Hollywood films dared to depict Islamic jihadists waging war against American citizens. Peter Berg's *The Kingdom* (2007), starring Jamie Foxx, Chris Cooper, Jennifer Garner, and Jason Bateman, proved a notable exception. Berg's film depicts terrorist bombings at the Riyadh compound on May 12, 2003, and the Khobar housing complex on June 26, 1996, in Saudi Arabia. The story follows a team of FBI agents, headed by Roland Fleury (Jamie Foxx), who investigate the bombing of a foreign-workers facility in Saudi Arabia. A trail of blood leads them to an apartment building that functions as a labyrinthine terrorist network. In his film Berg blames terrorism on Wahhabi extremism (a radical Islamic cult) as well as U.S. greed for Saudi oil. At times, his message appears heavy-handed. Ty Burr called Berg's film "Syriana for Dummies" but added that it's "fairly close to the truth ... a taut, slickly made thriller about an FBI team solving a terrorist bombing in Saudi Arabia." Burr speculated that the movie's "game plan" might involve "using a hard-boiled action flick as a Trojan horse to pick apart our assumptions and anxieties about the Middle East."[11] Although depicting the terrorists at work in Saudi Arabia, Berg's film also reminds viewers of another Saudi terrorist named Osama bin Laden.

Since their stunning failure to predict and warn officials of the September 11 attacks, and to protect the country against foreign agents, American intelligence agencies and operatives receive negative depictions even in mainstream films. Sydney Pollack's *The Interpreter* (2005) depicts Secret Service surveillance surrounding overheard plans to assassinate a foreign dignitary. Silvia Broome (Nicole Kidman), a U.N. interpreter, overhears whispers late one evening of an impending political assassination of Dr. Zuwanie (Earl Cameron), the president of Matobo, a mythical African country loosely based on Zimbabwe. She contacts the authorities, and Secret Service agent Tobin Keller (Sean Penn) heads the subsequent investigation. He becomes suspicious of Broome despite her innocence after learning of her Matobo citizenship and past involvement with a band of Matobo rebels. The Matobon government plants the bomb on a Brooklyn bus to assassinate Kuman-Kuman (George Harris), the exiled former president of Matobo. Despite Keller's heroic efforts, he fails to prevent the bus and all of its passengers from being blown up. This time, like September 11, 2001, the authorities fail to prevent a horrific act of terrorism.

Steven Spielberg's comedic airport drama *The Terminal* (2004) depicts the erosion and complete lack of human rights in U.S. airports after 9/11. Spielberg's film stars Tom Hanks as Viktor Navorski, a traveler from Krakozia, a mythical eastern European country. Upon arrival at New York's Kennedy Airport, Navorski learns that a military coup that just occurred in his homeland rendered him officially a "man without a country." Frank Dixon (Stanley Tucci), airport security manager, refuses to allow Navorski to leave the terminal because the United States does not recognize the legality of the new Krakozia government, so he cannot enter U.S. soil or depart from the airport. Unable to return home or proceed into New York City, Navorski lives inside the United Airlines international terminal. There he survives for seven months by working at night as an airport construction worker, while winning the hearts of all the airport employees with whom he comes in contact, except for Dixon, who warns him at one point, "If you go to war with me, you go to war with the United States." Functioning like a paranoid bureaucrat, Dixon symbolizes public perceptions of the Transportation Security Administration (TSA). At one point a character explains sarcastically, "Compassion, Frank, that's the foundation of this country." If so, the TSA possesses none of it in this film, which foregrounds antiterrorism policies while highlighting official American cluelessness about real homeland security.

Fernando Meirelles's *The Constant Gardener* (2005, British) depicts a murder mystery in Kenya involving a powerful multinational drug company's plot to unleash a lethal epidemic and then enrich itself by selling an antidote to the pathogen. Inside this backdrop of corporate deception, aided and abetted by the British government, a seeming love triangle develops among the protagonist, Justin Quayle (Ralph Fiennes); his wife, Tessa Quayle (Rachel Weisz); and a Kenyan doctor named Arnold Bluhm (Hubert Kounde). At that point unknown people murder Tessa and Arnold.

As the story of Tessa's murder unfolds, what first appeared as an affair between Tessa and Doctor Bluhm turns out to be a friendship and political liaison between the beautiful young activist and a sympathetic (though gay) Kenyan. The plot turns on a scheme by a pharmaceutical company to sell tainted, dangerous drugs that maim and kill. After Justin decides to investigate Tess's murder, he begins finding disturbing drug company links. He tries to tell others, including his friend and colleague Sandy Woodrow (Danny Huston), charging, "These pharmaceuticals are right up there with the arms dealers." Sandy replies, "We're not paid to be bleeding hearts; you know that, Justin."

At one point the film becomes political as Justin recalls his relationship with Tessa. During a lecture back in England, Quayle exclaims to his students, "Democracy is the very map and marker of civilization." He starts to leave when Tessa, then a student, asks, "What map is Britain using when it completely ignores the United Nations and decides to invade Iraq? Or do you think it is more diplomatic to bend to the will of a superpower and politely take part in Vietnam, the sequel?" As the rest of the class files out nervously, Tessa continues, "Why would we be killing some thousands of people just for barrels of oil and a photo opportunity on the White House lawn? Why?" As she continues her rant, she appears less and less rational, preparing the audience for the next scene, when she jumps into bed with Quayle.

The terror in *The Constant Gardener* stems from drug company officials who gladly assassinate anyone who stands in their way of reaping huge profits by murdering thousands of innocent people. Meirelles's film makes the point that terror stems from greedy corporations and compliant governments, not from zealots intent upon advancing their cause. Danger lies not in crazed terrorists attempting to destroy peaceful nations but in cruel, greedy corporations willing to stop at nothing to amass huge profits. The real villain turns out to be unfettered capitalism, not Islamic militancy.[12] Even with these anticapitalist themes, *The Constant Gardener* fared well at the box office, earning over $82 million from a production budget of only $25 million.

Stephen Gaghan's *Syriana* (2005) proved one of the more popular post-9/11 terrorism thrillers. *Syriana* stars George Clooney as Bob Barns, a cynical CIA agent operating in the Middle East, along with Matt Damon as Bryan Woodman, a financial analyst advising Prince Nasir (Alexander Siddig), the heir to an oil-rich emirate. It also includes a young Pakistani laborer named Wasim (Mazhar Munir), who studies radical Islam in a madrasa. In fact, this film includes a large cast of supporting actors. After Prince Nasir decides to recommend to his father, the emir, that he approve a natural gas contract with a Chinese company over an American one, the CIA orders Bob to assassinate Nasir. Later, the agency places Barns under investigation and harasses him. These narratives intertwine to present an ensemble portrait of U.S. economic interests in the Middle East. It depicts a rogue CIA ordering assassinations, corrupt oil company executives, and Islamic jihadists. It also depicts an alienated, radicalized prince who could represent a young Osama bin Laden. Like *The Constant Gardener*, *Syriana* proved attractive to audiences, though it did not rank among the top twenty in box office receipts. Nevertheless, Gaghan's film nearly doubled in profits its $50 million production budget, grossing almost $94 million by 2010.[13]

Like many post-9/11 terrorist films, *Syriana* includes graphic torture scenes, popular tropes in the wake of CIA torture techniques used in the war on terror. This time a CIA agent endures torture from a Hezbollah agent, who tears out the CIA agent's fingernails with a pair of pliers in an attempt to force him to unmask his local contacts, thereby symbolically turning the tables on the spy agency for its use of harsh interrogation techniques in the war on terror.

Robert De Niro's *The Good Shepherd* (2006) follows the exploits of charter members of the fledgling Central Intelligence Agency at the start of the cold war. Matt Damon plays Edward Wilson, who becomes a senior operative in the agency, and De Niro plays Bill Sullivan, an agency director. Sullivan visits Wilson at home to inform him of misgivings about the formation of the CIA. In his frank conversation he suggests that unscrupulous intelligence officers might exaggerate or lie about potential enemies for personal or selfish reasons. Wilson tortures a Soviet defector suspected of lying about his identity, at one point using waterboarding (a medieval torture technique in which subjects experience simulated death by drowning), an obvious reference to techniques used in the war on terror. The tortured man, unable to convince his attackers of his innocence, finally leaps out a window to his death, driven to suicide by the cruelty.

De Niro's film evokes several post-9/11 references. One reviewer observed, "*The Good Shepherd* is eerily relevant to our post-9/11 climate with the CIA running covert prisons and reportedly torturing terrorists; the National Security Agency conducting wiretaps without warrants; and columnist Robert D. Novak's July 2003 article revealing Valerie Plame as a CIA operative after an administration source reportedly gave her name. All of these incidents made the material in the film more relevant."[14] The film reveals a flawed, venal, and racist intelligence agency that abuses captives and betrays its closest friends. This description could describe public perceptions of contemporary intelligence agencies after their underwhelming performance on September 11, 2001.

Martin Campbell directed *Casino Royale* (2006), a post-9/11 James Bond thriller starring Daniel Craig. In this film Bond, understatedly depicted by Craig, combats a criminal syndicate that raises funds for international terrorism by creating panic in financial markets and cashing in on "put options" in which buyers can reap huge profits from a drop in stock prices. Incredibly, the film's villains, consisting of a shadowy organization, reaped immense profits by placing put options on stocks on September 10, 2001.

They must have been aware of 9/11 happening the next day, and they may well have ordered the attacks in order to manipulate the stock market.

Bond plays high-stakes poker with Le Chiffre (Mads Mikkelsen), one of the criminals, that ends after he receives a dose of poison. Later the chief villain, Mr. White (Jesper Christensen), tortures a naked, bound Bond, who, of course, survives to face future villains. Bond captures White at the end, so it seems that international terrorism suffers a damaging blow. However, the film never presents any links to Islamic religion or jihadist ideology or even to any plausible motivation for the villains, apart from the two standbys: greed and megalomania. Bond takes care of business, implying that the solution to international terrorism lies with lone secret agents.

Torture, which features so prominently in post-9/11 films, always evokes terrorism and the war on terror. Paul Greengrass's *The Bourne Ultimatum* (2007), the third installment in this popular thriller series, sets most of the action in Europe and North Africa. In this film Greengrass follows up on his *United 93* success and depicts both illegal assassinations and torture. Bourne, an intelligence agent assuming a new, created identity as a CIA undercover operative, experiences flashbacks to his real identity as David Webb that send him on an epic identity quest in which he learns that he was tortured by his handlers. The villain, Deputy Director Noah Vosen (David Strathairn), operates a supersecret agency that systematically violates the Bill of Rights by assassinating suspected foreign and American terrorists without due process. Vosen touts the currently prevailing permissive atmosphere regarding human rights and government oversight: "That's what makes us special: no more red tape!" No more red tape also means no more civil liberties or rule of law. Bourne exposes the rogue operation outside of government supervision and casts aspersions on its tactics of "rendition" (spiriting away captives to secret foreign prisons) and waterboarding. Bourne steals the files from the CIA and releases them to the world, setting off congressional hearings into intelligence excesses and occasioning the arrest of Deputy Director Vosen for conspiracy to assassinate Americans.

Waterboarding and rendition leave lasting scars on Bourne's psyche. He agonizes over his hidden identity until he rediscovers his true identity as a potent warrior and uses his martial arts skills as well as his expert motorcycle driving, car driving, lock picking, hot wiring, and other feats of technical acumen to defeat his torturers. He displays a mastery of technology and navigates successfully through the shadowy world of intelligence

Scene still: *The Bourne Ultimatum,* 2007. In this revenge thriller, former CIA operative Jason Bourne (Matt Damon) flees from attackers while attempting to regain the memories of his training as an assassin. Along the way he exposes an illegal CIA operation, similar to real intelligence operations inaugurated during the war on terror. (Universal / The Kobal Collection / Boland, Jasin)

agents. He embodies contemporary fears of out-of-control intelligence agencies and dictatorial and corrupt military. To Ross Douthat, "Bourne marries the efficiency of James Bond to the politics of Noam Chomsky. He's imperial overreach and blowback personified—the carefully brainwashed product of a covert CIA program that goes off the reservation and starts taking down his superiors, a succession of jowly, corrupt agents of the American empire."[15]

Breach (2007), directed by Billy Ray, depicts intelligence misdeeds committed by FBI agent Robert Hanssen (Chris Cooper), arrested in 2001 after selling agency secrets to the USSR and other governments for the previous twenty-five years. His spying is finally cracked by FBI agent Eric O'Neil (Ryan Phillippe), who resents being pulled off of investigations of terrorists for this internal security case. Although Ray's film ends with Hanssen's capture and arrest, it reminds viewers of the most unfortunate intelligence leak in the bureau's history, while it engenders additional doubts about the trustworthiness of intelligence agencies in the Iraq war era. With traitors like Hanssen peddling military secrets to the Soviets, the intelligence community's lapses in the wake of 9/11 appear less than surprising. *Breach* is reminiscent of *The Good Shepherd, The Bourne Ultimatum,* and other recent films in its bleak assessment of the intelligence community. Although Hanssen was not a conventional terrorist, his traitorous commerce with intelligence secrets helped undermine U.S. intelligence efforts and provided indirect assistance to terrorists. And as the biggest double agent in U.S. history, Hanssen himself becomes a major terrorist.

Ridley Scott's *Body of Lies* (2008) features Leonardo DiCaprio as Roger Ferris, a CIA agent operating in Jordan, and Russell Crowe as Ed Hoffman, his stateside operator. They track a terrorist network headed by Al-Saleem (Alon Aboutboul), a stand-in for Osama bin Laden, who heads a very nasty terrorist organization that stages terrorist bombings across Europe and plans future attacks in the United States. He explains to his followers that the bombings will increase: "As we destroyed the bus in Sheffield last week, we will be ready and prepared for the operation in Britain. We avenge the American wars on the Muslim world." However, Al-Saleem's megalomania, not his political views, proves his undoing. At least this quality provides the terrorist in chief with a measure of complexity, unlike the other jihadists depicted in this film.

A "good cop/bad cop" schism soon develops between Ferris and Hoffman after Hoffman ignores Ferris's advice and compromises an Al-Saleem safehouse in Amman, Jordan. Hani (Mark Strong) plays the sophisticated head of Jordanian intelligence, a man who demands loyalty and obedience, which Ferris refuses to provide. Hoffman personifies the corrupt intelligence agent common in post-9/11 terrorist thrillers, while Ferris rebels, Bourne-like, against agency corruption. Hoffman spends most of his time in Langley, Virginia, with his family until he confronts Ferris with an ultimatum: to return with him to CIA headquarters and accept a desk job. Ferris refuses and walks out, and Hoffman says, "You know that if you walk out on me you walk out on America."

Ultimately, Ferris chooses to "walk out on America" by opting for his love interest instead of "duty" and "obligation." In this case, love, in typical Hollywood fashion, triumphs as Ferris severs his allegiance to the CIA and attempts to find his own "separate peace" amid brutal wars and corrupt policies. Roger Ebert, in comparing Scott's film with earlier James Bond thrillers, observed that "increasing numbers of thrillers seem to center on heroes who are masochists surrounded by sadists, and I'm growing weary of the horror! Oh, the horror!"[16] Although Ebert may long for a return to more upbeat, pre-9/11 thrillers like the Bond series, the realities of post-9/11 audiences suggest that he may be in for a long wait.

Scott's villain, Al-Saleem, resembles the deceased Osama bin Laden in many respects, yet reverts back to pre-9/11 terrorist stereotypes in other ways. Al-Saleem, like bin Laden, leads a worldwide terrorist group dedicated to retaliation against the West for neocolonialist policies in the Middle East and the current wars in Muslim nations. Al-Saleem possesses a fatal weaknesses—megalomania. He lowers his guard and takes the bait after Ferris and Hoffman invent a fictitious terrorist group. Scott's film makes it appear that Al-Saleem cares more about his media image as a powerful jihadist than he does about his actual mission. Unfortunately for the United States, however, for decades bin Laden revealed no such weakness, allowing him to elude capture until his death in Pakistan at the hands of U.S. Navy Seals announced on May 1, 2011, nearly ten years after 9/11.

Body of Lies (2008) became one of only a few films depicting Islamic jihadists. Warner Brothers gambled that Scott's directorial skills, coupled with high-profile stars like Leonardo DiCaprio and Russell Crowe, would entice audiences toward a film dealing more directly with contemporary issues. The film ended up supporting this gamble—the original $70 million investment had grossed over $115 million by 2010.[17]

In 2008 another film appeared depicting Islamic terrorism. *Traitor,* directed by Jeffrey Nachmanoff, stars Don Cheadle as Samir Horn, a rogue U.S. special agent with Middle Eastern and African roots. Horn, a devout Muslim who infiltrates an Islamic terrorist organization waging a war of terrorism against the United States, finds himself in typical post-9/11 fashion forced to become a rogue officer because of official incompetence. In order to prove himself a jihadist, Horn bombs the U.S. Consulate in Nice (with covert assistance from the CIA). Then, along with a confederate, he goes to the United States to help organize the simultaneous bombing of fifty Greyhound buses (one for each state) to terrorize the American people and convince them "that nowhere is safe." However, FBI agents catch wind of the upcoming attacks and close in on the group, targeting Horn, whom they regard as a terrorist.

In the end, Horn's dual roles almost get the better of him when his undercover accomplice winds up dead. At that point he becomes a prime suspect and the subject of an FBI manhunt. Despite that, he never wavers in his loyalty to the United States. Finally, after a fierce gunfight in which he receives a shoulder wound, the FBI surrounds the terrorists and orders medical attention for Horn. After he recovers, he decides to leave the intelligence community because it kills innocent people. He explains, "You know that the Qur'an says that if you kill an innocent person it's as if you've killed all mankind?" Roy Clayton (Guy Pierce), his former FBI handler, replies, "It also says that if you save a life its like you've saved all mankind.... You're a hero Samir." Despite his hero status, Horn, like so many post-9/11 special ops heroes, walks away from the agency and retains his integrity. The FBI and the CIA come across as deeply flawed and broken.

Pete Travis's *Vantage Point* (2008) depicts a serious act of terrorism: the assassination of the president of the United States. President Ashton, played by William Hurt, falls victim to gunshots at the start of a speech in Spain promoting a treaty on international terrorism. Travis's film shows the assassination, as well as a subsequent large explosion pulverizing surrounding buildings, from a variety of different perspectives. Dennis Quaid plays Secret Service Agent Thomas Barnes, who failed to protect the president, along with Agent Kent Taylor (Matthew Fox). The constantly repeating assassination and bombing transforms this film into a post-9/11 *Rashomon* that forces viewers to relive the shocking assassination and devastating explosion numerous times, as if to remind viewers of America's vulnerability in the age of terrorism. Although the film falls short artistically, its modest success at the box office provides yet another clue about audience interest in terrorism, especially when it occurs far from the United States.

The James Bond franchise reappeared in 2008 with *Quantum of Solace*, directed by Marc Forster. Forster chose Daniel Craig to play Bond after his popularity in *Casino Royale* (2006). Bond seeks vengeance against a killer but discovers a plot by self-styled environmentalist Dominic Greene (Mathieu Amalric) to control Bolivia's water supply and its government. Unlike *Casino Royale's* massive put orders placed on the world's stock markets shortly before 9/11, the villains in this film engage in neocolonialism first and terrorism only as a means to their economic ends.

Domestic Terrorists

As ultraviolent features began appearing after 9/11, a number of them focused on domestic terrorism set in seemingly placid, peaceful communities. Like superhero films, these films feature powerful heroes and equally potent villains. David Cronenberg's *A History of Violence* (2005) depicts a seemingly typical small businessman, Tom Stall (Viggo Mortensen), who owns a café in Millbrook, Indiana, along with his wife, Edie (Maria Bello). One night Stall encounters two killers in his café, who brandish a pistol and threaten to kill a waitress. He scalds one with coffee, leaps over the counter, wrestles a gun from one of the killers, and shoots them both dead. The media seize upon the story of a small-town man defeating a pair of killers, but the wide publicity generated brings fresh killers to Stall's café, who claim that Stall is actually a gangster from Philadelphia named Joey Cusack. Stall/Cusack eventually confronts and kills the gang of criminals. He then heads to Philadelphia to confront his older brother, Robbie (William Hurt), who has become a mob leader. Robbie attempts to kill Joey, but the younger Cusack turns the tables, killing all of his brother's henchmen and his brother as well. After which, Stall/Cusack returns to Millbrook and resumes his identity as Tom Stall. Cronenberg's film serves as a classic example of post-9/11 thrillers, filled with characters as duplicitous as they are dangerous. In such a chaotic, deadly world only masters of the art of killing, like Joey Cusack, survive. Not until he takes out all of his antagonists can Stall resume his self-imposed anonymity. As such, he serves as a perfect post-9/11 hero. Like classic Western heroes, Cusack possesses better killing and fighting skills than anyone else, justifying not only his personal vengeance but also, by extension, America's war on terrorism, including the invasions of Afghanistan and Iraq.

Clark Johnson's *The Sentinel* (2006) depicts an assassination threat against President Ballentine (David Rasche). Veteran Secret Service Agent Pete Garrison (Michael Douglas) attempts to discover the identity of an alleged traitor within the Secret Service involved in the plot to assassinate the president while he conducts an illicit relationship with First Lady Sarah Ballentine (Kim Basinger). When everyone in the agency must take lie detector tests, Garrison fails because he conceals his relationship with the first lady, and he quickly falls under suspicion. He escapes custody and goes underground to discover the identity of the real traitor. Eventually, Garrison exposes Secret Service Agent William Montrose (Martin Donovan) and saves the president's life. In Johnson's film government agents barely manage to prevent unknown agents from assassinating the president, but audiences may not feel comforted when they realize that the threat to national security comes from within the government, not from fanatical foreigners. Secret moles ready to wreak havoc in America represent only one horrific scenario depicted in contemporary movies.

In homage to the 9/11 terrorist attacks, Tony Scott's *The Taking of Pelham 123* (2009) depicts a New York subway train taken hostage by domestic terrorists. Scott's film, like many post-9/11 movies, is a remake of an earlier thriller (1974) of the same name. In Scott's film a ruthless, violent criminal named Ryder (John Travolta) hijacks a New York City subway train and takes eighteen passengers hostage. He murders a hostage, then demands a $10 million ransom to be delivered within one hour; he threatens to kill one hostage for each minute the ransom fails to appear. Denzel Washington plays Walter Garber, a transit official under suspicion of receiving a bribe. Ryder refuses to negotiate with anyone except Garber, gradually bonding with him as an adversary. The New York mayor, played by James Gandolfini, agrees to the ransom, but then the question becomes whether it will arrive in time to prevent Ryder from killing any more hostages.

Prior to the hostage incident Ryder defrauded a government pension fund out of millions and went to prison for nine years rather than return $2 million of the stolen money. The hostage crisis ignites a precipitous decline on Wall Street, which Ryder counted on to allow him to realize over $300 million from his $2 million investment, making him a kind of Bernard Madoff precursor. Eventually, Ryder and his gang exit to a subway station underneath the Waldorf Hotel while sending the hostage-filled train speeding off to probable derailment. Finally, however, Garber singlehandedly captures Ryder while the stalwart New York Police Department nabs the other two gang members.

With the film's bleak, gritty images of New York City's streets and rat-infested subway tunnels and its hijacking motif, many critics acknowledged its artistic debt to the 9/11 terrorist events. Colin Covert of the *Minneapolis Star Tribune* observed that Scott's film establishes a somber tone that "forgoes cynicism and humor for pure post-9/11 anxiety."[18] The *Village Voice* reviewer called it "an explicitly post-9/11 movie. Make that post-post-9/11: The chief bad guy only looks like a terrorist, when in fact he's an even scarier foe—a commodities trader!"[19]

Revenge

Revenge thrillers, revenge sci-fi, and even revenge comedies revealing seething anger and resentment dominate post-9/11 cinema. Some of the most memorable films exude revenge from beginning to end. Examples include *Mystic River* (2003), *Spider-Man 2* (2004), *Troy* (2004), *Kill Bill: Volumes 1 and 2* (2003, 2004), *V for Vendetta* (2006), *Munich* (2005), *The Bourne Ultimatum* (2007), *Sweeney Todd* (2007), *The Brave One* (2007), *Death Proof* (2007), *Iron Man* (2008), *The Dark Knight* (2008), *Quantum of Solace* (2008), and *Inglourious Basterds* (2009).

Steven Spielberg's *Munich* (2005) depicts a secret Israeli hit squad sent by Mossad on a mission to track down and assassinate the Palestinian terrorists who massacred eleven Israeli athletes at the 1972 Munich Olympics. Of course, critics noted allusions to the war on terror as Israel responded with a covert military operation against the perpetrators. Suzanne Fields commented, "The movie's less than subtle subtext invokes the Iraq War, suggesting that the violent American response to Islamist violence, like the violence required of Israel to protect itself, can only beget a circle of blood and death in which nobody wins."[20]

No film depicts the motivations and consequences of revenge more vividly than Tim Burton's musical *Sweeney Todd: The Demon Barber of Fleet Street* (2007). Burton's hero, Benjamin Barker (aka Sweeney Todd), played by the versatile Johnny Depp, develops an insatiable desire for human slaughter in a twisted quest to avenge the rape of his wife and his own false imprisonment by villainous Judge Turpin (Alan Rickman). Barker/Todd resumes his old profession of barbering, establishing an elaborate, secret chamber below his barber's chair. He proceeds to slit his customers' throat and slides the now dead customers through a trapdoor to the secret chamber, where he processes and then cooks the dead bodies. Todd eventually commits suicide, a victim of his own unbridled vengefulness. This film sends a cautionary message—that vengeance becomes all-consuming and ultimately leads to self-destruction. Burton's film received an R rating for graphic violence, and indeed few films can equal the copious amounts of blood spilled in this movie by Todd's razorblade. By wallowing in violence and revenge and then depicting their dire consequences, Burton's film makes an indirect comment on other acts of vengeance, including the war on terror.

Serial Killers

In the years following 9/11, Hollywood churned out many films depicting real-life domestic terrorists, including serial killers, like *Dahmer* (2002), *Ted Bundy* (2002), *Speck* (2002), *Gacy* (2003), and *Ed Gein* (2007). These killers, all males, appealed to audiences fascinated with horror after the September 11 attacks. Wisconsin serial killer Edward Theodore Gein (1906–1984) inspired *The Silence of the Lambs*'s (1991) Buffalo Bill, *The Texas Chainsaw Massacre*'s (1974, 2003) Leatherface, and the 2000 film *Ed Gein: In the Light of the Moon*. A novel about his life appeared a year after his arrest, and in 1960 Alfred Hitchcock incorporated some of the details into his classic horror film *Psycho* in the character of Norman Bates.

In 2007 Michael Feifer released a post-9/11 version of Gein's exploits in *Ed Gein: The Butcher of Plainsfield*. In this film Gein (Kane Hodder) commits two murders and nine grave robberies in and around his rural Wisconsin home during the 1950s after becoming mentally unhinged by the death of his mother and deciding to become a woman in order to honor her. Accordingly, he exhumed several female bodies from the local cemetery and killed two other females. He may have also murdered other missing neighbors and family members. Feifer's film follows the main details of Gein's crimes as they are known by authorities. Gein's notoriety arose largely from the contents of his home. After his arrest in 1957 authorities discovered a bizarre collection of human body parts there, including female skins he tanned and sewed into a garment, masks made from human heads, bowls made from human skulls, and a variety of other human artifacts obtained from his grave robberies and murders. Feifer's depiction of Gein's house and its contents must have been inspired by the news photos of the real Ed Gein's house.

Unfortunately, despite its verisimilitude, Feifer's film did not fare well with critics and audiences, but its presence in a crowded field of other serial killer movies signals the rising appeal of the genre after September 11, 2001. David Schmidt argued that after the terrorist attacks, filmmakers turned to serial killer movies because they "provided a way to present the figure of the terrorist to the American public in a way that was both familiar enough to keep public fear and paranoia at manageable levels, and deviant enough to mobilize the necessary level of public support for the systematic dismantling of civil liberties in the United States, and the invasions of Afghanistan and Iraq."[21] The distinctions between vigilantism and serial murderers become increasingly difficult to delineate after 9/11 as filmmakers craft a large number of melodramas that tap into the public's desire for revenge. The thirst for vengeance, as witnessed in superhero films, also drives a number of other melodramas produced after 9/11.

Femmes Fatales

Bold, violent female killers emerged along with male serial killers, perhaps reflecting fears of rising female power. Although violent, these strong femmes fatales became popular with post-9/11 filmmakers and audiences. In 2003 Patty Jenkins's *Monster,* one of the most celebrated of the thrillers featuring murderous females, depicts real-life serial killer Aileen Wuornos (Charlize Theron), a Daytona Beach prostitute who initially kills in self-defense, later murdering men, most of them clients, for money and ultimately for a kind of vengeance. The film focuses on a nine-month period between 1989 and 1990, during which Wuornos has a lesbian relationship with Selby (Christina Ricci) and then begins murdering her clientele. Theron's depiction of Wuornos proved so poignant that she received the Academy Award for Best Actress in a Leading Role. Her character serves as an apt example of the post-9/11 fascination with dangerous females.

Quentin Tarantino's *Kill Bill: Volume 1* (2003) and *Kill Bill: Volume 2* (2004) present graphic evidence of the new breed of powerful post-9/11 femmes fatales. Tarantino's twin revenge thrillers feature Beatrix "The Bride" Kiddo (Uma Thurman). Betrayed by Bill (David Carradine) on her wedding day, shot, and left for dead, she lives to exact retribution on her attackers, all members of Bill's squad of assassins. The Bride undergoes spiritual and symbolic death by being buried alive in a coffin after being severely wounded. However, she escapes thanks to advanced martial arts training at the hands of a Chinese master and proceeds to defeat all of her attackers one by one in hand-to-hand combat. Her transformation occurs near the end of the second act when she encounters ex-lover Bill in a compromising position with another woman. Kiddo fatally wounds Bill by using a secret five-point attack that causes his heart to begin rupturing. Bill tells her, "You're not a bad person. You're a terrific person. You're my favorite person. But every once in a while you can be a real cunt." Her eventual triumph over Bill and his gang testifies to her strength as a character. *Kill Bill* films earned the term "splatter films" because of their images of graphic violence; they also qualify as revenge thrillers. The Bride wreaks vengeance against Bill, her teacher-nemesis, for his past actions.

In Jeff Stanzler's *Sorry, Haters* (2005) Robin Wright Penn plays Phoebe, who works for a cable music channel in New York City. In the first scene she hails a taxi driven by Ashade Mouhana (Abdel Kechiche), originally from Syria. Initially, she bonds with Mouhana and offers to assist him in freeing his brother, a Syrian Canadian kidnapped by the CIA while changing planes at JFK Airport and redacted (sent to a foreign country) to Syria for torture and eventual execution.

Despite her seemingly close relationship with Mouhana, Phoebe turns out to be a secret terrorist who, acting from vague personal motives, detonates a powerful explosive in New York City and blames it on Mouhana, a Muslim, so that the act will assume greater media importance. In an obvious role reversal a white, middle-class woman becomes a terrorist while a Middle Eastern Islamic man plays the role of innocent bystander. Audiences begin to realize her true character after Phoebe steals the money Mouhana plans to use to rescue his brother. In the final scene she murders Mouhana by pushing him in front of a subway, then prepares to detonate a powerful explosive in the subway station and blame it on Mouhana. This film, despite its ideological appeal and the high quality of Wright Penn's performance, grossed only $7 million by 2010.[22] Apparently, audiences found the film's powerful 9/11 themes unattractive.

Jodie Foster portrayed a memorable serial killer in Neil Jordan's *The Brave One* (2007). Foster plays Erica Bain, a popular New York City radio host who becomes the victim of a vicious street gang, who ends up stealing her dog, beating her boyfriend to death, and leaving her broken, beaten body for dead. After she recovers, she contacts the police to discover if they have any leads in the case, only to be rebuffed and ignored. Disappointed by law enforcement, she buys an illegal pistol and begins to stand up to bullies and robbers, killing a notorious street thug who robs a convenience store, as well as some subway thugs who threaten her. Eventually, she finds and executes the gang who abused her. By this time she has become a popular folk hero dubbed by media as "the Vigilante." Even the police turn the other way as she proceeds to even up the score.

Post-9/11 terrorist thrillers inspired satirical parodies. John Dahl's *You Kill Me* (2007) transforms the current fascination with death and destruction into a refreshing black comedy that spoofs post-9/11 violent thrillers. Dahl's film chronicles the exploits of Frank Falenczyk (Ben Kingsley), an improbable alcohol-addicted, professional assassin who works for a Polish mob in Buffalo, New York. One night Frank gets drunk and sleeps away his opportunity to kill an enemy. In response, mob bosses banish him to San Francisco, where he enrolls in Alcoholics Anonymous. He must overcome his addiction to regain his professional prowess. His ultimate test comes after a rival gang leader assassinates most of his old gang, forcing him to play the role of avenger. Dahl's neonoir thriller embraces black comedy as it revels in the details of assassinations and prowess with tools of the trade, including guns and knives. Frank soon finds a young, beautiful girlfriend, Laurel Pearson (Téa Leoni), who becomes a reluctant apprentice in the craft of killing. Dahl takes a satirical look at society's obsession with violence and murder in this film. His flawed assassin may remind viewers of the military's unresolved wars in Afghanistan and Iraq, where, like Frank's efforts to overcome his addiction, the military must first forswear its addiction to outmoded policies in order to regain its former glory.

* * *

In 2007 the wave of 9/11-inspired films like *The Bourne Ultimatum, Rendition, Ed Gein, Lions for Lambs, In the Valley of Elah,* and *Redacted* testified to the continuing media fascination with the terrorist attacks. Richard Allen noted that 9/11 themes and issues recently began percolating through pop culture in earnest. "There's the shock, and then it becomes part of the culture and it becomes the thing to do. Filmmakers are trying to be as contemporary as possible as they deal with issues like terrorism. It's an age-old thing. Think of the '50s Cold War and how it inspired science fiction."[23] Hollywood's post-9/11 movies underwent a transformation at least as dramatic as that following the Japanese bombing of Pearl Harbor in 1941.

Post-9/11 terrorist films depict families, corporations, governments, and even entire countries spiraling out of control, victimized by vendettas and personal greed or simply caught up in a world where it is no longer possible to control one's destiny. In fact, the destiny of financial institutions, intelligence agencies, and countries appears increasingly tenuous and dangerous in recent films. Revenge figures prominently in the thriller genre, and characters like Jason Bourne are stand-ins for real-life intelligence agents sent on secret, even illegal missions. Ultimately, these film characters all turn on their handlers, who appear increasingly corrupt, violent, and dangerous.

Thematically and visually, post-9/11 terrorist films strongly resemble neonoir movies of past decades, except that many appear even darker, bleaker, and more cynical. Night shots often predominate, along with neonoir settings and devious, violent characters. Villains of post-9/11 thrillers include an assortment of psychopaths, rogue intelligence agents, and Wall Street traders. Linked together by extreme violence and arrogance, these dangerous characters supply audiences with stand-ins for real terrorists like Osama bin Laden, Mohammad Atta, and Khalid Sheikh Mohammad, deemed too sensitive for cinematic depictions by nervous producers.

Ridley Scott's *Body of Lies* (2008) was the only successful commercial thriller featuring jihadist villains; Paul Greengrass's *Green Zone* (2010), a combat film starring Matt Damon, billed as a new installment of the Bourne saga, proved disappointing at the box office. Months after release Greengrass's film failed to earn back its $100 million production budget.[24] Audiences, with few exceptions, still seem wary of realistic depictions of the 9/11 attacks and subsequent wars.

Post-9/11 terror thrillers testify to Hollywood's and audiences' continued fascination with domestic and international terrorism. Hollywood seldom depicts terrorists on a purely ideological or religious mission, like the real 9/11 attackers. Instead, movie terrorists might be rogue intelligence officers, corrupt Wall Street traders, criminals, or even officials of the Transportation Security Administration. Hollywood terrorists also include femmes fatales. Even Hollywood's recent Islamic terrorists conform to pre-9/11 stereotypes of psychotic megalomaniacs who terrorize for fame and fortune, not for Islam. Filmmakers seemingly have trouble humanizing their movie terrorists.

CHAPTER SEVEN

Paranoia

Fear transforms into terror when amplified to an extreme. From Darwin: "*Fear, Terror.* The word 'fear' seems to be derived from what is sudden and dangerous."[1] Extreme fear transforms into paranoia, an emotion reflected particularly well in films of the sci-fi genre. Post-9/11 sci-fi expresses fear, anxiety, panic, and outright paranoia about humanity's fate in a violent, chaotic universe. A number of significant sci-fi films referencing the terrorist attacks surfaced after 9/11. Apocalypse is the form paranoia assumes in the genre. In apocalyptic films, paranoia symbolically stems not from fear of terrorists but from fear of outside forces poised to annihilate humanity and the entire earth.

Apocalypse

The word "apocalypse" literally means "lifting the veil," a veil that shrouds humanity's fateful encounter with the end of the world, often expressed as the Christian End of Days prophecy in the Book of Revelation. The notion of an impending world-ending catastrophe becomes especially appealing, according to Denis Dutton, because of widespread guilt for the wastefulness of contemporary life, "a sense that modernity and its wasteful comforts are bringing us closer to a biblical day of judgment."[2] Overindulgence leads to guilt, which implies punishment, penance, and eventual reconciliation.

Pre-9/11 Science Fiction

During the cold war, science fiction films gained large audiences with classics like *The Day the Earth Stood Still* (1951), *War of the Worlds* (1953),

It Came from Outer Space (1953), *Them!* (1954), and *Invasion of the Body Snatchers* (1956). These films express paranoia about world events; at that time it was communist conspirators. The post–World War II era's fears of atomic warfare and competition from the USSR remind us of contemporary fears of Islamic militants, corrupt government agents, and immoral or unethical conduct on the part of the U.S. military and corporations. Both the cold war era and the post-9/11 era inspired science fiction films depicting earth's devastation by extraordinary, often extraterrestrial, beings and forces. The popularity of the sci-fi film skyrocketed and transformed the genre from B-budget exploitation films to A-budget blockbusters offering abundant examples of genre changes in the wake of 9/11. Although the sci-fi genre reflects current fears about terrorism, it also showcases advancements in cinematography, 3-D projection, and computer-enhanced technologies.

Post-9/11 Science Fiction

Danny Boyle's *28 Days Later* (2002, British) provides audiences with a terrorist-themed disaster: the outbreak of a deadly microbe in the heart of London. Jim (Cillian Murphy) awakens in a deserted hospital and discovers an apparently empty city strewn with signs of catastrophe. He finds himself pursued by mad, infected people before being rescued by two other survivors, Selena (Naomie Harris) and Mark (Noah Huntley). They reveal that during his coma a deadly virus spread uncontrollably among the populace, turning most people, referred to as "the Infected," into vicious, robotlike creatures that prey on healthy humans. Selena and Mark fear that the outbreak has resulted in global catastrophe. Despite attacks by the Infected and even some healthy soldiers, Jim and Selena survive. An alternative ending substitutes an unhappy ending in which Jim perishes. The studio released the film with the happy ending in 2003. Boyle's film surpassed box office expectations and spawned a sequel, *28 Weeks Later,* in 2007 in which characters barely survive a zombie attack.

Zachary Weintraub's *Dream Warriors* (2003) sets the tone for many postapocalypse sci-fi features. *Dream Warriors* stars Daniel Goddard as Rage, a hybrid human survivor of a huge asteroid that destroyed most of humanity. He possesses superpowers, including extrasensory perception. The survivors divide between mutants with special powers and "pure" humans without special powers. The pure elements gather under the protection of Parish (Lance Henriksen), himself gifted with superhuman persuasive powers. Rage challenges Parish's dictatorial regime and finds himself the target of a massive manhunt by Parish's motorcycle-riding private army of hunters. Parish's "pure" humans are actually duped, brutalized, and selfish, especially Parish himself.

Rage's mutant friends hold far more interest for viewers. One possesses supernatural healing powers; another radiates electromagnetic radiation. These superpowerful mutants appear far more humane than Parish's pure human hunters. A child born to Parish becomes the prophetic messiah, destined to lead everyone to a peaceful community by a river. Ultimately, Rage overcomes Parish and saves the child. He and his followers start a village beside a peaceful river, far from Parish's hunters. Symbolically, Weintraub appears to be saying that humanity needs to reestablish ancient patterns of riparian rural development and eschew modern cities and postindustrialism.

Kerry Conran's *Sky Captain and the World of Tomorrow* (2004) depicts an apocalypse, complete with nostalgia, magic, giant bird-shaped flying robots, supervillains, an attack on New York City circa 1939, and stars Jude Law, Gwyneth Paltrow, and Angelina Jolie. The action begins in retro yet futuristic New York City in 1939, complete with vintage cars, clothes, and skyscrapers. Seemingly advanced technologically to the twenty-second century, these 1930s-era characters live in an age with space travel, amphibious aircraft, and jet packs. The resulting campy mise-en-scène brims with hidden messages about today's events. Eventually, the protagonists save the world from a sinister plot by the evil Dr. Totenkopf (Lawrence Olivier from archival footage). Totenkopf plans to destroy the earth by detonating deadly bombs. The film also raises issues owing to its nostalgic setting. As Henry Jenkins asked, "Are we living at a moment when yesterday's ideas about the future are more attractive than our own?" He labeled this blend of future and past "retro-futurism" and observed, "Science fiction, post-9/11, has offered little by way of alternative visions of the future beyond more of the same. Perhaps the only way forward is to retrace our steps."[3] Other sci-fi and horror films make use of retro-futuristic settings, including *The Breed* (2001) and *The Dark Knight* (2008). In fact, many vampire films, and most Batman films as well, tend toward retro. Count Dracula, or Count Orloff or whatever name he uses, often appears in an outdated tuxedo, as he does in *Dracula 3000* (2004). Perhaps these films convey a message about loss of faith in today's technology.

Scene still: *Sky Captain and the World of Tomorrow,* 2004. The plot ultimately involves the destruction of the entire planet by a mad scientist. After 9/11, science fiction films became more apocalyptic as well as more pessimistic about the dangers threatening humanity. (Paramount / The Kobal Collection)

Computer-Generated Imagery

Sky Captain raised the bar for computerized graphic imaging. For much of the movie, actors played against green screen backgrounds devoid of scenery or props. Technicians and engineers later added the retro-futuristic settings with graphic imagery. The artifice looks surprisingly realistic at times, although the computer-generated imagery (CGI) of the robotic monsters eventually becomes tiresome. *Sky Captain*'s artifices remind viewers of Hollywood movies during the golden age when rear projectors created the illusions of location shots in Hollywood studios. Other recent films utilizing computer-generated backgrounds include *Fantastic Four* (2005), *Beowulf* (2007), *Star Trek* (2009), and *Avatar* (2009). Disney/Pixar films consist almost exclusively of animation, starting with *Toy Story* in 1995 and including more recent creations like *Cars* (2006), *Ratatouille* (2007), *Wall-E* (2008), and *Up* (2009).

CGI comprises a major stylistic element for post-9/11 sci-fi films. Peter Jackson's *King Kong* (2005) reprises the 1933 classic by coproducers and documentarians Merian C. Cooper and Ernest B. Schoedsack. Jackson, best known for his Academy Award–winning adaptations of J. R. R. Tolkien's *Lord of Rings,* begins the film with the horrors of prehistoric Skull Island and ends with Kong's flight through the streets of New York and ultimately to the top of the Empire State Building. Though Jackson's film contains romantic elements, the final scene with the twenty-five-foot Kong astride a New York skyscraper recalls the air attacks on the World Trade Center. In the end New York recovers from its encounter with the giant ape, and life returns to normal. The danger arose not from terrorists but from intense human emotions, especially romantic love. As protagonist Carl Denham (Jack Black) explains, in the end "it wasn't the airplanes, it was beauty killed the beast!"

Although critics normally place *King Kong* in the sci-fi genre, Jackson's film also relies on horror for much of its energy. Skull Island, with its antediluvian monsters, giant cockroaches, enormous spiders, and centipedes serves as a perfect setting for supervillains and fantastical experiences. It also represents an incredibly hostile environment outside the borders of traditional society, even after substituting dinosaurs and other primitive monsters for jihadists.

Conspiracy

James McTeigue's *V for Vendetta* (2006), listed as an action-sci-fi thriller, possesses elements of a quintessential post-9/11 drama and acts as an indirect indictment of the Blair/Bush leadership during the war on terror. In the film, a starkly Orwellian England, ruled by fascistic Chancellor Adam Sutler (John Hurt) and a retro government reminiscent of Nazi Germany, uses terroristic threats to magnify its powers. The plot includes a militarized virus, created and accidently released during a secret government project that kills 100,000 Britons, and an out-of-control government that seizes absolute power and denies basic human rights to citizens. Instead of taking the blame for releasing the weapons-grade virus from a secret laboratory, Sutler capitalizes on the resulting outbreak and mass killing to wrest dictatorial control of Great Britain. The film satirizes Evangelical and neoconservative characters who complain about supposed American permissiveness. One popular progovernment commentator rants against "immigrants, Muslims, homosexuals, terrorists. Disease-ridden degenerates. They had to go. Strength through unity. Unity through faith. I'm a God-fearing Englishman and I'm

Scene still: *V for Vendetta,* 2006. A masked and costumed V (Hugo Weaving), looking like a combination of Batman and Zorro, brings down a fascist government headed by Adam Sutler (John Hurt) that has seized power in Great Britain. After 9/11, many films arose depicting corrupt, fascist governments. (Warner Bros. / The Kobal Collection / Carpi, Claudio)

goddamn proud of it!" V (Hugo Weaving) is a secret operative planning to bring down the entire British government. He fights back by bombing and destroying Old Bailey prison, executing various high party officials, and eventually killing Sutler.

Critics quickly associated the film with 9/11, especially the followers of the conspiracy theories that postulate Bush administration complicity in the terrorist attacks and condemn the widespread use of torture in interrogating suspects. Several independent films quickly appeared linking *Vendetta* with 9/11 conspiracy theories, including *9/11 Vendetta: Past, Present, and Future* (2006) and *9/11 Vendetta* (2006). These short films use *Vendetta* dialogue to illustrate connections to 9/11 conspiracy theories. *Vendetta* resonates with audiences already deeply suspicious of government antiterrorist policies, and several anarchist groups endorsed the antigovernment message of this film.[4] On the other side of the spectrum, conservative spokesperson Dr. Ted Baehr, editor of *Movietimes,* called the film "a vile, pro-terrorist piece of neo-Marxist, left-wing propaganda filled with radical sexual politics and nasty attacks on religion and Christianity."[5] McTeigue's film serves as a dramatic post-9/11 call for rebellion against corrupt governments.

Super Disasters

In Robert Emmerich's *The Day After Tomorrow* (2004), Jack Hall (Dennis Quaid), a climatologist, discovers that a huge iceberg has sheared off in Antarctica, which then causes a climatic catastrophe that triggers a new ice age. The abrupt climate shift submerges New York City in seawater and then buries it in snow and ice. New York as well as much of the developed world is devastated. Does climate change serve as a substitute for the 9/11 terrorists in this film? Both climate change and terrorists threaten that vulnerable metropolis, and climate change has become part of the post-9/11 paranoia.

Francis Lawrence's *I Am Legend* (2007), set in New York City, depicts the aftermath of a deadly virus that wipes out 90 percent of humanity and turns almost all of the survivors into psychopathic zombies. Will Smith plays Robert Neville, a biologist who survives but faces nightly dangers from zombie attacks. Seemingly alone, with only a dog for companionship, Neville, who works tirelessly on an antidote to the zombie infection, eventually encounters some other normal humans. They head for a secret fortress where most remaining humans now reside. He succeeds in synthesizing the antidote that renders the zombies harmless, but they murder him before the antidote takes effect. Earth's remaining inhabitants honor him with a plaque in the final scene. In this film, science ultimately saves humanity.

Michael Bay's *Transformers* (2007) delivers swipes at the U.S. military. Producer Don Murphy originally planned to produce a new version of *G.I. Joe* but changed his mind after the U.S. invaded Iraq in 2003.[6] Steven

Spielberg joined as executive producer and hired Bay as director. The film features CGI live-action versions of the Transformer cartoon characters, giant robots that possess the ability to transform themselves into mechanical objects. The film makes full use of CGI technology in its depiction of a savage war waged on earth between rival groups of superpowerful robots. It references an ancient war on the planet Cybertron between the Autobots, "good" robots, and the Decepticons, a group of "evil" robots. Both Autobots and Decepticons utilize their ability to transform themselves.

As war erupts between the robots, a human teenager named Sam Witwicky (Shia LeBeouf) receives his first car as a gift from his father, a vintage Camaro that is actually one of the friendly Autobots, named Bumblebee. Bumblebee defends Sam and his girlfriend, Mikaela Banes (Megan Fox), from a Decepticon named Barricade as other Autobots begin arriving to assist. Both Autobots and Decepticons battle over possession of the Allspark, an omnipotent cube that assures victory to whichever side possesses it.

Bay's film, inspired by twistable plastic toys, attracted mass audiences when it was released and inspired *Transformers II: Revenge of the Fallen* (2009). Both films depict the war between rival robots fought on battlefronts jumping from Qatar to the Hoover Dam and eventually to New York City. During the battle scenes two armies of massive robots topple buildings and wreak untold havoc until the Autobots' hero, Optimus Prime, defeats Megatron, leader of the Decepticons. Jon Voigt plays Secretary of Defense John Keller (symbolizing Donald Rumsfeld), who unofficially runs the country. The president, a stand-in for George W. Bush, never appears onscreen and takes no action except to order a Ding Dong cupcake, a characterization corresponding to a popular view of President George W. Bush as a mental lightweight dominated by authoritarian elements in his administration. Massive civilian casualties become a by-product of the war against Decepticons, a reference to the high death tolls of the Afghanistan and Iraq wars. The robot wars in the two films represent the classic struggle of "good" (enlightened humanism) against "evil" (malevolent greed and lust for power) in reference to events of 9/11 and their aftermath. The use of robots as whimsical war characters provides comic relief for the audiences.

Scott Derrickson's *The Day the Earth Stood Still* (2008) threatens an apocalypse while evoking post-9/11 rage, guilt, and violence. Derrickson's adaptation of Robert Wise's classic *The Day the Earth Stood Still* (1951), one of the best sci-fi films ever made, updates Wise's cold war version with post-9/11 themes. The basic plot revolves around an extraterrestrial named Klaatu (Keanu Reeves). In the 1951 film Klaatu's spacecraft lands in Washington, DC, whereas the 2008 craft lands in New York's Central Park, evoking Ground Zero. The U.S. military dispatches forces to Central Park to confront the extraterrestrial object, and the glowing orb emits Klaatu and later Gort, a giant robot with an impenetrable metal skin and immense destructive powers. The military greets Klaatu with gunfire, inflicting wounds requiring emergency treatment in a local hospital. A hastily assembled team of scientists gathers to study the alien, including Dr. Helen Benson (Jennifer Connelly), an astrobiologist who makes the initial contact with Klaatu. In the hospital Secretary of Defense Regina Jackson (Kathy Bates) grills Klaatu about his visit on earth and, in an obvious reference to the Bush-era interrogation practices, orders the use of "intensive interrogation techniques" to learn more from the alien. Dr. Benson empathizes with Klaatu and decides to facilitate his escape.

Klaatu's sinister mission eventually emerges after extraterrestrial "orbs" collect samples of the earth's fauna and flora. Aliens detect earth's delicate ecosystem on the verge of collapsing and decide to capture and save representatives from every species of life except humans, which they plan to annihilate immediately as punishment for mismanaging earth's ecosystems. However, Klaatu becomes charmed by Helen Benson and her young son, Jacob (Jaden Smith), and decides that humans deserve to survive. So a small boy and his mother save earth from destruction at the hands of aliens. Human failure to protect the environment and government interference with civil liberties, the film's main themes, resonate with post-9/11 fears.

Alex Proyas crafted an apocalyptical narrative in his 2009 science fiction thriller *Knowing*. Nicolas Cage plays John Koestler, a professor of astrophysics at MIT whose young son, Caleb (Chandler Canterbury), receives a letter from his school's recently unearthed time capsule consisting of hundreds of enigmatic numbers. Soon after Caleb receives the letter, mysterious strangers wearing overcoats visit him. His father studies the document and notices a familiar date: "09112001." Other numbers on the letter correspond with past dates on which notable disasters occurred, including terrorist bombings. Even more disturbing, some of the dates appear to reference future events. After Koestler witnesses the crash of an airliner on one of the predicted dates and a massive Boston subway accident on another, he fears that the other dates also foretell disasters. One in particular may foretell a final world apocalypse. John and Caleb discover other coordinates scratched into a closet wall in the former home of the now deceased girl psychic who originally wrote the mysterious manuscript. While at the home, they both encounter mysterious strangers who instantly transform into towering light-radiating figures. The film ends as a massive solar flare destroys New York City and then obliterates the rest of the planet. Prior to the destruction, the extraterrestrials (or are they angels?) invite Caleb and a few others of the "elect" into their spacecrafts, an obvious reference to the Apocalypse prophesy in the Book of Revelation. Proyas's film references biblical scripture foretelling the appearance of mysterious heavenly beings, including the Hebrew prophet Ezekiel's "wheels," rotating glowing wheel-shaped objects. Evangelicals found this PG-13 film appealing, especially because it lacked sex, profanity, and nudity. They might relate to its special effects, particularly the disaster scenes as prophecy. A sufficient quantity of moviegoers propelled Proya's film to the top of the box office charts and to a sizable profit.[7]

Andy Fickman's *Race to Witch Mountain* (2009), produced by Disney, reprised a 1970s film *Escape to Witch Mountain* (1975). This film appeals to conspiracy theorists who believe the government keeps the UFO issue secret. In the film, those caught trespassing on the "Witch Mountain" secret base risk a twenty-year prison sentence. Dwayne Johnson ("The Rock") stars as Jake Bruno, an ex-felon turned Las Vegas cabbie. He picks up two extraterrestrial children, Sara (AnnaSophia Robb) and Seth (Alexander Ludwig), at the site of a mysterious state highway closure in the Nevada desert. Sara and Seth persuade Bruno to assist them while they recover their spacecraft and elude an alien assassin. They originate from a dying planet where hostile aliens plan to take over the earth. The aliens want to destroy all earthlings so that they can then inhabit the planet. Sara and Seth have an alternative plan. They intend to convince their alien brethren to occupy a barren planet instead. *Race to Witch Mountain* became an instant blockbuster, displacing *Watchmen* (see Chapter 5) from the top spot in box office sales. The film's 9/11 tropes, imminent disasters, and xenophobic, misguided military appealed to audiences.

Neill Blomkamp's *District 9* (2009) performs an about-face on the stereotypical plot of diabolical aliens attacking terrified humans and delivers a thought-provoking sociopolitical parable about what humans might do to weak aliens if given the opportunity. Blomkamp, a protégé of *Lord of the Rings'* director Peter Jackson, chooses to set his film in his native South Africa. The plot begins twenty years earlier as a giant alien spacecraft stalls in the skies over Johannesburg. Disoriented insectlike bipeds, labeled "Prawns" by the local media because of their crustaceanlike appearance, escape the disabled craft. Local authorities consign them to a special area of the city called District 9 but provide them with little sustenance. The area eventually fills with a seedy Prawn-built shantytown reminiscent of Soweto. The Prawns become victimized by local officials and by Nigerian gangsters, who peddle cases of cat food, which Prawns find addictive. Despite their current low status, Prawns originated from a civilization considerably more advanced than earth's, and they possess superior technology. Their futuristic assault weapons incorporate biological mechanisms that render them inoperable by humans.

The film then fast-forwards to the present, where the Multi-National United (MNU) corporation assumes responsibility for the oppressed Prawn population. MNU plans to perform secret experiments to unlock Prawn technology, particularly for weapons. In an act of nepotism, MNU appoints one of its officials, Wikus van der Merwe (Sharlto Copley), a smiling, officious relative of MNU's CEO, to head the Prawn Relocation Project. Van der Merwe inspires little confidence in his paramilitary underlings until he accidently becomes infected by an alien microorganism that begins to transform him into a Prawn. MNU researchers capture and imprison him to force him to use his Prawnlike hand to fire Prawn weapons. Van der Merwe escapes from the laboratory and becomes the focus of a massive manhunt. *District 9* sides increasingly with the Prawns' insurrection. The film depicts the aliens as civilized, intelligent, creative, and courageous. After van der Merwe escapes his tormentors in the MNU laboratory, his fate intertwines with that of the Prawns, especially one called Christopher Johnson (Jason Cope), who becomes van der Merwe's protector as MNU paramilitary forces close in on the fugitive. Johnson repairs the Prawns' starship, disabled for twenty years, and flies away. Although unable to join the Prawns, van der Merwe radiates with joy as his friend escapes, delighted that he had assisted in the escape.

Disney XD network created its first feature in 2009 with the science fiction thriller *Skyrunners,* directed by Ralph Hemecker. This made-for-television production appeals to teenage audiences, but what is interesting for this study is the film's almost complete reliance on popular post-9/11 tropes. The plot surrounds a fourteen-year-old boy named Tyler Burns (Joey Pollari), who, along with his older brother, finds a small spacecraft and takes it for a spin in space, where he is hit with cosmic radiation that stimulates changes in his body and instills superpowers. Meanwhile, evil aliens have been tampering with earth's climate, causing extreme global climate change. And, as Burns's superpowers develop, his eventual confrontation with and defeat of the evil aliens become apparent. This plot contains nearly every post-9/11 trope: reliance on a superhero, inclusion of supervillains, references to an impending superdisaster, evil aliens, and a duplicitous and phony intelligence. All of these elements congeal in a movie about teenage encounters with voracious monsters intent on humanity's complete destruction. Special computer graphics propel the plot forward as the boys fly around in the spacecraft confronting monstrous beings from outer space. The resulting film perfectly epitomizes post-9/11 science fiction.

Shane Acker's 9 (2009) adds an animated thriller, starring rag dolls, to the growing list of apocalyptic films. Acker's film features a small, rag-doll-sized cyborg named 9 who comes to life in a postapocalyptic universe after a disastrous war between machines and humans left all humanity dead. Only burlap dolls like himself and terrible machines exist, with voices supplied by Christopher Plummer, Martin Landau, John C. Reilly, and Crispin Glover. The postapocalyptic setting of blasted buildings and twisted metal evokes the most primal 9/11 fears, while the cute burlap and metal characters add charm to this imaginative film. Armed with needles and thread, the burlap doll cyborgs battle monstrous machines that look like huge mechanical spiders and bats. A human scientist designs an intelligent machine capable of recreating itself and of inventing new devices, but an evil government misuses it. These machines possess minds of their own and soon destroy all of humanity in a brutal war. Only the doll-like creatures remain, each possessing precious remnants of their inventor's soul. These doll beings become the closest thing next to humanity available on planet earth.

The film's message arrives at the end, after the dolls defeat the giant machines. The dead dolls return as spirits, and as they depart, they bring life-giving rain. The dawn arrives on a new era in which machine-human hybrids inherit the planet from weak humans. The message, as in so many other post-9/11 apocalyptical thrillers, is "repent before it is too late." The lessons for today appear clear: Avoid extremism and overreliance on military weaponry.

Roland Emmerich's *2012* (2009) presents the now familiar doomsday scenario as predicted by Mayan mythology in which a massive destruction of the planet occasioned by gigantic earthquakes and volcanic eruptions occurs on a scale not witnessed since the biblical flood. The latest installment resonates with the era's deep pessimism and rising expectation of the end of the current civilization. As the film develops, it become increasingly darker and more pessimistic, yet it ends, as Hollywood movies often do, with a ray of hope as a boatload of humans discover refuge on the tip of Africa.

The retro spoof *Alien Trespass* appeared in 2009, written and directed by R. W. Goodwin. Goodwin sets his film in the 1957 desert town of Mohave, California. The film features teenagers sporting ponytails and ducktail haircuts and rugged local policemen. Eric McCormack plays Ted Lewis, a local scientist who becomes "borrowed" by an alien marshal named Urp, who plans to capture and destroy the Ghodas—large, one-celled, rubberized monsters—before they devour all life on earth. The entire film appears as a combination tribute-spoof of the classic science fiction genre. For example, advanced extraterrestrial Urp wears a surprisingly amateur-looking silvery spacesuit. And the rubberized Ghodas resemble crude monsters of classic 1950s sci-fi. *Alien Trespass* presents a naïve world in which nothing ever happens. Then one day, during a meteor shower, a spacecraft crashes to earth and an alien emerges. Audiences enjoyed the film's campy qualities and cheered as rubberized phallic-shaped Ghoda monsters suck the life from humans. With its campy, retro appearance and attractive characters, *Alien Trespass* ranks among the more creative of the post-9/11 science fiction genre. In post-9/11 sci-fi films such as this one, local law enforcement agents appear clueless, autocratic, and, ultimately, irrelevant. Underneath the film's campiness and semicomic tone lurks a serious depiction of impending doom and reliance on superpowerful aliens for protection.

Christian Alvart's *Pandorum* (2009) depicts the sole survivors of future wars on earth. Dennis Quaid and Ben Foster play Lieutenant Payton and Corporal Bower, who awaken from a hibernation disoriented and on board a starship. As they struggle to regain their memories and control of the ship, they must overcome hostile mutants possessing superpowers. The film's tagline aptly summarizes its message: "Don't fear the end, fear what happens next." As humanity's last remnants battle for their survival, the message could not be gloomier.

Albert and Allen Hughes's *The Book of Eli* (2010) envisions a postapoca-lyptic world in which ecological disaster transforms the planet into a waste-land. In a landscape reminiscent of *Mad Max Beyond Thunderdome* (1985), the Hughes brothers' film paints an especially bleak portrait of the future. Denzel Washington plays Eli, who travels across a blasted, parched land-scape headed west. Along the way he encounters scores of villains, some of which desire to possess his book, a King James version of the Bible. The film depicts a violent, desolate, postapocalyptic world in which the only solace turns out to be the Bible, serving as a road map for daily life. This message resonates with Evangelical and secular audiences alike.

The first Harry Potter film, *Harry Potter and the Sorcerer's Stone,* based on the novel by J. K. Rowling, appeared in 2001. This film belongs to the pre-9/11 canon. It inaugurated a series that currently consists of eight films:

- *Harry Potter and the Sorcerer's Stone* (2001)
- *Harry Potter and the Chamber of Secrets* (2002)
- *Harry Potter and the Prisoner of Azkaban* (2004)
- *Harry Potter and the Goblet of Fire* (2005)
- *Harry Potter and the Order of the Phoenix* (2007)
- *Harry Potter and the Half-Blood Prince* (2009)
- *Harry Potter and the Deathly Hallows, Part One* (2010)
- *Harry Potter and the Deathly Hallows, Part Two* (2011)

The films all feature Harry Potter (Daniel Radcliffe), a British wizard who begins the series as an eleven-year-old boy and ends it as a senior at Hog-warts School for Witchcraft and Wizardry in England. The films focus on a heroic struggle between evil forces, the "Dark Arts," and the students and faculty at Hogwarts School, especially Harry Potter, who learn and practice "good" magic.

By 2009 the series had become noticeably darker. David Yates reinvented the series in *Harry Potter and the Half-Blood Prince,* filming it as a neonoir with night-for-night shots, dark corners at Hogwarts, and scenes of Lon-don and other neighboring towns, evoking classic film noir cityscapes of the 1940s and 1950s. According to one critic, an ominous sensibility "pervades *Half-Blood Prince,* with its Dark Arts, dementors and Death Eaters, so Yates and his cinematographer Bruno Delbonnel borrow the *film noir* look. Hog-warts has never been so menacing—cathedral windows cast prison-bar shafts of light onto cold stone passages. Many scenes are staged at night. Even the posters for the film appear noirish, their texts askew, and their heroes half-hidden."[8] In true post-9/11 fashion, Yates also darkens the character of his youthful protagonist, Harry Potter, and includes war, revenge, pride, power, and greed—all well-used film noir devices. This episode pits Potter against the Dark Lord in a classic good versus evil confrontation. The Harry Potter series resonates with post-9/11 elements: superheroes, supervillains, and a struggle between the two sides, with the fate of the earth hanging in the balance.

James Cameron's much anticipated *Avatar* arrived just before Christmas 2009, and within two weeks it grossed a record $1 billion at the box office.[9] At two hours and forty minutes, the sci-fi epic contains a gung-ho military officer, Colonel Miles Quaritch (Steven Lang), hybridized characters with superhuman powers, a life-and-death struggle for existence, and a clash between scientists and military-industrial developers. Cameron's film, which he wrote and directed, stars Sam Worthington as disabled marine corporal Jake Sully and Sigourney Weaver as Dr. Grace Augustine, a botanist and head of the Avatar Program, which creates and employs hybrid human-Na'vi (blue humanlike aliens) called "Avatars" to research the Na'vi. Parker Selfridge (Giovanni Ribisi) serves as "company man" for the RDA mining corporation that plans to drive off the native humanoid Na'vi in order to mine for the precious mineral "unobtanium" scattered throughout their rich woodland. Sully inhabits a Na'vi avatar, endowed with superhuman strength and the ability to communicate with animals by day, and at night returns to his disabled human body (and the human base on Pandora). Sully and audiences readily identify with the forest-dwelling Na'vi, who mount powerful horselike steeds and fly atop giant beasts. They detest the harsh, greedy neocolonial mining company RDA and its military hirelings, who intend to expel the Na'vi from their holy "Tree of Souls" village nestled within a giant tree.

Placed in the context of 9/11, the film glorifies the indigenous population and demonizes RDA and the military, both in league to ruthlessly exploit Pandora's powerful minerals. Neocolonialism springs immediately to mind, with Pandora symbolizing developing nations (including Afghanistan and Iraq) and RDA evoking Halliburton and Blackwater. One critic noted, "As the marines rain bombs on the Na'vis, it is hard to miss the parallels with America's two ongoing wars. In *Avatar,* the aliens turn out to be victims of human (read American) greed. Replace unobtanium with oil and Na'vi with Iraqi and the film's anti-war message is clear."[10]

Post-9/11 science fiction thrillers like *King Kong* (2005), *Transformers* (2007), *Harry Potter and the Half-Blood Prince* (2009), *Cloverfield* (2008), *District 9* (2009), *Race to Witch Mountain* (2009), and *The Day the Earth Stood Still* (2008) evoke post-9/11 emotions: shock, rage, revenge, paranoia, terror, and horror. In addition, they resonate with film noir icons, including night-for-night shots, sleazy settings, damaged or nuanced protagonists, and implacable evil threatening to unleash chaos. They depict a venal, flawed society, far darker and more dangerous than in previous film cycles. In Wise's version of *The Day the Earth Stood Still* (1951), Klaatu appears predisposed to allow earth's humans one final opportunity to redeem themselves, whereas in Derrickson's 2008 adaptation a cynical Klaatu barely averts a preordained plan to annihilate the entire planet.

Instead of Islamic terrorists, post-9/11 science fiction depicts giant apes, monstrous reptiles, hostile aliens, and even heaven-sent angels, all bent on destroying social order and stability. Matt Reeves's *Cloverfield* (2008), also discussed in Chapter 3 and 8, represents a symbolic rendering of the 9/11 terrorist attacks on New York City, but instead of destroying the World Trade Center, the Cloverfield monster rips the head off the Statue of Liberty and heaves it into downtown Manhattan. Then the monster destroys high rises, subways, and other urban structures, sending the entire city into flight and forcing the military to contemplate using a nuclear bomb to destroy the monster. Is the cure better than the disease? This question appears frequently in current science fiction films. These filmmakers may be asking if the war on terror is really worth the expense in money and lives, a question remaining to be definitively answered.

After 9/11, science fiction films increasingly depict apocalyptic scenarios of earth's destruction. The planet faces catastrophic global climate change in *The Day After Tomorrow* (2004) and *The Day the Earth Stood Still* (2008). Earth faces attacks by solar flares in *Knowing* (2009) and hostile aliens in *War of the Worlds* (2005) and *Transformers* (2007). In *V for Vendetta* (2006) and *I Am Legend* (2007) plagues ravage humanity, and in *Megafault* (2009) a massive earthquake threatens to rend the earth in two. Whether the danger stems from plagues, natural disasters, bombardment from outer space, or hostile aliens, the films indirectly reference the terrorist attacks of 9/11 and subsequent attacks around the world. The notion of a civilization under

Scene still: *Cloverfield,* 2008. A prehistoric monster rips the head off the Statue of Liberty and flings it into the streets of Manhattan. As skyscrapers crash to the ground, audiences no doubt remember the 9/11 attacks as they view yet another "terrorist" attacking New York City. (Paramount Pictures / The Kobal Collection)

attack by extraterrestrials, climate change, or aliens resonates with hidden but widespread fears of Islamic militants spearheading jihadist wars against the United States. The 9/11 terrorist attacks transformed Hollywood's mood into pessimism verging on despair.

Current sci-fi films often incorporate biblical references and visions in lieu of political commentary, as in *War of the Worlds* (2005), *The Reaping* (2007), *2012* (2009), and *Legion* (2009). By referencing the Book of Revelation and the Book of Ezekiel, filmmakers tread safer ground than they would discussing Middle Eastern oil interests or Bush-era geopolitical ambitions. Unwilling to risk revenue by depicting the wars in Afghanistan and Iraq, filmmakers create conflicts generated by aliens or natural forces. However, these cinematic wars are not always resolved in earth's (or U.S.) favor. Some science fiction superhero thrillers, like *Push* (2009), predict difficult days ahead, whereas *Knowing* (2009) suggests the ultimate destruction of the surface of the earth, leaving only a few children left to grow and develop on an alien planet.

Post-9/11 sci-fi movies depict vengeance meted out against nefarious groups, but now these villains include the U.S. and British governments and the U.S. military. In fact, government and intelligence agencies are ridiculed and vilified in films like *I, Robot* (2004), *V for Vendetta* (2006), *Transformers* (2007), *I Am Legend* (2007), *The Day the Earth Stood Still* (2008), *Cloverfield* (2008), *Race to Witch Mountain* (2009), *Push* (2009), and *Avatar* (2009). The vilification of these agencies symbolizes agonizing doubts, conspiracy theories, and outright hostility toward military and political powers. Similar to the combat films and superhero movies previously discussed, post-9/11 sci-fi films seek vengeance against political evildoers who attempt to dupe the populace while engaging in mayhem and torture. The appeal of the post-9/11 genre suggests some of the reasons for Hollywood's recent box office bonanza in which movie sales rose dramatically (23 percent in 2008, 14 percent by spring of 2009). The surge in ticket sales appears even more surprising considering the stock market crash of 2008 and the recession of 2009 and mixed economic news of 2010.[11] Although box office receipts flattened in the United States during 2010, they rose an average of 8 percent worldwide.[12]

CHAPTER EIGHT

Post-9/11 Hollywood

The events of September 11 ushered in a new era in cinema. Films reflected highly emotional responses to the terrorist attacks, unleashing shock at the violence, grief for the victims, horror at the deaths and devastation, outrage against the perpetrators, thirst for vengeance against the attackers, fear of unknown terrorists, and paranoia about future attacks. Films from many genres became colored by these intense collective emotions. Post-9/11 films bear striking similarities in content, style, and mood and help define what I call the post-9/11 film movement. In post-9/11 films most genres rely on one or two dominant feelings. Science fiction, for example, relies on intense fear bordering on paranoia for its dramatic appeal. Horror films rely on revulsion and disgust through fierce antagonists, torture, and sleazy or disgusting settings. Melodramas depict undeserved misfortunes and elicit terror. Superhero films resonate with vengeance against evildoers. Combat films express outrage against a country, organization, or other group to justify warfare. Thrillers, like other melodramas, increasingly resonate with revenge against real or imagined outrages. After 9/11 they began including frank depictions of torture and other forms of prisoner abuse. September 11 affected the general movie culture and increased the popularity of horror, superhero, combat, sci-fi, and thriller genres, each reflecting the intensity of fear following the terrorist attacks and subsequent wars.

September 11 froze production on violent thrillers, including *Collateral Damage* and *Gangs of New York,* but they surfaced within a few months. Some media critics called upon Hollywood to abate screen violence, but post-9/11 audiences flocked to every violent thriller offered, whether horror, combat, or sci-fi. Shock emerged as a plot vehicle. Today's audiences demand plot twists involving disasters, murders, and massive violence, referencing 9/11. Films with surprising endings include *The Quiet American* (2002), *Dracula 3000* (2004), *A History of Violence* (2005), *Hostel* (2005), *The Interpreter* (2005), *Munich* (2005), *Sorry, Haters* (2005), *The Good German* (2006), *The Sentinel* (2006), *V for Vendetta* (2006), *Badland* (2007), *Blood Diamond* (2007), *Cloverfield* (2008), *District 9* (2009), and *Sherlock Holmes* (2009), and always involve violence.

Grief, as felt for the nearly 3,000 victims of the World Trade Center bombings, found expression in films like *United 93* (2006) and *World Trade Center* (2006). The wars in Afghanistan and Iraq provided fresh victims and fresh reasons to layer movies with strong doses of grief. In the midst of grief, sharp debate emerged. A series of documentaries, each presenting the filmmakers' perspective on 9/11, President George W. Bush, and the war on terror appeared after Michael Moore's controversial *Fahrenheit 9/11* (2004). The films present highly polemical depictions of the events and of the government's responses. Michael Wilson's *Michael Moore Hates America* (2004) and Alan Peterson's *FahrenHYPE 9/11* (2004) blast Moore's film as unpatriotic and anti-American. They praise and defend President Bush's leadership after the attacks.

Other post-9/11 films demonize monsters, zombies, and psychopaths instead of their ultimate targets, a government that appears disorganized, tyrannical, and incompetent. Recent depictions of corrupt military officers, sleazy executives, and ruthless intelligence operatives cast indirect reflections on George W. Bush, Dick Cheney, and Donald Rumsfeld, chief architects of the war on terror. A few daring filmmakers created movies critical of U.S. foreign policy in Afghanistan and Iraq even as these wars continued. *Redacted* (2007) grieves for the victims of American military in Haditha, Iraq; *In the Valley of Elah* (2007) grieves for an American soldier murdered by his own comrades. *Rendition* (2007) expresses the pain inflicted by U.S. intelligence agencies that order terrorist suspects to be abducted to other countries and tortured. *Badland* (2007) expresses grief and remorse for the massive killing of innocent civilians in the Battle of Fallujah. *The Hurt Locker* (2008) grieves for the brave soldiers assigned to defuse powerful explosives in Iraq; *Green Zone* (2010) grieves for the Iraqi people, doomed to endure a brutal civil war because of American lies about weapons of mass destruction. *The Hurt Locker*, which bears a strongly antiwar message ("war is a drug"), had barely earned enough revenue by 2010 to cover production costs, despite being awarded Best Picture at the 2009 Academy Awards.[1] *Green Zone* (2010) performed better than that, but even this highly touted action-adventure film, starring

Matt Damon and directed by Paul Greengrass, had not recovered its production budget months after release.[2] Post-9/11 movies now appear so grief-laden that many recent films could be labeled a "cinema of loss." The losses include loved ones, territory, money, innocence, and power. After 9/11 America lost its complacency about being beyond the reach of violent Middle Eastern antagonists and beyond the effects of blowback from U.S. foreign and military policies. Loss of innocence about the motivations of insurrectionists around the world also forms a part of this cinema of loss.

Vampires

Not since the Romantic age, when writers like Bram Stoker, Lord Byron, Samuel Taylor Coleridge, Mary Shelley, and Robert Southey penned vampire and other supernatural stories, have vampires enjoyed such popularity as currently. After 9/11 vampires suddenly became more popular than ever before. What special appeal do these creatures possess? To Delia Konzett, vampires experienced a spike of popularity after 9/11 precisely because these characters blend sex, hybridity, and diversity. Konzett explained that vampires today associate in viewers' minds with blood, which implies race as well as sexuality. For her, vampires represent postmodernism as well as cultural and ethnic diversity. She noted that vampire films may signal a positive development in American culture because "the 21st century American landscape once again appears open to discovery and adventure in the terms of multiculturalism, diversity, compulsive consumerism, and the decadent narcissism of the 'I want it now' generation."[3]

A poignant example of the passion that many now bestow upon vampire movies occurred in 2009 as approximately 2,000 young women set up a tent city outside the San Diego Convention Center in order to attend a panel on *New Moon,* the sequel to the vampire blockbuster *Twilight.*[4] When *New Moon* arrived in November 2009, it broke all previous box office records, and for a while it become the number one advance ticket seller of all time.[5] When *The Twilight Saga: Eclipse* appeared in the summer of 2010, it "ripped into the record books with its midnight launch, grossing over $30 million at more than 4,000 theaters. That surpassed *The Twilight Saga: New Moon*'s previous benchmark of $26.3 million."[6]

Far from the insidious monsters depicted in earlier vampire films, the vampires that appeared after 9/11 quickly transformed into superheroes protecting humanity. "Undead" movie characters fueled a box office bonanza after 9/11, along with more conventional superhero films. Changes already occurring in vampire films accelerated after the terrorist attacks as vampires transformed into human benefactors. The rise of so-called good vampires in notable films like *Van Helsing* (2004), *Underworld* (2003, 2006, 2009), and *Twilight* (2008–2010) relate to the tremendous popularity of superhero films. Because vampire characters possess superpowers, why not transform them into superheroes instead of supervillains? This transformation testifies to audiences' increasing demand for powerful movie characters that can provide the illusion of protection in an uncertain world.

After 9/11, vampires, along with mutants, became associated in movies with downtrodden human cultures and subcultures, including African Americans, Jews, American Indians, intellectuals, and youth. Instead of fiendish devils, vampires became sympathetic victims of official oppression and often represented oppressed minorities. Today's vampire characters may represent repressed minorities struggling for survival in a world that threatens at any moment to annihilate their entire "species." They might also represent a generation of youthful audiences that feel neglected or oppressed by their elders. Because vampires exist beyond mainstream society, they come off as attractive outsiders attempting to survive in a hostile world. Post-9/11 audiences find vampire alienation remarkably similar to their own.

Rage

Outrage, expressed in warfare and violent clashes between armed groups, became one of the post-9/11 movement's defining elements. The wars depicted—far from the real ones in Afghanistan and Iraq—feature zombielike enemies, weak national governments, and corrupt multinational corporations. Rage creates dramatic tension in films like *Troy* (2004), *300* (2006), *Blood Diamond* (2006), *The Kingdom* (2007), *Rambo* (2008), *Defiance* (2008), and *Inglourious Basterds* (2009). Each of these films features dramatic wars against armed and dangerous antagonists. They each fairly drip with anger and outrage.

Combat films proliferated after 9/11, and interest in real wars in Afghanistan and Iraq transformed into the box office appeal of films substituting distant and often exotic locations for the real battlefields. Post-9/11 depictions of former, distant, or futuristic wars allow filmmakers to comment indirectly on current wars in which the United States finds itself involved, especially the war on terror. By setting films far away in time and space from the current conflicts, such filmmakers may avoid the financial disasters awaiting those filmmakers bold enough to criticize wars while hostilities still rage. Therefore, the wars depicted in recent Hollywood films include the Burmese civil war, the Soviet-Afghan war, instability in Sierra Leone, jihadist attacks on Americans in Saudi Arabia, the Trojan War, the Battle of Thermopylae, and star wars waged against extraterrestrials. Understandably, filmmakers wishing to avoid appearing unpatriotic by depicting current conflicts involving American military turn their attention to other combat theaters, the more distant from the war on terror the better.

The release of violent combat images in foreign and distant wars after 9/11 corresponds with a cinematic expression of "rage," one of the most prominent post-9/11 emotions. It also corresponds with the release of dozens of unsettling images of the wars in Afghanistan and Iraq. Gabrille Murray noted that "the media release of documentary images of US and UK military personnel torturing prisoners at Abu Ghraib helped feed the escalation of uninhibited images of torture, degradation and mutilation in fiction film."[7] Once again, art and reality commingle, providing the post-9/11 film genre with documentary-like qualities, along with the dark, brooding atmosphere of neonoir.

In addition to combat films like *We Were Soldiers* (2002), *Troy* (2004), and *Defiance* (2008), combat plot elements appear with increasing frequency in other genres, like horror, sci-fi, and thrillers. *Transformers* (2007) functions as a combat film as well as a sci-fi thriller, and *Avatar* (2009) contains abundant combat scenes. Real wars spark interest in fictionalized ones, as long as the latter avoid direct evocations of the painfully long, frustrating wars in Afghanistan and Iraq. Films that directly reference current conflicts tend to fare poorly at the box office, helping to assure Hollywood's continued neglect of today's all-too-real conflicts.

Supervillains

After 9/11 Hollywood's villains transformed into supervillains, often with extraordinary powers. Many possess immortality, superhuman strength, mind-reading talents, and the ability to deflect bullets or heal quickly from mortal wounds. The post-9/11 era produced a cinema featuring caustic villains possessing superpowers at least as potent as those of superheroes. Heroes require villains, and superhero characters demand superpowerful antagonists for maximum dramatic effectiveness. If Superman or any other superhero encountered no superpowerful villains, how could filmmakers justify his or her superpowers? Superheroes require antagonists at least as powerful as themselves. However, superpowerful villains often steal the show from superhero protagonists, like the character Satan does in John Milton's *Paradise Lost.* Did Milton unconsciously intend for Satan to overshadow God in his epic? English poet William Blake, himself greatly influenced by Milton's poem, charged that Milton was "of the Devil's party without knowing it."[8]

Like Milton's Satan, Hollywood's supervillains often rival in charisma and popularity the superheroes they oppose. Batman's antagonist, the Joker, assumes a larger-than-life persona in *The Dark Knight* (2008) with Heath Ledger's performance; some would argue the Joker steals the show from his Caped Avenger superhero, played by Christian Bale. Through Kevin Spacey's skillful acting, Superman's nemesis, Lex Luthor, becomes a compelling antagonist for the Man of Steel. Spacey's strong performance rivals Brandon Routh's depiction of Superman. With powerful supervillains threatening humanity, only superpowerful superheroes can protect us.

The rapid increase in supervillain power and prestige often comes at the expense of superhero antagonists. *The Dark Knight's* Batman endures a painful physical beating from the Joker, and *Superman Returns'* Superman struggles to survive Lex Luthor's kryptonite-laden continent, which threatens to lay waste to the rest of the earth. The Fantastic Four combat not only Victor von Doom (Julian McMahon), their nemesis in the 2005 film, but also the Silver Surfer (voice of Lawrence Fishburne) in *The Fantastic Four: The Rise of the Silver Surfer* (2007). Like Superman and Batman, the Fantastic Four suffer increased dangers as their series develops. Even Sherlock Holmes battles a supervillain in the 2009 thriller in the form of an evil British aristocrat named Lord Blackwood (Mark Strong), who seemingly rises from the dead to head a vast satanic empire that threatens the earth. And the list goes on and on. Today's movie villains rank as the most powerful in movie history.

Contemporary movie villains, like *Saw's* (2004) Jigsaw, *Superman Returns'* (2006) Lex Luthor, *The Dark Knight's* (2008) Joker, *X Men: The*

Last Stand's (2006) Magneto, *Watchmen*'s (2009) Ozymandias, and *Avatar*'s (2009) Colonel Miles Quaritch, closely resemble media stereotypes of terrorists like Osama bin Laden, Khalid Sheikh Mohammad, Mohammad Atta, and other al Qaeda operatives. In sci-fi these bin Laden–like villains often confront superpowerful heroes acting as "police vigilantes," extralegal personalized weapons of mass destruction. The struggle between these superterrorists and the heroes confronting them often results in graphic scenes of bloodshed and carnage. The battles of the titans in science fiction and superhero films add significant amounts of murder and mayhem to appeal to a public that demands such features.

September 11 evoked powerful feelings of horror and revulsion worldwide, which found expression in a newly revitalized horror film industry. Televised images of real terrorist attacks and wartime casualties translate into films featuring similar images, often in different or remote settings. Horror permeates post-9/11 movies and not only serves as the subject of many popular movies, including the *Saw* (2004–2010) franchise, *Hostel* (2005), *The Texas Chainsaw Massacre* (2003), and *The Last House on the Left* (2009), but also forms an increasingly important element in a variety of other melodrama subgenres, including thrillers, sci-fi, and combat films. Horror has always played a crucial role in literature and remains an essential element in melodrama, especially in tragedy. Horror films experienced a renaissance after 9/11, with notable directors like Tim Burton, Robert Zemeckis, Bryan Singer, and Neil LaBute contributing significant films to an often trite, artistically sterile genre. Freddy Kruger (1987–2010), Jason Voorhees (1980–2009), *The Texas Chainsaw Massacre*'s (1974–2003) Meathead, and other venerable villains join newcomers like *Saw*'s (2004) Jigsaw. Sometimes they don't even possess proper names, like *Hostel*'s (2005) Dutch Businessman. However embodied, post-9/11 horror villains often resemble composite portraits of Osama bin Laden, Mohammad Atta, and other al Qaeda terrorists. These horror villains remain dedicated to murder and mayhem and derive an almost psychosexual pleasure from inflicting pain and suffering on their not-so-innocent victims.

In addition to the horror genre itself, many other post-9/11 films contain horrific elements like torture, mayhem, gore, and blood, rendered all the more vividly through computer-generated imaging. Blood depicted in computer-enhanced high definition 3-D images becomes an even more powerful symbol for chaos and terrorism. Blood and gore may remind viewers subconsciously of the 9/11 attacks and the war on terror, and they may also symbolize retaliatory carnage against the "evildoers" behind the continuing series of terrorist attacks. Viewers grow increasingly drawn to movies featuring horror and violence because they reflect aspects of contemporary society impossible to ignore. Audiences' attraction to horror, violence, and revenge reflects the increasingly widespread presence of those elements in society.

A notable horror subgenre, the "versus" films, features superpowerful monsters battling weak humans *and* villainous equals armed to the teeth with deadly skills and cunning. *Freddy vs. Jason* (2003), *Alien vs. Predator* (2004), and *Aliens vs. Predator: Requiem* (2007) represent some of the more popular crossover films. In these movies the monsters, pitted against each other, overpower all of the other characters, especially humans. In *Freddy vs. Jason* Freddy Krueger (Robert Englund) releases fellow villain Jason Voorhees (Ken Kurzinger) from hell in order to frighten townspeople into remembering him in their thoughts, the only way he can remain "alive." By doubling the villains, the versus films appear even bleaker and more violent than the normal horror fare, which is fitting in the post-9/11 emotional climate, with its lingering post-traumatic stress.

The horror of the 9/11 attacks and the subsequent scrapping of former U.S. policies forbidding torture in the field fueled Hollywood's interest in torture and horror as the horror genre's popularity skyrocketed. David Edelstein observed that movies featuring torture exploded upon the scene after U.S. torture policies became publicly known. Edelstein noted that "we've engaged in a national debate about the morality of torture, fueled by horrifying pictures of manifestly decent men and women (some of them, anyway) enacting brutal scenarios of domination at Abu Ghraib." He concluded that according to box office receipts "a large segment of the population evidently has no problem with this."[9] After Edelstein coined the term "torture porn," its use became more widespread. Don Kaye observed that the new torture porn genre "expresses the idea that its viewers are intensely, pruriently aroused by the sight of human bodies—usually young, nubile ones, and quite often female—getting torn into bloody chunks in the most awful ways imaginable."[10]

After 9/11 even some religious-themed films featured scenes of graphic violence. Mel Gibson's *The Passion of the Christ* (2004) serves as a prime example. Some critics labeled Gibson's film a "Christian torture movie" and "Christian torture porn."[11] By graphically depicting the scourging and

Scene still: *The Passion of the Christ,* 2004. A flagellated, mutilated Jesus Christ (Jim Caviezel) bears his cross to the taunts of Roman soldiers in Mel Gibson's *The Passion of the Christ.* Critics condemned this film for excessive sadomasochism, with some calling Gibson's film an example of "Christian torture porn." (The Kobal Collection)

hanging of Jesus Christ, including every stinging blow of whip, fist, or nail, Gibson's film deserves the torture porn label. However, despite its violent content, the film received tremendous support from Evangelical Christian churches, which helped it achieve record opening gross ticket sales of over $76 million, making it the most profitable opening weekend of any film at that point in history. Currently, Gibson's film ranks in the top ten in total box office receipts.[12] The various controversies surrounding Gibson's film, including charges that it contains a strongly anti-Semite message, helped inspire audiences to watch it. Christopher Hitchens blasted Gibson's film as "homoerotic" and called it an "exercise in lurid sadomasochism." Hitchens charged that the movie appeals to audiences that "like seeing handsome young men stripped and flayed alive over a long period of time."[13] Even today, Gibson's film continues to provoke critical controversy for its violent images.

At approximately the same time that torture porn became a staple of horror films, graphic torture scenes began to appear in mainstream thrillers. Paul Greengrass's *The Bourne Ultimatum* (2007) chronicles the desperate quest of rogue CIA assassin and amnesia victim Jason Bourne/David Webb (Matt Damon) to uncover his hidden past and discover his true identity. His past involves Operation Blackbriar, a supersecret CIA program designed to assassinate terrorists instead of arresting and trying them in courts of law. It superseded Operation Treadstone, an earlier and less violent organization that first appeared in the novel *The Bourne Identity* by Robert Ludlum (1980). It turns out that a real-life assassination squad whose identity was kept secret even from members of Congress existed until 2009, when Secretary of Defense Robert Gates summarily abolished it. Here is a case of film depicting reality, perhaps to an uncomfortable degree.

Other post-9/11 films also depict the era's infamous torture practices, even films not officially ranked as "horror." Gavin Hood's *Rendition* (2007) details the torture of Anwar El-Ibrahimi (Omar Metwally), an Egyptian-born engineer who has lived his entire life in the United States. This film, and the Bourne series, exposes the military's interrogation techniques as sadistic and unconstitutional. Whether the torture springs from the acts of psychopaths, supervillains, or government agents, audiences flock to it in droves.

Current films depict the U.S. government as corrupt, brutal, and ineffective, especially the military and intelligence units. Those agencies failed to predict or prevent the September 11 terrorist attacks, despite what we now realize in hindsight were crucial bits of information already in the intelligence system. Now, these same intelligence agencies find themselves vilified in Hollywood movies. Their operatives often function as villains, and their missions often turn out to be secretive, illegal, and unconstitutional.

Super Disasters

If fear helps define pre-9/11 emotions, paranoia better expresses post-9/11 emotions. Viewers awoke on September 11, 2001, to witness the death of their feelings of insularity and invulnerability and the birth of new fears, anxieties, and uncertainty about the future. Many films depict the earth under attack from aliens (*Transformers, Alien Trespass, The Day the Earth Stood Still, Race to Witch Mountain, Cloverfield*). Others blame humanity's near annihilation and the earth's destruction on natural forces, including comets and meteors, earthquakes, global climate change, and plagues (*2012, The Day After Tomorrow, I Am Legend, The Book of Eli, Pandorum*). Films depicting mass destruction occasioned by comets and asteroids, massive earthquakes, catastrophic wars, deadly plagues, extraterrestrial invaders, severe climate change, and acts of terrorism proved popular. In addition to their symbolic depictions in films, the 9/11 attacks qualify as a horrific disaster unparalleled in movie history. Eventually, a few filmmakers created movies chronicling episodes from those events. Paul Greengrass's *United 93* (2006) became the first major film to address the 9/11 attacks on the World Trade Center directly. His film inaugurated a spate of disaster films that is still unfolding.

Oliver Stone's *World Trade Center* (2006) depicts the terrorist attacks on the World Trade Center from the perspective of Port Authority police officers, played by Nicolas Cage and Michael Peña. Stone's film certainly qualifies as a disaster movie, complete with a surrealistic setting amid the chaos and destruction of Ground Zero. And beyond the Trade Center destruction lurks another more threatening disaster—war. During the elaborate rescue of the two policemen, one of the rescuers announces, "I don't think you realize this, but this country is at war."

Matt Reeves's *Cloverfield* (2008) references 9/11 more directly—though symbolically—than most current melodramas. In it a monstrous reptile reminiscent of Godzilla attacks and destroys New York City. J. J. Abrams, the film's producer, noted that "stories in which the destruction of society occurs are explorations of social fears and issues that filmmakers, novelists, playwrights, painters have been examining for a long time. The theory of attack became the reality of attack seven years ago. It's no coincidence that so many stories are being told that grapple in different ways with 'us vs. them.'"[14]

Roland Emmerich ranks as the king of disaster movie makers. His *Independence Day* (1996) depicts the invasion of the earth by aliens, and his twin post-9/11 disaster films, *The Day After Tomorrow* (2004) and *2012* (2009) explore geological and climatic apocalypses that nearly destroy earth. According to Emmerich, "In *Independence Day* the world was something worth defending. In *Day After Tomorrow* the message was, 'We'll go down if we don't stop what we're doing,' and in *2012* 'We're going down no matter what.'"[15] Despite the demise of life on earth as we know it, the end of

Emmerich's film turns a bit optimistic as the arc carrying the film's protagonists heads toward safe land on South Africa's Cape of Good Hope.

David Michael Latt contributed a made-for-TV entry into the disaster genre with *Megafault* (2009), which threatens the earth with a seismic fault that splits the entire North American continent asunder. This entry suffers from an unimaginative script, poor acting, and less-than-stellar special effects, but despite these flaws, it conforms to the post-9/11 pattern by threatening total geological destruction of the planet.

Images of urban devastation proliferated in both American and British cinema after 9/11. Contrary to initial hesitation to depict violence in urban settings, filmmakers quickly discovered a gold mine of urban-disaster-related films, although at first few ventured to depict the 9/11 attacks directly, substituting deadly viruses, asteroids, and even monsters for terrorists. Films like *28 Days Later* (2002), *The Day After Tomorrow* (2004), *War of the Worlds* (2005), *28 Weeks Later* (2007), *Cloverfield* (2008), and *2012* (2009) depict different apocalypses striking the earth or at least a significant portion of it.

Although disasters may originate on earth, descend from outer space, or be ordained by ancient prophecy, in post-9/11 movies human characters also inflict mass destruction and mayhem. The destruction may result from science or technology gone awry, as in the doomsday bombs invented by evil Dr. Totenkopf in *Sky Captain and the World of Tomorrow* (2004), the weaponized virus destroying much of London in *V for Vendetta* (2006), the human-created virus destroying most of humanity in *I Am Legend* (2007), and a menacing new continent created by Lex Luthor in *Superman Returns* (2006). Each of these disasters threatens humanity's complete destruction. In film after film produced after 9/11, major disasters threaten the earth, or at least New York, Gotham City, and other assorted U.S. and foreign locations.

Repressed Superheroes

As is the case with vampires, "mutant" superhero characters like the X-Men (2000–2009), Spider-Man (2002–2012), Daredevil (2003), Hellboy (2004, 2008), Elektra (2005), and Catwoman (2004) face organized discrimination and threats of extinction. The X-Men comic and film series depict U.S.-led efforts to regulate and ultimately decimate the X-Men as potential menaces to the public well-being. The Mutant Registration Act first appeared in Marvel comics in *X-Men* #181 (May 1984), although Marvel introduced the concept of government regulation of superheroes and mutants a few years earlier. The Watchmen comic series introduced the Keane Act, another version of the Mutant Registration Act, in comics released between September 1986 and October 1987. The controversial act first appeared in the 2004 Pixar-animated feature film *The Incredibles,* but other films, such as *Watchmen* (2009), also reference antivigilante legislation and agencies charged with protecting the nation against homegrown superheroes, including mutants.

Vampires and mutants face official discrimination and symbolize widespread fears that the government discriminates actively against its true heroes. Antimutant and antivampire legislative acts suggest government repression of other minorities, like African Americans, Hispanics, and gays. Mutants and vampires with extralegal superpowers constitute the only hope left to defeat terrorists bent on destroying America. These characters' popularity comes at a time when public support of military and intelligence operations has been plummeting to an all-time low. By 2005 it became apparent that previous rationales for using U.S. military to overthrow dictatorial governments no longer held sway in the public mind. A public opinion poll that year revealed that "a majority of Americans reject the idea of using military force to promote democracy. Only 35% favored using military force to overthrow dictators. Less than one in five favored the US threatening to use military force if countries do not institute democratic reforms."[16] These numbers reveal public dissatisfaction and disillusionment with war as a means for political change, debunking Prussian historian Karl von Clausewitz's famous dictum that "war is a continuation of politics by other means." With war increasingly losing public support, vigilante-style protectors consisting of superheroes, vampires, and mutants may satisfy current yearning for security.

Terror

Terror plays a special role among post-9/11 emotions. As a noun it means "intense, overpowering fear" or "anything that instills such a fear." It also means "violence toward private citizens, public property, and political enemies."[17] The word has come to signify a paramilitary strategy for attacking often much larger and better-equipped foes. After 9/11 Hollywood began disguising political-religious terrorists like al Qaeda and the Taliban, transforming these villains into crime organizations, domestic terrorists, rogue Wall Street day traders, or even aliens from distant planets. The thriller genre especially witnessed terrorist-inspired villains who labor, often from the inside, to totally control and, if possible, destroy the infrastructures of civilization.

Violent political events readily find artistic expression. For example, late Renaissance Europe suffered wars, plagues, and assassinations, which eventually found expression in a genre of plays now called "revenge tragedies."[18] The events of September 11, 2001, stimulated a spate of revenge films that remain popular today. After the September 11 attacks, public shock and anger soon transformed into rage and strident calls for revenge against al Qaeda, Osama bin Laden, and Saddam Hussein. In 2003, on the eve of the U.S.-led war against Iraq, country musician Darryl Worley released "Have You Forgotten?" in which he called for revenge against bin Laden and al Qaeda for the 9/11 attacks. P. J. Liberman and L. J. Skitka argued that in 2003 the desire for revenge for the 9/11 attacks resulted in a surge of public opinion in favor of war against Iraq.[19]

Notable post-9/11 revenge thrillers include *Mystic River* (2003), *Kill Bill: Volume 1* (2003) and *Kill Bill: Volume 2* (2004), *Man on Fire* (2004), *The Punisher* (2005), *Munich* (2005), *Sorry, Haters* (2005), *The Bourne Ultimatum* (2007), *Rambo IV* (2008), and *Quantum of Solace* (2008). Each of these films references terrorism, foreign or domestic. Why the sudden demand for these revenge films? One critic asked, "What are these dreams trying to tell us?"[20] Revenge featured so prominently in Hollywood movies by 2004 that Matthew E. Goldberg referred to post-9/11 movies as "a cinema of revenge."[21]

Post-9/11 themes and tropes come into sharper focus when we compare these films with earlier pre-9/11 movies. Thrillers constitute the most popular genre. Pre-9/11 representatives like the adaptations of Tom Clancy novels featuring Jack Ryan—*The Hunt for Red October* (1990), *Patriot Games* (1992), *Clear and Present Danger* (1994), and *The Sum of All Fears* (2002)— and even those depicting terrorist attacks against the United States, including *Passenger 57* (1992) and *Executive Decision* (1996) now seem dated. Each of these now appears hopelessly naïve in the wake of the real attacks. The Clancy adaptations feature American intelligence agent Jack Ryan

(Harrison Ford), who, like Captain America, always saves the day and prevents World War III, while the CIA basks in the credit. Currently, few positive depictions of the CIA, the National Security Agency, or the FBI exist in Hollywood films.

Post-9/11 thrillers including the Bourne series (2002–2007), *Rendition* (2007), *Redacted* (2007), *The Quiet American* (2002), and *Breach* (2007) depict U.S. military and intelligence officers as sadistic, manipulative, cruel, selfish, duped, and hopelessly out of touch with the people. Science fiction and fantasy films also depict the American military as cruel, duplicitous, and intent on illegal covert actions, as in *The Day the Earth Stood Still* (2008), *Fantastic Four: Rise of the Silver Surfer* (2007), *X-Men 2* and *X-Men: The Last Stand* (2003, 2006), *Jumper* (2008), *Push* (2009), and *Avatar* (2009).

Wealthy psychopaths, demented scientists, rogue military officers, and criminal bosses served as villains in pre-9/11 thrillers. Witness the 1960s and 1970s James Bond villains in *Dr. No* (1962) and *Goldfinger* (1964), as well as *Collateral Damage*'s (2002) Lobo and *Air Panic*'s (2001) Cain. These villains act primarily for personal greed or aggrandizement, and they seem far removed from today's suicide bombers and airplane hijackers.

Post-9/11 villains continue to exhibit avarice and megalomania, but now they exhibit those characteristics on a much grander scale. For example, the shadowy villains of *Casino Royale* (2006) launch the 9/11 attacks and then reap huge gains from their previously placed put options in stock markets. The attacks, and the resulting deaths of nearly 3,000 people, simply serve to manipulate the world's financial markets. The attacks served no ideological or political purpose beyond someone making a killing on Wall Street.

Another quintessential post-9/11 villain appears in *The Dark Knight* (2008). The Joker (Heath Ledger) takes sadistic pleasure in forcing passengers in two ferryboats to blow up each other. This character represents media stereotypes of Osama bin Laden and other Islamic terrorists as consummately evil for no apparent reason. However, unlike jihadists who employ terror tactics to combat the "Great Satan," the Joker terrorizes not because he seeks political or even financial gain but simply because "some men just like to watch the world burn." He becomes a kind of pyromaniac who enjoys destruction far more than creation, and his desire to smash things and people makes him almost a pagan god of war.

Post-9/11 Hollywood villains often resemble popular conceptions of a depoliticized al Qaeda. *Saw*'s (2004) Jigsaw places individuals in elaborate traps; *Sherlock Holmes*'s (2010) villainous Lord Blackwood (Mark Strong) plots to seize power in England by attacking Parliament with poison gas and then intends to rule the world. These villains act out of megalomania and sadism. They do not wage jihad against the United States for political reasons. *Superman Return*'s (2006) Lex Luthor and *Transformers*' (2007) Decepticons also threaten the earth and all of its inhabitants. These powerful characters evoke associations with bin Laden and other terrorist leaders who seemingly operate with impunity despite massive military, police, and intelligence efforts to capture and kill them. As they remain untouched in their hidden sanctuaries, movie villains become increasingly more threatening and pose more dire risks to humanity.

Demonized Politicians

Political leaders in post-9/11 films often function as villains. Examples include fascistic Chancellor Adam Sutler in *V for Vendetta* (2006), cruel Secretary of Defense Regina Jackson in *The Day the Earth Stood Still* (2008), duplicitous CIA Deputy Director Noah Vosen in *The Bourne Ultimatum* (2007), and ruthless CIA agent Corrine Whitman in *Rendition* (2007). And the list goes on. These government operatives in post-9/11 movies obsess over gaining and retaining power, not over protecting and serving citizens. Bad government, instead of good government, prevails. This cinematic distrust of American interests corresponds to a worldwide diminution of trust in the U.S. government. After the 2003 U.S.-led invasion of Iraq, respect for the United States declined steeply overseas as measured by public opinion polls. A Pew Global Attitudes Project Poll revealed that "favorable opinions" of America between 2000 and 2006 dropped from 83 to 56 percent in the United Kingdom, from 62 to 39 percent in France, from 78 to 37 percent in Germany, and from 50 to 23 percent in Spain. Even in Japan, a staunch U.S. ally, support for American policies declined from 77 percent in 2000 to 62 percent in 2006.[22]

While the United States inspires negative depictions in Hollywood movies, foreign governments fare no better. Post-9/11 movies cynically and savagely attack them, depicting all as evil, sinister, and dictatorial. *Rambo IV* (2008) demonizes the military and government of Burma (Myanmar); *V for Vendetta* (2006) depicts the British government as a fascist dictatorship, and the film ends with a citizen revolt. *Vendetta's* tagline reads, "People should not be afraid of their governments. Governments should be afraid of their people." *Blood Diamond* (2006) exposes greedy African warlords; *District 9* (2009) reveals a clueless UN taskforce that contracts with a multinational corporation to provide brutal, inept security forces. *Avatar* (2009) depicts an over-the-top marine colonel plotting to illegally extract a valuable mineral resource from a planetlike moon while laying siege to the local inhabitants. Many saw this plot as a veiled reference to American neocolonial policies throughout the world. Conservative critic Ted Baehr complained about the film's underlying anti-American, anti-imperialist message and added that the film "has an abhorrent New Age, pagan, anti-capitalist worldview that promotes goddess worship and the destruction of the human race."[23]

Rogue Corporations

Like government agencies, globalized corporations receive scathingly negative depictions in post-9/11 movies. Films like *Syriana* (2005), *Blood Diamond* (2006), and *District 9* (2009) depict with deeply negative connotation the inner workings of corporations. *Syriana's* oil company, *Blood Diamond's* gem official (reminiscent of the De Beers company), and, especially, *District 9's* evil Multi-National United evoke viewer antipathy toward large corporations. Post-9/11 movies depict corporate interests as venal, self-serving, and oblivious to any human suffering that might arise from their actions.

Like movies, post-9/11 fiction also savages corporations. Literary critic Benjamin Bird examined contemporary fiction and found that authors called for "the need for the contemporary US to sharpen its sense of history, in particular, to develop greater understanding of the prehistory of 9/11 and reconsider the past in light of the Al-Qaeda attacks." In addition, contemporary fiction focuses attention on "the body" as a microcosm of human history. Finally, fiction writers "insist on the need to consider the close connection between American corporations and violence, especially that which is abetted or provoked by corporations in the wider culture."[24] This attention to the role of American corporations in violent events equates quite well to filmmakers' depictions of rogue corporations and the havoc they wreak.

Religion

After the intensity of the 9/11 attacks, no one should be surprised by the strength of the religious themes that flooded post-9/11 movies. Prior to 9/11 mainstream audiences generally shied away from religious-themed movies while Evangelical Christians lamented the dearth of religion-friendly movies.[25] One critic recalled that prior to 9/11 many Hollywood commentators assumed "religion was spent as a social force." After the September 11 attacks, however, "suddenly, no one was saying that religion was done for."[26] A decade before September 11, 2001, Samuel P. Huntington, noted Harvard historian, predicted that in years to come "the principal conflicts of global politics will occur between nations and groups of different civilizations." Huntington predicted violent culture wars between nations and other entities, often fought over competing religious values. "Conflict between civilizations will be the latest phase in the evolution of conflict in the modern world," replacing the now dated cold war ideological clashes. In the coming conflicts religion would emerge from backstage to play a central role.[27] After September 11, 2001, few doubted the power of religion to inspire violence.

Although pre-9/11 films tended more toward a vague spirituality, religion currently permeates many Hollywood films. President George W. Bush himself raised the religion issue when he described the war on terror as a "crusade" for American values against terrorists and other "evildoers." Bush created a maelstrom of controversy in his September 19, 2001, speech when he stated, "This crusade, this war on terrorism, is going to take awhile." Muslims worldwide condemned Bush's choice of words. One mullah complained that the president's speech "recalled the barbarous and unjust military operations against the Muslim world" by Christian armies intent on capturing Jerusalem over the course of several hundred years.[28]

The vast majority of Americans now view religion as a primal factor in world events, contributing to wars and other conflicts between nations, ethnicities, and regions. Six months after 9/11, 51 percent of Americans reported that the attacks prove there is too little religion in the world, not too much.[29] In 2009 a subsequent Pew Forum report indicated that the vast majority of Americans believe that religion plays a powerful role in world events. According to a July 2005 poll by the Pew Forum, Americans say that religion has a great deal (40 percent) or a fair amount (35 percent) to do with most wars and conflicts in the world, which is similar to the 79 percent who expressed these views in 2003. In addition, Americans' opinions about recent events in the Middle East also reflect a religious bias. A July 2006 poll by the Pew Forum revealed that a substantial amount of Americans indicate that they sympathize more with Israelis (44 percent) than with Palestinians (9 percent) in the current conflict between these entities.[30] Religious values now appear regularly in movies.

Interest in apocalyptic religion spiked after September 11, 2001, and films found mass audiences in theaters across the country. In 2004 Mel Gibson's *The Passion of the Christ,* a film documenting Christ's scourging and death by crucifixion, made the biggest splash at the box office. Gibson appeared at many churches to publicize his film, which premiered at churches across the nation. By 2009 Gibson's film had earned more than $370 million, a startling amount even among mainstream films. *The Chronicles of Narnia: The Lion, the Witch, and the Wardrobe* (2005) has earned more than $291 million to date; *The Chronicles of Narnia: Prince Caspian* (2008) has earned more than $141 million.[31] These sales represent typical Hollywood "blockbuster" attendance and demonstrate the recent popularity of religious-themed movies.

Movies with religious themes need not relate directly to Evangelicalism. Superhero films like *Spider-Man* (2002), *Catwoman* (2004), *The Fantastic Four* (2005), *Superman Returns* (2006), *The Dark Knight* (2008), and *Avatar* (2009) contain subtle but noticeable religious themes. Superpowerful characters able to fly, stop bullets with their bodies, deflect giant asteroids, knock jet fighters out of the air, and leap over buildings, amid other miracles, function as quasi-religious beings, or gods. Many of today's superheroes exhibit godlike qualities, especially the ability to protect humanity against evildoers. And many of these characters, like Superman, possess immortality, an important divine quality. Vampires, too, possess immortality, and some appear omnipotent, and mutants possess sparks of divinity compared with ordinary humans. In short, Hollywood movies today increasingly resemble religious stories with divine characters enacting superhuman deeds.

Along with the phenomenal success of James Cameron's *Avatar* came some highly critical commentary about the film's alleged anti-Christian pantheistic message. Ross Douthat noticed pantheistic elements in *Avatar* and many other contemporary films. He asserted, "Many self-professed Christians hold beliefs about the 'spiritual energy' of trees and mountains that would fit right in among the indigo-tinted Na'vi (human-like beings in *Avatar*)."[32]

Despite abundant examples of the influence of 9/11 and the war on terror in films, some critics disagree about their meaning. In 2009 David Germain described what he perceived as an escapist movement in contemporary movies in which filmmakers feature lighter, less pessimistic fare. Germain postulated the existence of a "decade of escapism" in which many filmmakers eschewed depictions of harsh realism for "lighter" fare, including fantasy, sci-fi, and superheroes, thereby distracting audiences from uncomfortable references to the seemingly interminable war on terror and domestic and international terrorist attacks. "The past decade solidified the fan boy as Hollywood's key audience, with the final installments of George Lucas' 'Star Wars' chronicle joining comic-book heroes (Batman, Spider-Man, the X-Men), toy stories ('Transformers'), and revived franchises ('Indiana Jones,' 'Star Trek') to produce a succession of colossal opening weekends."[33] What Germain failed to note, however, is that many of the "escapist" films he notes in his article, including *Lord of the Rings* (2001), *Harry Potter and the Half-Blood Prince* (2009), *The Dark Knight* (2008), *Spider-Man* (2002, 2007), *X-Men* (2009), and *Transformers* (2007, 2009), bear the earmarks of the post-9/11 movement. A closer examination of these films reveals deep-seated pessimism and cynicism, elements not of escapism but of the post-9/11 milieu. These films feature darker, more flawed protagonists than in previous eras, and their villains are far more potent and menacing than those of earlier epochs. Although these films may appear escapist on the surface, they each reflect the harsh realities of post-9/11.

Special Effects

No feature of post-9/11 films identifies them better than their reliance on digital, 3-D, and green screen technology. Advances in digital filmmaking, computer graphics, and other techniques help explain the look and content of many post-9/11 movies. Films like *Sky Captain and the World of Tomorrow* (2004), *Beowulf* (2007), *The Fantastic Four* (2005), *Spider-Man* (2002–2007), *The Day After Tomorrow* (2004), *I Am Legend* (2007), and *Avatar* (2009) reflect not only post-9/11 psychology but also the state of contemporary filmmaking technology. Techniques like 3-D and Performance Action render superhero and superdisaster films more realistic than they would have been in previous decades. They also allow for greater flexibility in set design or mise-en-scène. In the hands of some directors these new techniques result in highly imaginative films like *Spider-Man 2* (2003), *Sky Captain and the World of Tomorrow* (2004), *Transformers* (2007, 2009), *The Day After Tomorrow* (2004), *I Am Legend* (2007), *Twilight: New Moon* (2009), and *2012* (2009). Recent technological advances often provide directors with additional elements with which to endow their movies.

The recent proliferation of fantasy-based movies, a hallmark of post-9/11 movies, corresponds to the rise of computer imaging techniques, resulting in a proliferation of computer-generated imagery (CGI). Films like *Beowulf* (2007), *Transformers* (2007), and *Harry Potter and the Half-Blood Prince* (2009) rely on computer-created characters that look increasingly realistic as the technology improves. Post-9/11 filmmakers rely on computer-generated imagery to create realistic-looking props, settings, and even characters. Robert Zemeckis's *Beowulf* (2007), for example, relies extensively on computer-generated settings and props. Zemeckis shot the entire film with his characters performing in front of green screens (uniformly green-colored backgrounds allowing filmmakers to import whatever settings and props they wish) and later added the fantastic settings of Viking mead halls and dragon's lairs.

By employing green screens, filmmakers may create either 2-D or 3-D films. *Beowulf*, for example, appeared simultaneously in a 3-D 70-millimeter Imax version and a 2-D edition. Other CGI movies include the Terminator series, especially the last two installments (2003, 2009); *Pirates of the Caribbean* (2003); *The Day After Tomorrow* (2004); *War of the Worlds* (2005); *WALL-E* (2008); *Transformers* (2007, 2009); *Underworld* (2003, 2006, 2009); and *Avatar* (2009). The practice of computer enhancements continues to accelerate, reflecting widely accessible technology and audience demand for fantasy and surrealism.

Technological advances in the wrong hands, however, weaken movies. Too much CGI induces technological overload. Too many CGI Starship Troopers, Orcs, demons, vampires, or werewolves may tire audiences or, worse yet, break their willing suspension of disbelief that movies must inspire. Too much of anything may prove distracting. Rob Logato, director of the Howard Hughes biopic *The Aviator* (2004), explained that, although computer graphics technology allowed him to shoot several striking scenes in the movie, including a spectacular scene in which Hughes, played by Leonardo DiCaprio, crashes his plane in the middle of a Beverly Hills neighborhood, he avoided overusing the computer technology. "For me, future is going backwards," said the Oscar-winning director. "Of course, the computer technology helped me take 30 to 40 shots in a few hours, but once you see all these movies trying to top each other, all those huge CG-driven effects can lose their magic. It's good to go under the top, instead of over the top. Use the technology to tell a good story, don't overuse the tools and go towards the artistic side."[34]

But what does Logato mean by "go towards the artistic side"? Who can say how much CGI is going to push a film over the top? Fans of computer animation, for example, may possess a higher tolerance for computerized settings and characters than typical audiences do. Perhaps a sufficient temporal distance will one day resolve the issue of how much of the "artistic side" is enough. But whether critics ever fully embrace the remarkable proliferation of CGI, HD, 3-D, and other innovations, they constitute a signature or hallmark of post-9/11 movies. Genres as widely disparate as science fiction, horror, thrillers, and combat films increasingly contain computer-generated imagery.

The transformation of films through CGI, green screens, 3-D, and other computer technologies add many new elements of unreality to the post-9/11 genre. As filmmakers increase their use of these technologies, their films emit an aura of artificiality as well as fantasy. *The Movies Made Me Do It* online magazine charged that Patrick Tatopoulos's *Underworld: Rise of the Lycans* (2009) relied excessively on CGI techniques to the film's detriment. As the reviewer noted, "One of my favorite aspects of the original movie was Wiseman's insistence that CGI be kept to a bare minimum. Sadly, director Patrick Tatopoulos has no such qualms after taking the hand off. The majority of the werewolf action here is primarily computer imagery, and the results aren't always pretty."[35]

Technology also plays a crucial role in today's real-world conflicts and their depictions in films. Superheroes like Batman, Iron Man, the Terminator, Wolverine, and the Hulk owe their superpowers to technology. These heroes must defeat superpowerful antagonists possessing similar technology. But films like *Terminator 3* (2003); *I, Robot* (2004); and *Sky Captain and the World of Tomorrow* (2004) warn of the catastrophic consequences of the forces unleashed by military and surveillance technology. Technology provides the advanced weapons necessary to defeat the forces of terrorism and their movie surrogates, yet in today's films it also provides the greatest challenge to order and stability. Technology in the wrong hands often proves catastrophic, as evidenced in many movies, like *Superman Returns* (2006), *The Dark Knight* (2008), and *Iron Man* (2008, 2010). Technology therefore functions as a double-edged sword in post-9/11 films.

Post-9/11 Heroes

Not since the rise of film noir during the 1940s and 1950s have movie heroes become so dark. Pessimism and cynicism now pervade the entire culture. Even Walt Disney's mild cartoon protagonist Mickey Mouse, long a youth icon (Mickey Mouse Clubs), underwent a dramatic makeover in 2009. *New York Times* writer Brooks Barnes warned viewers of upcoming Disney movies to adopt a more nuanced view of Mickey, advising audiences to "look for a little less Mr. Nice Guy."[36] Increasingly, post-9/11 movie characters, even cartoon characters aimed at children, seem defeated, tormented, and fragile.

Few filmmakers presented the conflicted post-9/11 individual as effectively as Spike Lee in *The 25th Hour* (2002), a filmic romp into degradation, defeat, and despair. Lee's protagonist, Montgomery Brogan (Edward Norton), could not be more defeated and doomed. Caught by the Drug Enforcement Administration in possession of cocaine, Brogan finds himself sentenced to seven years in prison. Much like the victims of the Twin Towers attacks, Brogan discovers that his former life as prosperous, hip drug dealer has drawn to a close, and he must sacrifice his relationship with his father (Brian Cox); his beautiful young Puerto Rican girlfriend, Naturelle (Rosario Dawson); and his closest friends. At one point two friends gather in friend Frank Slaughterly's (Barry Pepper) Manhattan apartment, overlooking Ground Zero. As Slaughterly talks about Brogan's impending prison sentence with teacher Jacob Elinsky (Philip Seymour Hoffman), another longtime friend, the camera zeros in on Ground Zero, drawing unmistakable parallels between the terrorist attacks and the disruption and devastation faced by Brogan. In the end he makes up with Naturelle and, following his father's suggestion, flees to the Southwest and assumes a new identity. An epilogue shows the couple many years later surrounded by a large family. In Lee's film one must renounce one's old aggressive, irresponsible lifestyle and create an entirely new identity, one much simpler, less urban, and more family-oriented. The only problem is if you break the law like Brogan and then flee you become a fugitive from justice. His new identity and seemingly idyllic life comes at a price: he could land in jail or prison if recognized.

The protagonists of Oliver Stone's *World Trade Center* (2006), Will Jimeno (Michael Peña) and John McLoughlin (Nicolas Cage), two New York City Port Authority policemen trapped under falling World Trade Center wreckage, symbolize the courageous aspect of the post-9/11 self. The two trapped officers, attempting to rescue victims, become victims themselves, experiencing pain, agony, and frustration as they lie pinned under tons of debris. Valiant rescue workers eventually free the two men, who certainly symbolize tenacity and determination in the midst of carnage and devastation. The rescue workers who labored long hours to free victims became 9/11 icons, and McLoughlin and Jimeno best symbolize the immediate responses to 9/11.

Jason Bourne (Matt Damon), the protagonist of the Bourne series, qualifies as the quintessential post-9/11 hero. Bourne, the product of secret (and illegal) behavior modification techniques, emerges much like *Manchurian Candidate* (1962) assassin Raymond Shaw (Lawrence Harvey). The difference between Bourne and Shaw, however, is that Bourne functions as the protagonist, whereas Shaw functions as the villain. In the post-9/11 world, villains transform into heroes. These two categories morph into each other. When vampires can be heroes, why not rogue agents like Bourne? In fact, Jason Bourne serves as a particularly appropriate post-9/11 protagonist because he finds himself duped by the government, manipulated through torture and technology, and pursued by government agents intent on his destruction. The Bourne series (2003–2007) demonizes the U.S. intelligence community in the same way that North Korean intelligence agents become demonized in *The Manchurian Candidate*. The difference is that during the cold war Soviet or other communist agents became demonized, but after 9/11 U.S. agents, not enemy operatives, serve as villains.

Edward Cullen (Robert Pattinson)—the traditional "good guy" (though vampire) of *Twilight* (2008), *The Twilight Saga: New Moon* (2009), and *The Twilight Saga: Eclipse* (2010)—also represents post-9/11 self-conceptions, as revealed in the unprecedented popularity of the *Twilight* series. Cullen possesses the power to run at blurring speeds, climb the tallest trees with ease, deflect speeding vans using only one hand, and leap onto high ceilings. He never ages and possesses immortality. And he subsists not on the blood of human victims but on animal blood obtained through the sport of pursuing wild game through the forest. His very bite transforms ordinary humans into immortal beings like himself. Cullen's virtual invulnerability epitomizes contemporary fears of vulnerability, while his superpowers express an overwhelming need for protection in an uncertain world. Cullen's perpetual youth captures the Romanticism of Byronic heroes while serving as a foil against growing fears of personal inadequacy in the face of contemporary uncertainty.

Each of these heroes illustrates distinct aspects of the post-9/11 psyche, including feelings of paranoia, vulnerability, and mortality. As we stare into the face of death, why not fantasize about perpetual youth and superhuman powers? In a sense post-9/11 heroes allow viewers to escape their personal fears and anxieties while feeling comfort from heroes battling the same inexplicable forces as we all are. For all of the pessimism, many post-9/11 heroes, like *The 25th Hour*'s (2002) Monty Brogan (Edward Norton), eventually overcome the forces of chaos surrounding them and carve out a small piece of paradise for themselves, or at least they resolve their trauma and return to a peaceful existence like *The Bourne Ultimatum*'s (2007) Jason Bourne (Matt Damon) or to the warmth and comfort of their homes like *World Trade Center*'s (2006) 9/11 victim John McLoughlin (Nicolas Cage). These characters succeed in the midst of social and political chaos.

Post-9/11 Neonoir

Critics herald the arrival of a newly minted version of the venerable film noir style in many post-9/11 movies. Genres as disparate as sci-fi, horror, thrillers, and combat assume a darker aspect after 2001. Night-for-night shots and other dimly lit scenes reveal neon-splashed cityscapes, rain, and snowstorms and doomed, duplicitous, amoral characters. These are all icons of the film noir genres of the 1940s and 1950s as well as the neonoir films of the 1980s and 1990s. The newest additions to the film noir repertoire receive their dystopic worldview and jaded cynicism from the emotional shock of the 9/11 attacks. Even today, many years later, audiences flock to the darkest, saddest, and bleakest films in years. These films reveal a public with deep-seated emotional scars resulting from the 9/11 attacks and the interminable war on terror that followed. The administration of George W. Bush inspired dozens of noirlike movies, and the administration of Barack Obama continues to do the same.

The list of prominent post-9/11 films bears surprising similarities to the earlier film noir genres. First, the docudramas depicting the terrorist attacks, like *World Trade Center* (2006) and *United 93* (2006), resonate with film noir icons and cinematography. Dark shots and bleak settings characterize these films. Other films depicting the attacks, including *DC 9/11* (2003), *The Heroes of Flight 93* (2005), *Flight 93* (2006), and *Twin Towers* (2006), rely on film noir icons to a greater or lesser extent. In fact, how could it be otherwise? Images of Ground Zero and of the planes hitting the World Trade Center seem especially noir. Smoke-filled streets, piles of rubble, and a frightened populace in a city brought nearly to a standstill as a result of the attacks seem to leap out of a film noir textbook.

In addition to the relatively few films depicting the actual September attacks and their aftermath, scores of others make oblique references to 9/11, either by depicting terrorists, New York City, or horrific dangers awaiting not-so-innocent victims. Horror films, for example, which experienced a spike in popularity in the aftermath of 9/11, continue to grow even darker. Suddenly, viewers find themselves mesmerized by more diabolical characters than they grew accustomed to in the years prior to 9/11. They face demonic villains like Leatherface, Jason, Jigsaw, the Dutch Businessman, and Freddy, including entire families of serial killers like the Firefly family. And the settings become even more disgusting, including Leatherface's meatpacking plant, the Dutch Businessman's abandoned factory, and both inner-city and rural slums. After 9/11 cinematography, too, grows darker as victims (rarely innocent) pile upon the stage in greater numbers than ever before.

Science fiction also experienced a renaissance with such films as *Sky Captain and the World of Tomorrow* (2004), *King Kong* (2005), *Cloverfield* (2008), *I Am Legend* (2007), *Transformers* (2007), *Race to Witch Mountain* (2009), *District 9* (2009), *Pandorum* (2009), and *Avatar* (2009), which all feature cinematic elements derived directly from film noir, including dark, dimly lit settings; duplicitous, evil villains; and deeply flawed and often doomed protagonists. Monsters arise to destroy New York and other cities and landmarks, much like the science fiction noirs of the 1950s that were remade after 9/11: *Invasion of the Body Snatchers* (1956, 1978, 2007), *The Day the Earth Stood Still* (1951, 2008), *Them!* (1954, 2006), and *The Blob* (1958, 1988, 2009). Long after these films appeared in theaters, critics began to realize their debt to the film noir visual and thematic style, with their doomed, flawed protagonists and superpowerful villains.

Superhero films also resemble neonoir, including *Superman Returns* (2006), *Iron Man* (2008, 2010), and *The Dark Knight* (2008). These films feature night-for-night shots, sleazy cityscapes, and flawed characters battling superpowerful villains. Instead of the confident, godlike superheroes of the past, post-9/11 superhero films feature protagonists who suffer from deep traumas, experience personal crises, and spend much of their time looking confused and vulnerable. *The Dark Knight* (2008) finds himself powerless and in jail; the Man of Steel in *Superman Returns* (2006) descends into a deep funk and disappears from earth for years. He languishes powerless on an island until he makes a miraculous recovery and defeats supervillain Lex Luthor. Even James Bond endures torture in *Casino Royale* (2006).

Vampire films, a post-9/11 mainstay, naturally appear noirish because their characters generally frequent the night, shirk from bright lights, and, on occasion, blend into the shadows and completely disappear. Films like *Van Helsing* (2004), *The Lost Boys* (1987, 2008), *Twilight* (2008, 2009, 2010), and *Queen of the Damned* (2002) share many characteristics of neonoir thrillers, including crazed supervillains, femmes fatales, sleazy settings (along with opulent ones), and dark cinematography. Vampires are nearly synonymous with film noir protagonists, and post-9/11 vampires morphed into extremely complex characters, at times saving humans from evil versions of themselves.

War films, too, share many characteristics with classic and neonoir films, including obligatory night scenes, smoke-filled battlefields, angst-ridden protagonists, and violence. Images of violence actually help define film noir, and no genre displays more violence than combat films. *Rambo IV* (2008) epitomizes the post-9/11 combat genre, although other memorable ones include *Charlie Wilson's War* (2004), *Troy* (2004), and *300* (2006).

Blurred Genres

Post-9/11 films often defy traditional genre definitions by referencing more than one genre. Blending and changing genre conventions link post-9/11 films with postmodernism, a movement that began in the last decades of the twentieth century and continues to date. In postmodernism genres blend into each other so that fiction films resemble documentaries, thrillers resemble sci-fi, and horror appears in a variety of other genres besides horror films.[37] *Cloverfield* (2008), for example, qualifies as both a disaster movie and a science fiction thriller, with strong elements of horror thrown into the mix for good measure. Matt Reeves's film, shot with jerky hand-held cameras, depicts the complete destruction of New York City not by terrorists in airplanes but by a huge reptilian monster that stands twenty stories tall, breathes fire, and appears to have a maniacal desire to destroy the entire city, including its inhabitants and its skyscrapers. In one never-to-be-forgotten scene that occurs early in the film, the monster actually flings the head of the Statue of Liberty into downtown Manhattan. It takes only a small imaginative jump to replace the monster with the 9/11 terrorists, who also wreaked destruction in New York City. Jessica Wakeman wrote that "*Cloverfield* nails what that morning [September 11, 2001] felt like: the confusion at first, and then fear overwhelms and all you can think about is the possibility of dying and needing to escape by getting *out-out-out* but where can you go because the subways and trains aren't running?" She added that the movie "gets what it *looks* like and *feels* like to believe there's eight planes in the air, that the president ordered any non-grounded aircraft to be shot down, they could be shot down above your city and kill you, and what if there's a ground attack?" Finally, the film's mood of utter despair "depicts what it's like to be convinced that that day is the day you are going to die."[38]

Horror, a genre once neatly categorized, now spills over into many others, including thrillers, sci-fi, and combat films. Horror infuses post-9/11 sci-fi films like *Cloverfield* (2008) and *I Am Legend* (2007), terrorist thrillers like *The Bourne Ultimatum* (2007) and *Rendition* (2007), and superhero movies like *X-Men: Origins* (2009) and *Iron Man* (2008), and vampire films like *Queen of the Damned* (2002), *Van Helsing* (2004), *Dracula 3000* (2004), *Twilight* (2008), and *Lost Boys: The Tribe* (2009). Vampire films, with their depictions of fanged beings slurping human blood, always resonate with horror and often become classified as horror films.

Horror also forms the basis for monster films like *Cloverfield* (2008) or human monsters like Hannibal Lecter (*Hannibal Rising,* 2007). Zombies in films like *The Hills Have Eyes* (2006), a traditional horror film, and *I Am Legend* (2007), a sci-fi/horror blend, routinely decapitate, disembowel, and otherwise eviscerate their victims. Today's science fiction and thriller supervillains routinely disembowel, set fire to, eviscerate, or cause their victims to explode all over the stage. Awash in horror, post-9/11 cinema reeks with blood and singed (and sometimes cooked) human flesh. By infiltrating other genres, horror films now account for a significant percentage of Hollywood movies.

Post-9/11 films also resonate with Gothic and Romantic elements. As in Romanticism, nature itself seems to have gone awry, and post-9/11 films serve as wake-up calls on issues like global climate change. In addition, torture, rendition, rogue intelligence operatives, and violations of civil and human rights are depicted. These films speak of widespread disillusion with official sources of power, including President George W. Bush, Vice President Dick Cheney, and Secretary of Defense Donald Rumsfeld.

Vietnam

One of the most remarkable features of post-9/11 movies turns out to be their connection with films of the 1970s and 1980s, or the post–Vietnam War era. Many post-9/11 horror films, including *The Texas Chainsaw Massacre* (1974, 2003), *The Hills Have Eyes* (1977, 2006), *The Last House on the Left* (1972, 2009), *The Fog* (1980, 2005), and *The Wicker Man* (1973, 2006), reprise popular post–Vietnam War horror movies. The 1970s and 1980s witnessed the rise of neonoir, with such classics as *Chinatown* (1974), *Night Moves* (1975), *Taxi Driver* (1976), and *Body Heat* (1981). Horror films, like neonoir, also feature graphic violence, libidinous sexuality, and pessimistic zeitgeists. With numerous references to the films of post-Vietnam America, today's cinema reflects both eras' distrust of political, military, and corporate power. Like the wars in Iraq and Afghanistan, the Vietnam War became very unpopular with filmmakers and audiences.

Post-9/11 Style

A dark, dystopic, and violent filmic style developed rapidly after September 11, 2001, even after producers promised to concentrate on lighter fare. Reflecting the mass trauma that 9/11 caused among thousands, movies since 9/11 dramatically darkened and became increasingly more violent and paranoid. This transformation occurred in response not only to the terrorist attacks themselves but also to related events, like wars in Afghanistan and Iraq, enactment of the Patriot Act, establishment of the Department of Homeland Security, and increased security measures throughout the country. After 9/11 the United States transformed into a surveillance and security society in which secret government operatives kidnapped and tortured suspected terrorists and placed thousands of others under covert surveillance.

As the temporal distance between the 9/11 events and contemporary movies expands, it becomes increasingly possible to identify the thematic and stylistic elements common to post-9/11 movies. Although the terrorist attacks inspired movies in every genre, the general parameters of the new post-9/11 movement now appear with increasing clarity. The elements of post-9/11 style continue emerging, with increasing clarity, as time goes by. They include the following:

1. *Despair.* Post-9/11 films often possess a dark, depressing atmosphere. Borrowing from film noir, post-9/11 filmmakers learned to shoot many of their films at night in sleazy, depressing settings. Films as varied as *The Hills Have Eyes, Munich, Syriana, The Taking of Pelham 123, The Dark Knight, Hellboy, Hostel,* and *I Am Legend* feature bleak, dystopic, devastated settings and a dark, dimly lit atmosphere.

2. *Violence and horror.* Current films drip with violence like never before in film history. The entire torture porn genre, for example, and the larger horror genre all appear drenched in rape, brutality, torture, and murder. This period easily qualifies as film history's most blood-soaked era.

3. *Vengeance.* Revenge is one of the most popular post-9/11 themes, usually linked to feelings of outrage. Since 9/11 a group of films called "revenge thrillers" have become one of the most popular contemporary genres.

4. *Superheroes.* In addition to "leap[ing] tall buildings in a single bound," today's superheroes and supervillains have harnessed the power of cosmic radiation, scientific formulas, and even toxic pollutants and become the strongest, most potent protagonists in film history.

5. *Disasters.* Disasters of major proportions have been in public awareness since 9/11, and they still seem to remain on the minds of filmmakers and audiences alike. Many varieties of disasters entertain audiences in post-9/11 Hollywood, ranging from asteroids striking the planet to global climate change, deadly viruses, and aliens and zombies threatening to destroy humanity. One hallmark of post-9/11 movies, therefore, is the persistence of disasters as plot devices. Violent, flaming images of destruction grace post-9/11 disaster films, rendered all the more realistic through digital technology.

6. *Film noir.* Urban fog, relentless rain, neon lights, sleazy settings, and deteriorating walls have become icons of post-9/11 films. So many

neonoirs belong or bear a striking resemblance to post-9/11 films that it becomes impossible to separate the two styles. Post-9/11 films exhibit seedy settings, dystopic themes, dark lighting, duplicitous situations, and powerful, often devious characters. These constitute the essential components of film noir. In retrospect it becomes clear that many post-9/11 films could easily be classified as neonoir, and nearly all feature films have noir icons and characters.

7. *Cynicism.* A growing body of post-9/11 films expresses cynicism of government, the military, and, especially, American intelligence agencies. Agents are depicted as ruthless, unprincipled, and out of touch with common people.

8. *Satire.* A growing number of post-9/11 films contain elements of social and political satire, as well as self-satire. Many, like *Sky Captain and the World of Tomorrow, Alien Trespass,* and *The Men Who Stare at Goats* appear campy. *Team America* satirizes both President George W. Bush's foreign policy and liberal opponents of his policies. *Alien Trespass*'s rubber monsters function as self-satire, whereas *Hancock* satirizes the entire superhero genre.

9. *Computer enhancements.* A large number of post-9/11 movies feature extensive computer enhancements like green screens, digital effects, and 3-D.

Post-9/11 films emerged as a dominant Hollywood style, and eventually the term "post-9/11 movies" will become as familiar to critics and movie enthusiasts as are earlier stylistic terms like "film noir" and "neonoir." In fact, these three styles seem like continuations of the same film noir movement that began in the early decades of the twentieth century.

The Age of Paranoia

Like the "age of anxiety" of the 1950s and 1960s, when films reflected cold war paranoia, many of today's movies, like *The Road to Perdition* (2002), *The 25th Hour* (2002), *Mystic River* (2003), *The Texas Chainsaw Massacre* (2003), *War of the Worlds* (2005), the Bourne trilogy (2002–2007), *The Wicker Man* (2006), *Cloverfield* (2008), and *The Taking of Pelham 123* (2009), exude shock, grief, rage, horror, vengeance, and terror. These 9/11 emotions resonate in many contemporary films. They help define what could be called the age of paranoia. They project physical and emotional dystopias haunted by dangerous characters, faded dreams, and lost opportunities. They herald social instability, insecurity, fear, and a sense of impending doom. Despite a few escapist films with upbeat messages, a large number of today's films exude pessimism, cynicism, and paranoia. They feature harder, more ruthless, and far more violent protagonists than those of earlier eras.

Paranoia also results from the failure of the news media and the U.S. government to adequately tamp down widespread conspiracy theories and doubts about official government statements regarding terrorism and, especially, 9/11. A 2006 Scripps poll revealed that one-third of all Americans believe that the U.S. government either carried out the 9/11 attacks or intentionally allowed them to happen in order to provide a pretext for war in the Middle East.[39] That means that tens of millions of Americans believe that their government might be responsible for the 9/11 attacks. No wonder the U.S. government receives a largely negative portrayal in post-9/11 movies.

Visually, these films often appear dark, with familiar film noir icons like reflecting panes of glass, sheets of ice, or pools of water. They resemble neo-noir films, enhanced with computerized graphics, nostalgic settings, dark lighting, and duplicitous characters. Some of these films demonstrate artistic excellence, whereas others are tasteless and repellent.

Future Trends

The events of September 11, 2001, transformed movies as profoundly as the bombing of Pearl Harbor did on December 7, 1941, casting a bleak emotional pall on film content and film style for years. However, although World War II resulted in a massive output of war movies, 9/11 inspired few war films. Instead, it gave life and new direction to revenge thrillers, torture porn, and disaster films. Films emerged featuring vengeance, terror, horror, and paranoia, although these elements also suggest the classic film noir genre. After 9/11 a new film noir genre with post-9/11 themes, issues, and images arose and now dominates Hollywood movies.

How will future historians characterize Hollywood movies since 9/11? In 2001 some predicted little tangible impact from the terrorist events, especially after initial hopes of a gentler, more-family-oriented cinema proved unfounded. Subsequent developments proved these predictions all wrong.

Instead of producing gentler movies or remaining untouched by the attacks and their aftermath, filmmakers responded to the 9/11 attacks by producing some of the most pessimistic, violent, cynical movies in history. Warren Epstein noted that, despite producers' vows to eliminate or reduce violence and depictions of terrorist acts, post-9/11 movies became loaded with greater-than-usual levels of violence and cataclysmic scenarios. Epstein observed that instead of retreating from graphic depictions of violence, movies produced during the first year after 9/11 contained even higher doses of violence than pre-9/11 fare had.[40]

Post-9/11 movies resonate with highly charged emotions, along with critical examinations of intelligence and security agencies and a cynical perspective on a variety of social institutions, particularly U.S. corporations, military, and government. Fear verging on paranoia runs rampant through many post-9/11 movies.

However, even in the midst of pessimism, fear, and all of the rest, recent melodramas, even apocalyptic ones, end with idyllic visions of the future of humanity. *Pandorum* (2009) ends with the beautiful planet Pandorum and a hopeful experiment in seeding it with humanity's last survivors. *Avatar* (2009) ends with a victory for the Na'vi people of the moon Pandora. And *2012* (2009) ends as a watercraft full of future colonists strikes untouched land near southern Africa, providing a verdant new world to populate. As the events of 9/11 recede further into the past, the question of influences on filmmaking arises. Possibilities include Hollywood's current fascination with the genre passing into obscurity; the genre morphing into wry, witty parodies of today's popular movies; or an evolution of the genre into something as yet unseen.

The history of Hollywood's popular genres suggests future directions. Westerns, the quintessential genre, emerged during the twentieth century, with popular studio films starring Tom Mix, Roy Rogers, William S. Hart, and Gene Autry. Early fans thrilled to Cecil B. DeMille's *The Iron Horse* (1939), John Ford's *Stagecoach* (1940), and Fred Zinnemann's *High Noon* (1952). A decade later fans watched "revisionist" Westerns like John Sturges's *The Magnificent Seven* (1960); Sergio Leone's *The Good, the Bad, and the Ugly* (1965); Sam Peckinpah's *The Wild Bunch* (1969); and George Roy Hill's *Butch Cassidy and the Sundance Kid* (1969). These later films relied on multiple heroes, elevated levels of violence, and realistic depictions of Western characters. Examples of parodies include Eliot Silverstein's *Cat*

Ballou (1965) and Mel Brooks's *Blazing Saddles* (1974). Clint Eastwood's *Unforgiven* (1992), Edward Zwick's *Legends of the Fall* (1994), and Kevin Costner's *Open Range* (2003) present nuanced, revisionist themes and late-Western time frames. Westerns never passed into obscurity.

Post-9/11 movies now exhibit unmistakable signs of revisionism and parody. Jon Favreau's 2010 *Iron Man 2* parodies his earlier version of the superhero film *Iron Man* (2008). Rob Letterman and Conrad Vernon's *Monsters vs. Aliens* (2009) satirizes sci-fi thrillers like *Transformers* (2007, 2009) and R. W. Goodwin's *Alien Trespass* (2009) pokes fun at sci-fi thrillers like *War of the Worlds* (2005). These parodies signal a turning point in recent cinema by utilizing satire and irony to enliven the otherwise dystopic post-9/11 genre.

Some films embrace a sense of futility and tenuousness. Mel Gibson's *The Passion of the Christ* (2004) depicts Jesus' scourging in literalist biblical terms, but Christian audiences knew that Christ would return. The Hughes brothers' *The Book of Eli* (2010) depicts a postapocalyptical world in which only the Bible offers salvation. James Cameron's *Avatar* (2009) suggests deeper truth lies in paganism. Ultimately, apocalypse itself evokes biblical as well as pagan themes and continues to prove popular with post-9/11 audiences, and so many of these apocalyptic epics now end on an optimistic note. According to these films, humanity might survive its current crises, though vast numbers of people must die in the process.

Terrorism continues to dominate headlines at home and abroad, so terrorists are likely to continue to be film villains. Issues, including the continuing effects of the great recession, political polarization, and ecological disasters like the gulf oil spill, keep films' messages pessimistic. But the optimism seen recently suggests sunnier films in the future. The neonoir style promises to remain popular. Its dark settings, night shots, and nuanced characters still resonate with viewers and filmmakers alike.

When will Hollywood emerge from its lingering post-9/11 trauma? The answer depends in part on public perception about terrorism and U.S. responses. At present, movies still contain symbolic references to the attacks, while media largely ignore these attacks. *Washington Post* columnist Brad Hirschfield complained in 2009 about disappointingly little media attention paid to the anniversary of the September 11, 2001, attacks. He noted, "We need to figure out how to keep memory alive in ways that helps us to build a better and more secure future without dredging up hurt and rage to mobilize us." He admitted this may prove an impossible goal, "but if we cannot do so, we are positioning ourselves for one of two futures: either we continue to be victims or we become just another version of those who victimized us."[41]

Given that post-9/11 themes continue to inspire popular movies, there seems little likelihood that the movement will disappear anytime soon. Instead, movies may continue for a long time to come to reflect the events of September 11, 2001, and the violent and costly wars that followed. The post-9/11 style, as the most recent manifestation of the film noir/neonoir cycles demonstrate, should remain in vogue with filmmakers and audiences alike as long as it continues to deliver shocks and thrills and continues to depict our greatest fears and hopes in entertaining forms.

The current crop of post-9/11 films reveals an increasing ambivalence about traditional concepts of good and evil. Characters once stereotyped as villains, like vampires and werewolves, emerge as humanity's protectors and benefactors and even our conscience. Paradoxically, as superheroes gained popularity, they also became more complex as characters, moving away from earlier comic book–type flat depictions. Today, even superheroes experience defeats, injuries, and romantic setbacks. No longer representing moral and physical perfection, they represent more powerful yet fatally flawed versions of ourselves. Everyone functions as their own imaginary superhero at times, and today's movie villains represent our deepest fears and most persistent paranoia. In post-9/11 movies heroes don't always win and they often lose more than they gain. These flawed, doomed heroes affect audiences' own imaginary heroes, rendering them more realistic but at the same time more troubled and sad. Audiences coming out of post-9/11 movies remind me of the cartoon character Pogo's famous line: "We have met the enemy, and he is us."

Notes

Chapter One

1. Nicholas L. Carnagey and Craig A. Anderson, "Changes in Attitudes Towards War and Violence After September 11, 2001," *Aggressive Behavior* 33 (2007).

2. Marc Bekoff, "Emotions Gone Wild," *Mysteries of Science,* U.S. News and World Report Special Collector's Edition, 2009.

3. Elaine Herscher and Psyche Pascual, "Special Report: Coping with the Trauma of 9/11," www.cvshealthresources.com/topic/trauma.

4. Matthew Tull, "Did Media Coverage of 9/11 Increase Risk for PTS in Children?" ptsd.about.com/ad/infoforfriendsfamily/a/children_Sept.11

5. Michael A. Cohn, Matthias R. Mehl, and James W. Pennebaker, "Linguistic Markers of Psychological Change Surround September 11, 2001," *Psychological Science* 15, no. 10 (October 2004).

6. Stephen Keane, *Disaster Movies: The Cinema of Catastrophe* (London: Wallflower Press, 2001).

7. Roger Ebert, "Collateral Damage," *Chicago Sun Times,* February 8, 2002.

8. Todd McCartney, "Collateral Damage," *Variety,* February 7, 2002.

9. Roger Ebert, "Big Trouble," *Chicago Sun Times,* April 5, 2002.

10. Jennifer Netherby, "Late Knight Release," *Video Business,* September 17, 2001.

11. Stephen Holden, "Film; Post-9/11 and Pre," *New York Times,* January 5, 2003.

12. Simon Reynolds, "'Forrest Gump' Sequel Halted by 9/11," *Movies,* December 8, 2008.

Chapter Two

1. www.911docs.net/—46k.

2. J. Hoberman, "Lights, Action, Exploitation," *Village Voice,* August 26, 2003.

3. Robert Ebert, "Fahrenheit 9/11," *Chicago Sun-Times ,* June 24, 2004.

4. http://boxofficemojo.com/movies/?id=fahrenheit911.

5. Dan Jewell, "'Homeland Security': Duck, Run for It," *Media Life Magazine,* August 2005.

6. John Zigler, "The Continuing Censorship of 'The Path to 9/11,'" Fox News, September 11, 2008

7. www.yale.edu/lawweb/avalon/sept_11/911Report.pdf.

8. www.thepriceofliberty.org/06/05/22/rockyd.htm.

9. Brian Lowry, "World Trade Center," *Variety,* July 31, 2006.

10. Ed Gonzalez, "9/11: Press for Truth," *Slant,* August 31, 2006.

11. www.youtube.com/watch?v=7E3oIbO0AWE www.loosechange911.com/.

12. Dan Gibson, "Are Any 9/11 Conspiracy Films Plausible?" *Mother Jones,* September–October 2008.

13. Paul Joseph Watson and Alec Jones, "David Lynch Questions 9/11 on National Radio," *Prison Nation,* January 25, 2007, http://infowars.com/articles/sept11/lynch_questions_911_national_radio.htm.

14. Roger Ebert, "Gunner Palace," *Chicago Sun-Times,* March 11, 2005.

15. Drew Tillman, "Iraq for Sale," *Village Voice,* August 29, 2006.

16. Matt Zoller Seitz, "A War Hero's Terror, Tragedy, and Rescue," *New York Times,* November 20, 2007.

17. http://boxofficemojo.com/movies/?id=badland.htm.

18. http://movies.nytimes.com/2007/12/07/movies/07grac.html.

19. www.nytimes.com/2009/03/19/ . . . /19gates.html.

20. Roger Ebert, "Green Zone," *Chicago Sun-Times,* March 10, 2010.

21. "Mixed Reviews for Green Zone," *Right Wing News,* March 12, 2010.

22. John Anderson, "Gambling with a Return to the Mideast," *New York Times,* December 5, 2008.

23. www.remoteviewed.com/remote_viewing_history_military.htm.

Chapter Three

1. Charles Darwin, "The Expression of the Emotions in Man and Animals," darwin.literature.com/Expression_of_the_Emotions_in_Man_and_Animals/index/html.

2. www.thefreedictionary.com/horror.

3. www.academic.brooklyn.cuny.edu/english/melani/ . . . /tragedy.

4. J. Gerald Kennedy, *Poe, Death, and the Life of Writing* (New Haven, CT: Yale University Press, 1987).

5. Isabela Christina Pinedo, "Recreational Terror and the Postmodern Elements of the Contemporary Horror Film," paper delivered at Living in Terror: Post-9/11 Horror Films, Sixth Annual RMMLA Conference, Alberta, Canada, October 4–6, 2007.

6. "Susan Burggraf Explores the Appeal of Horror," *Bowdoin Campus News,* May 15, 2000.

7. www.cnn.com/2006/US/09/08/911.overview/index.html.

8. Tim Dirks, "Horror Films," www.filmsite.org/horrorfilms.html.

9. Roger Ebert, "The Blair Witch Project," Rogerebert.com, July 16, 1999.

10. www.the-numbers.com/movies/ . . . /NighmareOnElmstreet.php.

11. www.the-numbers.com/movies/series/FridayThe13th.php.

12. *Freddy vs. Jason* summary of box office results, charts, release information, and related links, www.boxofficemojo.com/movies/?id=freddyvsjason.htm.

13. L. Vincent Poupard, "9/11 Changes That Affected the Movie Industry," AC News, September 10, 2009, www.associatedcontent.com/ ... /911_changes_that_affected_the_ horror.html.

14. Mathew Leyland, "The Fog," *BBC Movies,* February 26, 2006.

15. David Edelstein, "Now Playing at Your Local Multiplex: Torture Porn," *New York Movies,* January 28, 2006.

16. Roger Ebert, "The Devil's Rejects," *Chicago Sun-Times,* July 22, 2005.

17. James Rocchi, "The Wicker Man, James' Take," *Cinematical,* September 2, 2006.

18. Robert Koehler, "The Hills Have Eyes," *V-Film,* March 2, 2006.

19. Alexander Zaitchik, "*Beowulf:* War-Porn Wrapped in a Chippendale's Body," Alter-Net, November 27, 2007, www.alternet.org/movies/68959.

20. Roger Friedman, "Cloverfield: Horror Film Not Sensitive About 9/11," FoxNews. Com Home Entertainment, January 16, 2008.

21. Alain Silver and James Ursini, *The Vampire Film: From* Nosferatu *to Bram Stoker's* Dracula (New York: Limelight Editions, 1993).

22. http://boxofficemojo.com/movies/?id=underworld2.htm.

23. Sharon Waxman, "At the Movies, at Least, Good Vanquishes Evil," *New York Times,* May 10, 2004.

24. http://boxofficemojo.com/movies/?id=vanhelsing.htm.

25. Tim Goodman, "TV Review: True Blood," *San Francisco Chronicle,* September 5, 2008, www.sfgate.com/cgi-bin/article.cgi?f=/c/a/2008/09/05/DDTA12O4B1. DTL#ixzz0qx9ZzjfD.

26. Roger Ebert, "The Twilight Saga: Eclipse," *Chicago Sun-Times,* June 28, 2010.

27. http://boxofficemojo.com/movies/?id=twilight08.htm.

28. Foster cited in Ruth La Ferla, "A Trend with Teeth," *New York Times,* July 1, 2009.

29. David Ordona, "Why Horror-Movie Remakes Are Box-Office Gold," *San Francisco Chronicle,* August 26, 2007.

30. http://boxofficemojo.com/movies/?id=hillshaveeyes207.htm.

Chapter Four

1. Charles Darwin, "The Expression of the Emotions in Man and Animals," Darwin-literature.com/The_Expression_of_the_Emotions_in_Man_and_Animals/Index/html.

2. www.famousquotes.me.uk/speeches/George_W_Bush/.

3. http://onlinejournal.com/artman/publish/article_2026.shtml.

4. See Carl Boggs and Tom Pollard, *The Hollywood War Machine: U.S. Militarism and Popular Culture* (Boulder, CO: Paradigm Publishers, 2007).

5. Roger Ebert, "We Were Soldiers," *Chicago Sun-Times,* March 1, 2002.

6. *The True Story of Charlie Wilson,* History Channel, December 21, 2007.

7. www.nytimes.com/2010/06/14/world/asia/14minerals.html.

8. John Mueller, "Dead and Deader," *New York Times,* January 20, 2008.

Chapter Five

1. Nicholas L. Carnagey and Craig A. Anderson, "Changes in Attitudes Towards War and Violence After September 11, 2001," *Aggressive Behavior* 33 (2007).

2. Lois Gresh and Robert Weinberg, *The Science of Superheroes* (Hoboken, NJ: John Wiley and Sons, 2002).

3. Richard Corliss, "Kick-Ass: Redefining the Superhero," *Time*, April 26, 2010.

4. James Kakalios, *The Physics of Superheroes* (New York: Gotham Books, 2006).

5. "Popeye the Sailor," answers.com, www.answers.com/topic/popeye-the-sailor.

6. Gresh and Weinberg, *The Science of Superheroes*.

7. Kakalios, *The Physics of Superheroes*.

8. *Spider-Man* #36, February 2002.

9. Rudiger Heinze, "Trauma, Morality, and Conformity: American (Super) Heroes After 9/11," *EESE* 4, 2007, webdoc.gwdg.de/edoc/ia/eese/artic27/heinze/6_2007.html.

10. http://dictionary.reference.com/browse/mutant?jss=0.

11. http://en.wikipedia.org/wiki/Bryan_Singer.

12. Kanti C. Kotecha and James L. Walker, "Vigilantism and the American Police," in *Vigilante Politics,* ed. H. Hon Rosenbaum and Peter C. Sederberg (N.p.: University of Pennsylvania Press, 1976).

13. Brandon Grey, "*Spider-Man* Ties *Titanic*'s $400 Million Record," *Box Office Mojo,* July 8, 2002.

14. www.the-numbers.com/movies/series/SuperHero.php.

15. www.komar.org/hulk/president.

16. www.imdb.com/title/tt0770828/.

17. Lowell Goodman, "*Superman Returns*: It's All There, Including the 'Mission Accomplished' Moment," *Bright Lights Journal,* 2006, www.brightlightsfilm.com/54/superman1.htm.

18. Gregory McNeill, "Superman and Post-9/11 America," www.supermanhomepage.com/comics/comics.php?topic ... /.

19. http://boxofficemojo.com/movies/?id=catwoman.htm.

20. http://boxofficemojo.com/movies/?id=superexgirlfriend.htm.

21. Manohla Dargis, "Showdown in Gotham City," *New York Times,* June 18, 2008.

22. Steve Biodrowski, "Sense of Wonder: The Dark Knight—Gotham City's Politics of Noir," September 21, 2008, http://cinefantastiqueonline.com/ ... /sense-of-wonder-dark-knights-politics-of-noir/.

23. Insight Team, "Inside the Sect That Loves Terror," *Sunday Times,* August 7, 2005.

24. http://boxofficemojo.com/movies/?id=fantasticfour2.htm.

25. Roger Ebert, "Iron Man 2," *Chicago Sun-Times,* May 5, 2010.

26. Manohla Dargis, "Time-Space Continuum? No Big Deal. And the Swag ... ," *New York Times,* February 14, 2008.

27. A. O. Scott, "Wolverine: I, Mutant, Red in Face and Claw," *New York Times,* May 1, 2009.

28. Meridith Woerner, "How 9/11 Changed Watchmen," February 26, 2009, http://io9.com/tag/post_911.

29. Sandra Blakesley, "Researchers Train Minds to Move Matter," *New York Times,* July 21, 2009.

30. Jeff Dawson, "Has the New Batman Plundered Its Plot from 9/11?" *Sunday Times,* July 20, 2008.

31. A. O. Scott, "How Many Superheroes Does It Take to Tire a Genre?" *New York Times,* July 24, 2008.

32. Kakalios, *The Physics of Superheroes.*

33. Gresh and Weinberg, *The Science of Superheroes.*

34. "Iron Man: The Science Behind the Fiction," *NewScientist,* May 1, 2008, www .newscientist.com/ ... /dn13815-iiron-mani-the-science-behind-the-fiction.html.

35. Daniel Dumas, 'The Dark Knight: Where Does He Get Those Wonderful Toys?" *Wired,* July 18, 2008.

36. Adam Weiner, "The Physics of *Batman,*" Popsci.com, August 15, 2008, www.popsci .com/entertainment-%2526 ... /physics-batman.

37. www.militaryremoteviewers.com/.

38. Bill Christiansen, "Implants Create Insect Cyborgs," *LiveScience,* February 4, 2008.

39. Mark D. Norman, Julian Finn, and Tom Tregenzen, "Dynamic Mimicry in an Indo-Malaysian Octopus," *Proceedings of the Royal Society,* September 7, 2001, http://darwin .biology.utah.edu/PubsHTML/PDF-Files/mimic.pdf.

40. Gary S. Bekkum, "Inside the National Security Agency: Are Psychic Spies Watching You?" *American Chronicle,* September 20, 2007, www.americanchronicle.com/articles/viewArticle.asp?articleID=38134.

41. Hadley Leggett, "Make Like a Dolphin: Learn Echolocation," *Wired Science,* June 30, 2009, www.wired.com/wiredscience/2009/06/echolocation/.

42. Kotecha and Walker, "Vigilantism."

Chapter Six

1. Charles Darwin, "The Expression of the Emotions in Man and Animals," darwin-literature.com/The_Expression_of_the_Emotions_in_Man_and_Animals/Index/html.

2. Ibid.

3. www.thefreedictionary.com/terror.

4. www.reuters.com/article/idUSTRE61H4JI20100218.

5. http://dictionary.reference.com/browse/terrorism.

6. www.cbsnews.com/blogs/2010/02/18/ ... /entry6220055.shtml.

7. http://dictionary.reference.com/browse/thriller.

8. Martin Rubin, *Thrillers* (Cambridge, UK: Cambridge University Press, 1999).

9. www.leninimports.com/hitchcock_saboteur.

10. http://boxofficemojo.com/genres/chart/?id=terrorism.

11. Ty Burr, "Political Thriller with Plenty of Firepower," Boston.com, September 28, 2007.

12. http://boxofficemojo.com/movies/?id=constantgardener.htm.

13. http://boxofficemojo.com/movies/?id=syriana.htm.

14. "The Good Shepherd," http://rheaven.blogspot.com/2009/09/good-shepherd.html.

15. Ross Douthat, "The Return of the Paranoid Style," *Atlantic Monthly,* April 2008.

16. Roger Ebert, "Body of Lies," *Chicago Sun-Times,* October 8, 2008.

17. http://boxofficemojo.com/movies/?id=bodyoflies.htm.

18. Colin Covert, "On the Fast Track to Hell in Pelham 123," *Mineapolis Star Tribune,* June 15, 2009.

19. Jim Ridley, "Blood on the Tracks: The Taking of Pelham 1-2-3," *The Village Voice,* June 10, 2009.

20. Suzanne Fields, "Turning *Munich* into a Movie," *Jewish World Review,* January 3, 2006.

21. David Schmidt, "Serial Killing After 9/11," *Journal of American Culture,* March 1, 2005.

22. http://boxofficemojo.com/movies/?id=sorryhaters.htm.

23. Cited in Cary Darling, "Hollywood Goes to War: Mainstream Movies Focus on Iraq," McClatchy Newspapers, October 1, 2007.

24. http://boxofficemojo.com/movies/?id=greenzone.htm.

Chapter Seven

1. Charles Darwin, "The Expression of the Emotions in Man and Animals," darwin-literature.com/The_Expression_of_the_Emotions_in_Man_and_Animals/Index/html.

2. Denis Dutton, "It's Always the End of the World as We Know It," *New York Times,* January 1, 2010.

3. Henry Jenkins, "The Tomorrow That Never Was," *Technology Review,* October 1, 2004.

4. http://anarchistnews.org/?q=node/415.

5. Ted Baehr, "Time Warner Promotes Terrorism and Anti-Christian Bigotry in New Leftist Movie, 'V for Vendetta,'" WorldNetDaily, www.wnd.com/news/article.asp?ARTICLE_ID=49317.

6. Kellvin Chavez, "On Set Interview: Producer Don Murphy on Transformers," *Latino Review,* February 21, 2007, www.latinoreview.com/news.php?id=1502.

7. http://boxofficemojo.com/movies/?id=knowing.htm.

8. Keiran King, "New 'Harry Potter'; Grown-Up, Darker," *Jamaica Gleaner,* July 26, 2009.

9. http://news.yahoo.com/s/ap/20100103/ap_en_mo/us_box_office.

10. Shohan Saxena, "Hollywood's Fascination with Extra-Terrestrials as Villains," *Economic Times,* December 20, 2009, http://economictimes.indiatimes.com/news/ ... villains/ ... /5358793.cms.

11. Steve Mason, "Raining Cash in Hollywood," Hollywood.breitbart.com/smason/2009/03/03/2009-records/.

12. Richard Verrier, "Worldwide Movie Box Office Receipts Rise in 2010," *Los Angeles Times,* February 24, 2011.

Chapter Eight

1. http://boxofficemojo.com/movies/?id=hurtlocker.htm.

2. http://boxofficemojo.com/movies/?id=greenzone.htm.

3. Delia Konzett, "Cinematic Professor Comments on Popularity of Vampires as HBO's 'True Blood' Returns," *Beta Newswise,* University of New Hampshire, June 12, 2009.

4. Grady Hendrix, "Vampires Suck: And That's the Problem," Slate, July 28, 2009, www.slate.com/id/2223486/.

5. "*New Moon* Opening Night, Box Office Sales Go Wild, Advanced Tickets Help Break Records," Huffington Post, November 20, 2009, www.huffingtonpost.com.

6. Brandon Gray, "'Eclipse' Rises with Record Release, Midnight Launch," *Box Office Mojo,* June 30, 2010.

7. Gabrille Murray, "Under Construction," Monash University Arts, March 20, 2008, dialogic.blogspot.com/2009/ . . . /gabrielle-murray-images-of-torture.html.

8. William Blake, *The Marriage of Heaven and Hell* (London: Camden Hotten, 1868).

9. David Edelstein, "Now Playing at Your Local Multiplex: Torture Porn," *New York Movies,* January 28, 2006.

10. http://movies.msn.com/movies/torture.

11. "The Passion of the Christ," *Moria: Science Fiction, Horror, and Fantasy Review,* January 3, 2009, www.moria.co.nz/horror/passionofthechrist.htm.

12. Gil Kaufman, "'Passion of the Christ' Pulls Off Box Office Miracle," MTV Online, March 10, 2004, www.mtv.com/news/articles/1485426/20040301/index .jhtml?headlines=true.

13. www.jahsonic.com/PassionChrist.html.

14. Rebecca Winters Keegan, "*Cloverfield*: Godzilla Goes 9/11," *Time,* January 16, 2008.

15. Tyler Gray, "Destroying the Earth Over and Over Again," *New York Times,* November 8, 2009.

16. "U.S. Public Rejects Using Military Force to Promote Democracy," World Public Opinion.org, September 29, 2005, www.worldpublicopinion.org/ . . . /brunitedstates canadara/77.php.

17. *The American Heritage Dictionary of the English Language* (New York: Houghton Mifflin, 1969).

18. http://renaissance-theatre.suite101.com/article.cfm/revenge_tragedies#ixzz0Qvy4 NIWT.

19. P. J. Liberman and L. J. Skitka, "Just Deserts in Iraq: American Vengeance for 9/11," paper presented at the MPSA Annual Conference, Palmer House Hotel, Chicago, Illinois, April 3, 2008, http://www.allacademic.com/meta/p268312_index.html.

20. Matt Zoller Seitz, "Ribbons of Revenge," *New York Press,* April 23, 2004.

21. Matthew E. Goldberg, "Post-9/11 Films: A Cinema of Revenge," *The Raw Story,* 2004, www.rawstory.com/exclusives/contributors/cinema_of_revenge.htm.

22. "America's Image Slips, but Allies Share U.S. Concerns over Iran, Hamas," Pew Global Attitudes Project, June 13, 2006, http://pewglobal.org/reports/display .php?ReportID=252.

23. Ted Baehr, "*Avatar:* Get Rid of Humans Now," *Movieguide,* January 10, 2010, www
.movieguide.org/.

24. Benjamin Bird, "History, Emotion, and the Body: Mourning in Post-9/11 Fiction,"
Literature Compass, 4, no. 3 (2007).

25. See Tom Pollard, *Sex and Violence: The Hollywood Censorship Wars* (Boulder, CO:
Paradigm Publishers, 2009).

26. Eboo Patel, "Religion in the Post-9/11 World," *Worldview,* September 11, 2009,
www.wbez.org/Program_WV_Segment.aspx?segmentID=36720.

27. Samuel P. Huntington, "Clash of Civilizations?" *Foreign Affairs,* Summer 1993, www
.foreignaffairs.com/ … /samuel … huntington/the-clash-of-civilizations.

28. Peter Ford, "Europe Cringes at Bush 'Crusade' Against Terrorists," *Christian Science
Monitor,* September 19, 2001.

29. Pew Research Center for the People and the Press, press release, March 20, 2002,
www.witherspoonsociety.org/religion_after_9_11.htm.

30. Pew Forum on Religion and Public Life, July 2009, http://pewforum.org/world
-affairs/.

31. http://boxofficemojo.com/genres/chart/?id=christian.htm.

32. Ross Douthat, "Heaven and Nature," *New York Times,* December 20, 2009, www
.nytimes.com/2009/12/21/opinion/21douthat1.html.

33. David Germain, "Hollywood Counters Reality with Decade of Escapism," Associated
Press, December 8, 2009, http://news.yahoo.com/s/ap/20091208/ap_en_mo/us_decade_
film.

34. Ramin Zahid, "Experts Discuss VFX Future at Digital Studio Summit," *Animation
Magazine,* November 2, 2004.

35. www.moviesmademe.com/movie/review/2020.

36. Brooks Barnes, "After Mickey's Makeover Look for a Little Less Mr. Nice Guy," *New
York Times,* November 5, 2009.

37. www.colorado.edu/English/courses/ENGL2012Klages/pomo.html.

38. Jessica Wakeman, "On *Cloverfield* and 9/11," Huffington Post, January 21, 2008.

39. Christopher Hayes, "9/11: The Roots of Paranoia," *The Nation,* December 8, 2006,
www.thenation.com/doc/20061225/hayes.

40. Warren Epstein, "Despite Pundits' Predictions, 9/11 Had Little Impact on Hollywood," *The (Colorado Springs) Gazette,* September 12, 2002.

41. Brad Hirschfield, "For God's Sake," *Washington Post,* September 11, 2009, www
.newsweek.washingtonpost.com/onfaith/ … /2009/09/september_11_2009.html.

Selected Filmography

Alien Trespass (2009). This retro sci-fi spoof, written and directed by R. W. Goodwin, takes place in 1957 amid the 1950s horror movie craze. Set in the desert town of Mohave, California, the film features cute teenagers sporting ponytails and ducktail haircuts, hard-bitten local policemen, and assorted other characters. Eric McCormack plays Ted Lewis, a local scientist whose body becomes "borrowed" by an alien marshal named Urp, also played by McCormack.

Batman Begins (2005). Christopher Nolan presents a dark, post-9/11 superhero, Bruce Wayne (Christian Bale), combating domestic terrorists who threaten to overrun Gotham City. As a child, Wayne watched helplessly as his wealthy parents died at the hands of thugs. In later years he searches the world for skills and knowledge to defeat the dark forces besieging his city.

Beowulf (2007). Robert Zemeckis's version of this Old English dragon tale stars Ray Winstone as the Anglo-Saxon hero Beowulf, Anthony Hopkins as King Hrothgar, and Angelina Jolie as a dazzling shape-shifting dragon. Like the medieval epic, Zemeckis's film relates a dramatic struggle between forces of darkness and living heroes and delivers a subtle yet distinct post-9/11 message.

Blood Diamond (2006). Edward Zwick focuses audience attention on a forgotten civil war on Africa's west coast in 1999. Zwick's film stars Leonardo DiCaprio as Danny Archer, a white Rhodesian outwardly functioning as a diamond smuggler and secretly working for the CIA.

Body of Lies (2008). Ridley Scott's film depicts CIA operatives tracking down terrorism. Leonardo DiCaprio plays Roger Ferris, a CIA operative working under the direction of CIA officer Ed Hoffman (Russell Crowe). They both expend their efforts tracking down and cracking an Islamic terrorist organization led by Al-Saleem (Alon Aboutboul), an obvious Osama bin Laden surrogate, that plans and executes a series of deadly terrorist bombings in European cities.

The Bourne Ultimatum (2007). Paul Greengrass's third installment in this popular thriller series follows up on his *United 93* success and depicts assassinations and waterboarding. Bourne, an intelligence agent assuming a newly created identity as a CIA undercover operative, experiences flashbacks hinting at an earlier identity, sending him on an epic identity quest.

Breach (2007). Billy Ray provides yet another example of intelligence lapses in this film's depiction of the traitorous American FBI agent Robert Hanssen (Chris Cooper), arrested in 2001 after selling agency secrets to the USSR for twenty-five years.

Catwoman (2004). "Pitof's" (Jean-Christophe Comar) film features Halle Berry as Patience Phillips (a significantly named graphics designer) and her magical transformation into Catwoman, a superhero capable of almost unlimited feats of strength and agility.

Charlie Wilson's War (2007). Mike Nichols depicts the Soviet-Afghan war from the perspective of Charlie Wilson (Tom Hanks), a U.S. congressman who sits on two strategic committees responsible for funding covert operations and who adopts the cause of the Afghan mujahideen and begins to approve increasingly larger amounts of government funds to help them.

Cloverfield (2008). Matt Reeves represents a symbolic rendering of the 9/11 terrorist attacks on New York City, but instead of destroying the World Trade Center, like the real terrorists did, a giant reptilian monster rips the head off of the Statue of Liberty and heaves it into downtown Manhattan. Then, the beast attacks the Woolworth Building and skyscrapers, subways, and other buildings, sending the entire populace into flight and causing the military to consider using a nuclear bomb to destroy the monster.

Collateral Damage (2002). Directed by Andrew Davis, this film stars Arnold Schwarzenegger as Gordon "Gordy" Brewer, a Los Angeles firefighter who barely survives a terrorist bombing in New York City that kills his wife and son. Vowing revenge, "Gordy" tracks the terrorists to Colombia, then infiltrates their drug gang, and ultimately extracts vengeance from guerrilla leader Claudio "El Lobo."

The Constant Gardener (2005 British). Directed by Fernando Meirellas, this film depicts a murder mystery in Kenya involving a powerful multinational drug company's nefarious plot to unleash a lethal epidemic and then enrich itself by selling an antidote.

Daredevil (2003). Mark Steven Johnson bases his film on the popular Marvel comics superhero. Ben Affleck stars as Matt Murdock, a Hell's Kitchen lawyer who as a child ran into a container of toxic waste. The waste spurts onto his eyes, blinding him but, in the process, somehow endowing him with superpowers that allow him to navigate through the world as easily as a sighted person.

The Dark Knight (2008). Directed by Christopher Nolan, this film continues the Batman franchise with another post-9/11 rendition of the popular superhero. Christian Bale once again stars as Batman/Bruce Wayne, the dualistic superhero. Nolan refuses to glorify Batman, even though Bale's character possesses considerable charisma, especially when armed with his high-tech weaponry and other toys.

The Day the Earth Stood Still (2008). Scott Derrickson evokes post-9/11 angst, anger, guilt, and violence. Derrickson's adaptation of Robert Wise's 1951 classic, considered one of the best sci-fi films ever made, updates Wise's cold war thriller with typical post-9/11 themes.

Defiance (2008). Edward Zwick returns to World War II, "the good war," but this time he depicts not Americans but Polish resistance fighters battling the Nazi invasion of Belarus. Survivors of Nazi attacks in 1941 band together, hide deep in the forests, and wage a clandestine war of resistance.

District 9 (2009). Neill Blomkamp turns the stereotypical plot of diabolical aliens attacking terrified humans into a thought-provoking sociopolitical parable about what deeds humans might perpetuate on weak aliens if given the opportunity.

Dracula 3000 (2004). Directed by Darrell Roodt, this film functions as a poorly made reprise of the venerable Count Dracula, here called Orlock (Langley Kirkwood). In this blend of sci-fi and horror, a spacecraft on a routine mission in the year 3000 spots a long-lost transporter that appears uninhabited. When the ship beams the transporter aboard, however, the crew discovers Orlock ready to attack them and drink their blood.

Elektra (2005). Directed by Rob Bowman, this film was inspired by the 2003 movie *Daredevil*. Elektra Natchios (Jennifer Garner), Daredevil's superpowerful girlfriend in the earlier film, is the daughter of a Greek billionaire as well as a carefully trained superhero crime fighter.

Fahrenheit 9/11 (2004). Michael Moore indicts President George W. Bush for stealing the 2000 presidential election, for frittering away much of his time vacationing, for secretly siding with Saudi Arabia because of family business dealings with Saudi prince Bandar, and for waging unjust wars in Afghanistan and Iraq.

FahrenHYPE 9/11: Unraveling the Truth About Fahrenheit 9/11 and Michael Moore (2004). Alan Peterson condemns Moore's film as well as Moore personally and directly, charging him with attempting to belittle the threat posed by terrorists.

Fantastic Four (2005). Tim Story features not one but four characters with superpowers. Doctor Von Doom (Julian McMahon) finances a space voyage for himself, along with Reed Richards (Ioan Gruffudd), Sue Storm (Jessica Alba), Johnny Storm (Chris Evans), and Ben Grimm (Michael Chiklis). These superheroes battle supervillains in this sci-fi thriller.

Flags of Our Fathers (2006). Clint Eastwood's biopic examines the lives of the three flag-raisers at Iwo Jima and explores the long-range effects of combat on soldiers.

The Fog (2005). Rupert Wainwright reprises the 1980 John Carpenter classic about a supernatural fog that engulfs a small Pacific Northwest island village called Antonio, killing, maiming, starting mysterious fires, and generally perpetrating chaos and mayhem.

Gangs of New York (2002). Martin Scorsese comes uncomfortably close to actual 9/11 events, even though he sets his film in the mid-nineteenth century in New York's Five Points neighborhood. Producers withheld release of this film until months after 9/11.

The Good German (2006). Steven Soderbergh depicts postwar military operations in Germany on the eve of the 1945 Potsdam Conference, which divides Europe among the Allies. However, far from showcasing military virtues, Soderbergh's film depicts Americans as rife with corruption, ignoring and condoning Nazi atrocities at an underground missile plant.

The Good Shepherd (2006). Robert De Niro follows the exploits of charter members of the fledgling Central Intelligence Agency at the start of the cold war, exposing in the process some of the harsh tactics used by the agency.

Green Zone (2010). Paul Greengrass sets this film in Iraq in 2003 during the frantic U.S. search for weapons of mass destruction in order to justify to the world the 2003 invasion of Iraq. Chief Warrant Officer Roy Miller (Matt Damon) searches in vain for WMD, then learns that they haven't existed for many years. In the process he uncovers a U.S. plot to deceive the world about the presence of the contentious weapons in Saddam Hussein's arsenal.

Harry Potter and the Half-Blood Prince (2009). David Yates directs this installment of the Harry Potter series. This dark episode pits Potter against the Dark Lord in a classic good versus evil confrontation.

Hellboy (2004). This film by Guillermo Del Toro features yet another comic-book character on the big screen—a superpower-possessing human-demon hybrid who was conjured up by the Nazis during World War II but was raised and tamed on a U.S. military base.

The Hills Have Eyes (2006). Alexandre Aja's film epitomizes the post-9/11 horror film. In this remake of Wes Craven's 1977 classic, a family who is vacationing in a remote New Mexico desert is attacked by desert mutants deformed by atomic testing.

A History of Violence (2005). David Cronenberg depicts a seemingly typical small businessman, Tom Stall (Viggo Mortensen), who owns a café in Mill-brook, Indiana, along with his wife, Edie (Maria Bello). But is Stall really who he says he is? We are unsure after he handily dispatches two killers who attack patrons in his café.

Homeland Security (2004). Daniel Sackheim's film stars Scott Glenn as Joe Johansen, a CIA officer, and Tom Skerritt as Admiral Theodore McKee, appointed director of the Office of Homeland Security after the 9/11 attacks. *Homeland Security* skillfully depicts a series of missed cues and close calls in the days leading up to 9/11, including a suspicious flight instructor noticing his pupil apparently intent on learning to aim a plane at a target, not land and take off at an airport.

Hostel (2005). Directed by Eli Roth, this film features not vengeful ghosts but a secret organization named Elite Hunting that recruits and delivers unwitting victims to clients willing to pay dearly for torturing and murdering them.

Hulk (2003). Ang Lee pioneers the new superhero genre featuring darker, more complex characters than during previous superhero cycles. The protagonist, Bruce Banner (Eric Bana), a young biochemist accidentally exposed to intense radiation, discovers that when he is angered, his body transforms into a gigantic green character with superhuman powers.

The Incredibles (2004). This animated feature written and directed by Brad Bird for Pixar features the Parr family of superheroes, headed by Bob Parr (Craig T. Nelson), nicknamed "Mr. Incredible" for his superstrength and athletic abilities. Bob marries "Elastigirl" (Holly Hunter), who possesses an ability to stretch her pliable body around corners and flatten and elongate arms, legs, hands, and fingers in order to fight crime.

The Interpreter (2005). Sydney Pollack depicts Secret Service surveillance surrounding overheard plans to assassinate a foreign dignitary. A UN interpreter, Silvia Broome (Nicole Kidman), overhears whispers late one evening of the impending political assassination of Dr. Zuwanie (Earl Cameron), the president of Matobo, a mythical African country loosely based on Zimbabwe.

In the Valley of Elah (2007). Paul Haggis's film stars Tommy Lee Jones as Hank Deerfield, a retired army sergeant whose son disappears after returning from active duty in Iraq. Police detective Emily Sanders (Charlize Theron) helps Deerfield search for his son, who Deerfield suspects may have met with foul play after partying one night with fellow platoon members.

Iraq for Sale: The War Profiteers (2006). Paul Greenwald exposes the often chaotic practices of Blackwater and other private companies operating for the U.S. military in Iraq. Greenwald's documentary charges that private companies avoid government oversight and the rule of law by virtue of their special exempt status.

Iron Man (2008). Directed by Jon Favreau, this film stars Robert Downey Jr. as Tony Stark (aka Iron Man), a billionaire weapons manufacturer and inventor. Stark invents a huge flying exoskeleton that provides him with superpowers, which he uses to combat crime—eventually within his own corporation.

Jumper (2008). This film by Doug Liman depicts David Rice (Hayden Christiansen), a powerful mutant possessing the ability to teleport himself through willpower instantaneously to any part of the globe, including bank vaults, thereby allowing him to amass great material wealth.

Kill Bill: Volume 1 (2003) and *Kill Bill: Volume 2* (2004). In both films, Quentin Tarantino presents graphic evidence of a new breed of powerful post-9/11 femmes fatales. Tarantino's twin films feature a vengeful femme fatale named "the Bride," Beatrix Kiddo (Uma Thurman). Betrayed by Bill (David Carradine) on her wedding day, shot and left for dead, she lives to exact retribution on her attackers, all members of Bill's squad of assassins.

The Kingdom (2007). Peter Berg's film, starring Jamie Foxx, Chris Cooper, Jennifer Garner, and Jason Bateman, depicts terrorist bombings at the Riyadh compound on May 12, 2003, and the Khobar housing complex on June 26, 1996, in Saudi Arabia. The story follows a team of FBI agents, headed by Roland Fleury (Jamie Foxx), who investigate the bombing of a foreign workers facility in Saudi Arabia.

King Kong (2005). Peter Jackson reprises the 1933 classic by coproducers and documentarians Merian C. Cooper and Ernest B. Schoedsack. Jackson revives this classic thriller by injecting elements of a horror film, as well as a nontraditional love story between woman (Ann Darrow played by Naomi Watts) and beast.

Knowing (2009). This film by Alex Proyas stars Nicolas Cage as John Koestler, a professor of astrophysics at MIT whose young son, Caleb (Chandler Canterbury), receives visits from mysterious strangers in overcoats after discovering an enigmatic letter recently unearthed from a fifty-year-old time capsule.

The Last Sect (2006). Jonathan Dueck adds a modern twist to the vampire genre. These modern vampires infest an online dating service that provides fresh victims for the ever-ravenous vampires who inhabit it.

Lions for Lambs (2007). Robert Redford explores several controversial aspects of the war in Afghanistan. Redford's film stars Redford, Meryl Streep, Tom Cruise, and Derek Luke. Cruise plays Jasper Irving, an ambitious Republican U.S. senator who champions a new military strategy in Afghanistan that proves a disaster.

Lost Boys: The Tribe (2008). P. J. Pesce reprises Joel Schumacher's 1987 cult classic, *The Lost Boys*. Peace's film features Tad Hilgenbrink and Autumn Reeser as Chris and Nicole Emerson, two orphan siblings who visit an aunt living in Luna Bay, a seaside town with a large number of surfers as well as vampires.

A Mighty Heart (2007). Michael Winterbottom presents a fictionalized account of events surrounding the kidnapping and murder of American journalist Daniel Pearl. Winterbottom's film focuses on Pearl's wife, Mariane, in 2002 from the time of Pearl's disappearance until weeks later when a videotape revealed that he had been killed at the hands of Khalid Sheikh Mohammad and other terrorists associated with al Qaeda.

Munich (2005). Steven Spielberg depicts a secret Israeli hit squad sent by Israeli intelligence on a mission to track down and assassinate the Palestinian terrorists who massacred eleven Israeli athletes at the 1972 Munich Olympics. In Spielberg's film Israel acts much like the United States did after the September 11 attacks by choosing covert, possibly illegal military strikes against terrorists.

My Super Ex-Girlfriend (2006). This comedy by Ivan Reitman depicts superheroine "G-Girl" (Uma Thurman), who gains superpowers after touching a glowing meteorite while in high school. She employs superstrength, superhearing, laser vision, and the ability to fly in order to fight crimes and natural disasters. In the process, she makes life miserable for her ex-boyfriend and his new girlfriend.

9/11: Press for Truth (2006). Directed by Ray Nowosielski, this film attacks government responses to 9/11 from the perspective of the Jersey Girls, four 9/11 widows who become instrumental in questioning official government statements regarding 9/11. Their "press for truth," joined by many others, eventually leads to the formation of the 9/11 Commission.

Painful Deceptions (2005). Eric Hufschmid doubts the official version of the events of 9/11. His film questions Flight 77, the American Airlines flight that struck the Pentagon, and the attacks on the World Trade Center and Building 7.

The Quiet American (2002). Phillip Noyce depicts some very disturbing events in Vietnam prior to the war. Thomas Fowler (Michael Caine), a middle-aged British journalist living in Saigon, encounters Alden Pyle

(Brendan Fraser), a young aid worker from the United States. The two compete for the affections of Fowler's beautiful Vietnamese girlfriend, Phuong (Do Thi Hai Yen), but their triangular romantic relationship also symbolizes the three-way conflict among Britain, the United States, and the Vietnamese people over the eventual fate of Vietnam.

Race to Witch Mountain (2009). This film by Andy Fickman became an instant blockbuster, displacing *Watchmen,* a dark superhero film, from the first spot in box office sales. Fickman's film, produced by Disney, reprises the 1975 *Escape to Witch Mountain.* This film appeals to Area 51 fans who enjoy conspiracy theories about the government keeping the UFO issue under wraps.

Rambo (2008). Sylvester Stallone arrives twenty-six years after the premiere of the original *Rambo: First Blood* feature. He acts, directs, stars, and coscripts this fourth installment of the franchise, this time titled simply *Rambo.* In it John Rambo (Stallone) enjoys a curmudgeonly semiretirement in Thailand until a group of Christian missionaries persuade him to rent his boat to travel upriver to the war-torn Karen region of Burma (Myanmar).

The Reaping (2007). Stephen Hopkins's film exemplifies post-9/11 apocalyptic thrillers. Hilary Swank stars as Katherine Winter, a university professor and professional debunker of supernaturalism who confronts horrors that seem straight out of the Bible.

Redacted (2007). Brian De Palma chronicles a notorious case of American soldiers who raped and murdered a fifteen-year-old Iraqi girl and killed her family in 2006. *Redacted* evokes De Palma's 1987 *Casualties of War,* which also depicts wartime rape (in Vietnam).

Rendition (2007). Starring Reese Witherspoon, Jake Gyllenhaal, Peter Sarsgaard and Meryl Streep, Gavin Hood's film tells the story of Isabella Fields El-Ibrahimi's (Reese Witherspoon) increasingly emotional search for her Egyptian-born husband, Anwar El-Ibrahimi (Omar Metwally), kidnapped (renditioned) by American intelligence operatives and sent to a foreign prison for torture.

The Ring (2002). Gore Verbinski's is the first horror film released after 9/11. It reprises *Ringu,* a successful 1998 Japanese horror film based on a novel by Koji Suzuki about a diabolical videotape seemingly possessed with supernatural power that kills some viewers exactly seven days after they view it.

The Sentinel (2006). Clark Johnson depicts an assassination threat against President Ballentine (David Rasche). Veteran Secret Service Agent Pete Garrison (Michael Douglas) attempts to discover the identity of an alleged traitor within the Secret Service involved in a plot to assassinate the president while he conducts an illicit relationship with First Lady Sarah Ballentine (Kim Basinger).

Sky Captain and the World of Tomorrow (2004). Kerry Conran presents post-9/11 audiences with a science fiction thriller possessing nostalgia, magic, giant bird-shaped robots that flap metal wings while firing cannon shots, supervillains, an attack on New York City circa 1939, and stars Jude Law, Gwyneth Paltrow, and Angelina Jolie.

Spider-Man (2002). Sam Raimi's film features teenage geek Peter Parker (Tobey Maguire), who after being bitten by a radioactive spider turns into Spider-Man, a superhero sporting a splendidly muscled physique and able to craw up walls, shoot webs from his wrists, and travel through the air as if possessing the gift of flight.

Spider-Man 2 (2004). This sequel, also directed by Sam Raimi, features an older Peter Parker, who enrolls in college, where he continues to struggle in his relationship, renouncing his superpowers to try to become "normal," and finally deciding to use his powers to fight crime.

Spider-Man 3 (2007). The third installment directed by Sam Raimi depicts an even darker Spider-Man who assumes an alternate, black-costumed identity in order to defeat the powerful forces threatening humanity. The sequels become darker as Spider-Man transforms into a more violent, potent character, following the direction of post-9/11 superheroes. This episode features an attack on a New York skyscraper strongly reminiscent of the September 11, 2001, terrorist attacks on the World Trade Center.

Superman Returns (2006). Bryan Singer reprises the Superman franchise. In this film the venerable Man of Steel (Brandon Routh) battles a superpowerful foe, Lex Luthor (Kevin Spacey), with the fate of the earth hanging in the balance.

The Taking of Pelham 123 (2009). Tony Scott reprises the 1974 thriller of the same name in which a ruthless, violent criminal named Ryder (John Travolta) hijacks a New York City subway train and takes eighteen passengers hostage.

Team America: World Police (2003). Trey Parker satirizes U.S. geopolitical hubris in the war on terror, among other targets. Parker's film (cowritten by Matt Stone and Pam Brady) deliberately aims its satire not only on the Bush/Cheney war on terror by also at political positions regarding terrorism taken by both left and right.

The Texas Chainsaw Massacre (2006). Marcus Nispel updates the 1977 horror classic of the same name. Nispel's film takes place in a lonely and foreboding desert location in which a father and son embark on a killing spree, attacking, murdering, and even consuming their victims.

Transformers (2007). Michael Bay references an ancient war on the planet Cybertron between the Autobots, advanced robots led by Optimus Prime, and the Decepticons, a group of evil robots led by the satanic Megatron.

Transformers II: Revenge of the Fallen (2009). Also directed by Michael Bay, this sequel focuses on an intergalactic war between rival races of robots; the fate of earth depends upon the result.

Twilight (2008). Directed by Catherine Hardwicke, this film inaugurates an entirely new kind of character—the "good vampire." Hardwicke's film stars attractive Kristin Stewart as Bella Swan, a high school student who moves to the small town of Forks, Washington, to be with her father. While attending the local high school, she falls in love with handsome senior Edward Cullen (Robert Pattinson), a vampire.

Twin Towers (2003). Bill Guttentag's and Robert David Port's award-winning 34-minute documentary short profiles the New York Police Department's Emergency Services Unit located in the South Bronx.

Ultraviolet (2006). Kurt Wimmer's film presents Violet (Milla Jovovich), a young woman afflicted by a transformational blood disease that turned her and many others into superheroes and superheroines in the late twenty-first century.

Underworld (2003). Directed by Len Wiseman, this first installment of the Underworld series is about a vampire named Selene (Kate Beckinsale) who falls in love with a human named Michael Covin (Scott Speedman), who possesses an antibody in his blood that might allow a hybrid race of immortals who are part vampire, part werewolf.

United 93 (2006). Paul Greengrass's film focuses on the hijacked United Flight 93 that many have speculated was intended to crash into the White House on September 11, 2001. Instead, according to the film, the passengers revolt against the hijackers and attempt to retake the plane after learning about the other hijacked airliners that crashed into the World Trade Center.

V for Vendetta (2006). James McTeigue's film features a terrorist attack that kills 100,000 Britons by a militarized virus, which turns out to have been created and accidently released by a secret government project. This film depicts Great Britain in the hands of a cruel fascist dictator. It also depicts a revolution against this dictatorship,

Vantage Point (2008). Pete Travis depicts the assassination of an American president while visiting Spain. The film shows the president blown away by bullets, and shortly thereafter a huge bomb ignites, destroying much of the town. Travis's film depicts these same events from different perspectives, constantly reminding audiences of America's vulnerability to assassinations and other acts of terrorism.

W (2008). Oliver Stone's controversial film presents George W. Bush's reactions to 9/11. To some, disappointed by Stone's lack of Bush-bashing in this effort, the film functions more like a paean to the forty-third president than a criticism of the Bush approach to terrorism (invade, threaten, cajole). Bush (Josh Brolin) comes off better in this film than many felt he should, and Stone's empathy for a fellow Yale grad appears akin to camaraderie. Instead of a definitive documentary in the culture war over the war on terror, Stone's film serves as a benign chiding of the president's abilities. In it, Bush comes off as a disappointing failure, not an evil warmonger.

War, Inc. (2008). Joshua Seftel bitingly satirizes the wars in Iraq and Afghanistan. He casts John Cusack as Brand Hauser, a high-level assassin hired by the Viceroy (Dan Aykroyd), a former U.S. vice president who administers Turaqistan, a central Asian republic.

The War Within (2005). In this film directed by Joseph Castelo, Hassan (Ayad Akhad), a brilliant young Pakistani engineer living in Paris, finds himself arrested, knocked out, and smuggled out of the country to Pakistan by American agents who falsely accuse him of membership in a terrorist cell.

Watchmen (2009). This film directed by Zack Snyder, depicts a retro-futuristic 1980s America in which costumed superheroes assist law enforcement agencies in fighting crime. In the present day, however, the murder of one of the now retired superheroes inspires another superhero who goes by the name of Rorschach to launch an investigation. Snyder's film joined a growing number of science fiction thrillers based on comic books depicting superheroes protecting humanity.

We Were Soldiers (2002). This film, by Randall Wallace, begun prior to 9/11 but released later, paints a fairly positive portrait of U.S. military performance during the Vietnam War.

World Trade Center (2006). Oliver Stone focuses on the rescue of two Port Authority police officers trapped in wreckage at Ground Zero. John McLoughlin (Nicolas Cage) and William A. Jimeno (Michael Peña) manage to hang onto life, hoping to be discovered by rescue workers.

X-Men (2000). Bryan Singer's film exemplifies pre-9/11 "scientific" superheroes as few others have. Audiences are introduced to a collection of powerful yet kinky characters who have supposedly evolved rapidly in a rare instance of accelerated evolution.

X-Men 2 (2003). Bryan Singer directs this sequel with many of the original characters. However, the heroes in this film appear much weaker and more conflicted than those in the original, and the villains in Singer's sequel seem far more brutal and menacing.

X-Men: The Last Stand (2006). Brett Ratner directed this installment in which the clash between mutants and humans grows even darker and more violent than in *X-Men 2*. In this film, scientists discover an "antidote" to mutant powers, a drug so powerful that it will neutralize and possibly even kill mutants wishing to avail themselves of the new opportunity to renounce their superpowers and immortality in favor of a human existence.

X-Men Origins: Wolverine (2009). Director Gavin Hood explores the superhero's decision to live as an ordinary lumberman in Canada. His career ends, however, after his girlfriend dies, apparently at the hands of Sabertooth (Liev Schreiber). James Logan (Wolverine) played by Hugh Jackman vows revenge and voluntarily enters a secret government laboratory designed to vastly improve his body's weaponry.

Index

About the Author

Tom Pollard is Professor of Social Sciences at National University in San Jose and has collaborated on documentary films that have appeared on BBC, the Discovery Channel, the Life Network, Canadian Broadcasting System, and various PBS channels. His most recent book is *Sex and Violence: The Hollywood Censorship Wars* (Paradigm, 2010). He has coauthored, with Carl Boggs, *The Hollywood War Machine* (Paradigm, 2007) and *A World in Chaos: Social Crisis and the Rise of Postmodern Cinema* (Rowman & Littlefield, 2003).